SERGER SECRETS

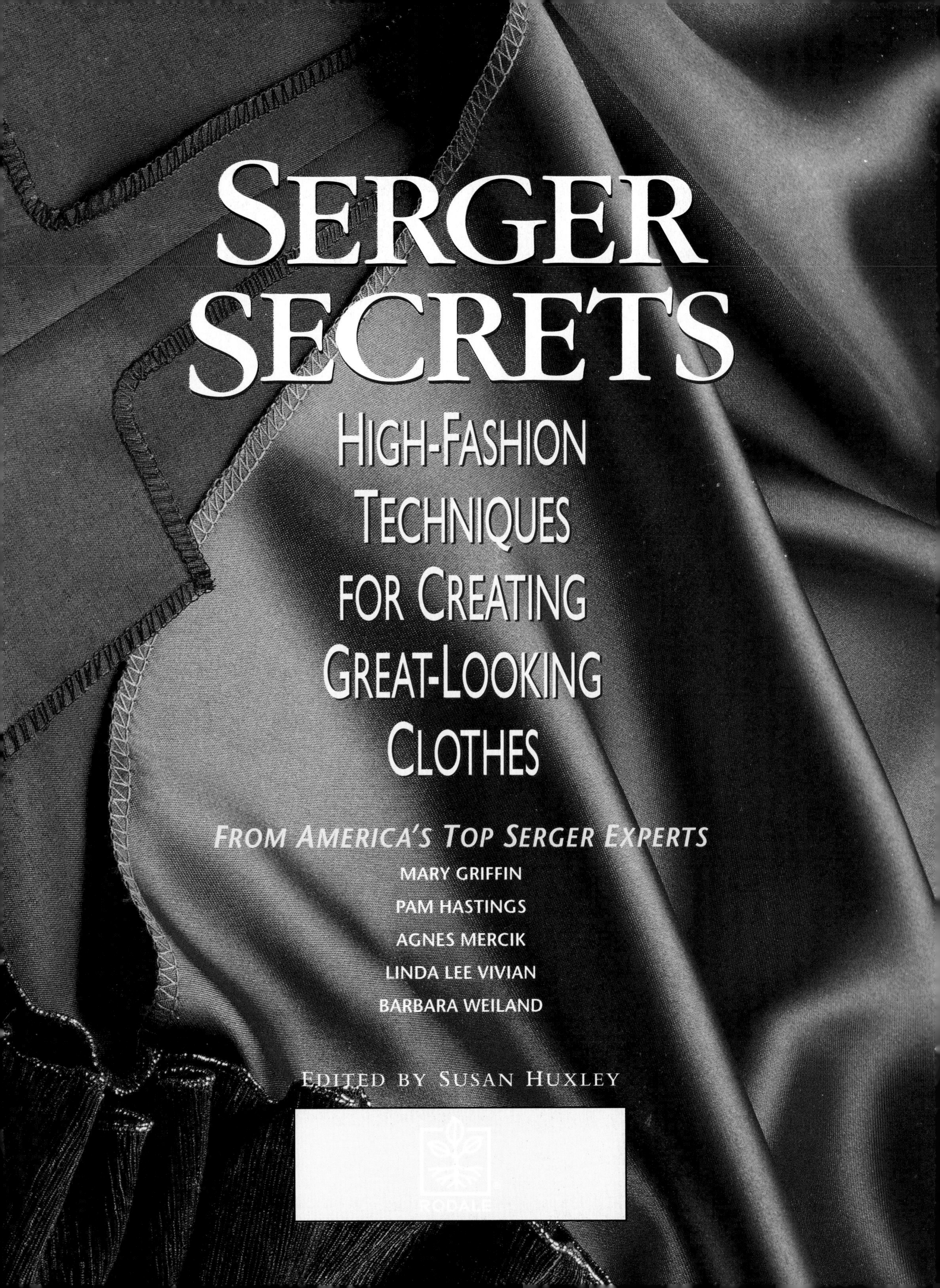

SERGER SECRETS

HIGH-FASHION TECHNIQUES FOR CREATING GREAT-LOOKING CLOTHES

FROM AMERICA'S TOP SERGER EXPERTS

MARY GRIFFIN

PAM HASTINGS

AGNES MERCIK

LINDA LEE VIVIAN

BARBARA WEILAND

EDITED BY SUSAN HUXLEY

RODALE

The authors and editor who compiled this book have tried to make all of the contents as accurate and as correct as possible. Illustrations, photographs, and text have all been carefully checked and cross-checked. However, due to the variability of materials, personal skill, and so on, neither the authors nor Rodale Inc. assumes any responsibility for any injuries suffered or for damages or other losses incurred that result from the material presented herein. All instructions should be carefully studied and clearly understood before beginning a project.

We're always happy to hear from you. For questions or comments concerning the editorial content of this book, please write to:

Rodale Inc.
Book Readers' Service
33 East Minor Street
Emmaus, PA 18098

Look for other Rodale books wherever books are sold. Or call us at (800) 848-4735.

For more information about Rodale and the books and magazines we publish, visit our Web site at:

www.rodale.com

Printed in the United States of America
Rodale Inc. makes every effort to use acid-free ∞, recycled paper ♻.

Library of Congress Cataloging-in-Publication Data
Serger secrets : high-fashion techniques for creating great-looking clothes from America's top serger experts Mary Griffin, Pam Hastings, Agnes Mercik, Linda Lee Vivian, Barbara Weiland.
p.   cm.
Includes bibliographical references and index.
ISBN 0–87596–794–9 hardcover
ISBN 1–57954–464–9 paperback
1. Serging.   I. Griffin, Mary.   II. Title: High-fashion techniques for creating great-looking clothes.
TT713.S34   1998
646.2'044—ddc21   98-19763

Distributed to the book trade by St. Martin's Press

| | 14 | 16 | 18 | 20 | 19 | 17 | 15 | | | hardcover |
| 12 | 14 | 16 | 18 | 20 | 19 | 17 | 15 | 13 | 11 | paperback |

Editor: Susan Huxley

Cover and Interior Book Designer, Photo Stylist, and Layout Designer: Stan Green/Green Graphics

Needle Illustrator: Barbara Field

Tip Box Illustrator: Sandy Freeman

Cover Photographer: Mitch Mandel

Interior Photographer: Mitch Mandel, except for: Photograph, page 11—Ed Landrock; Photographs, pages 14 and 209—Kurt Wilson

Seamstress and Researcher: Sue Nester

Photography Editor: James A. Gallucci

Hand Model: Anne Cassar

Copy Editor: Jennifer Hornsby

Manufacturing Coordinator: Patrick T. Smith

Indexer: Nan Badgett

Editorial Assistance: Jodi Guiducci

RODALE HOME AND GARDEN BOOKS

Vice President and Editorial Director:
Margaret J. Lydic

Managing Editor, Sewing Books:
Cheryl Winters-Tetreau

Director of Design and Production: Michael Ward

Associate Art Directors: Patricia Field and Carol Angstadt

Production Manager: Robert V. Anderson Jr.

Studio Manager: Leslie M. Keefe

Copy Director: Dolores Plikaitis

Book Manufacturing Manager: Mark Krahforst

Office Manager: Karen Earl-Braymer

A special thank-you is extended to the machine companies who so generously loaned us the sergers shown throughout this book: Bernina of America, Inc. (model 2000DE); Pfaff American Sales Corporation (sewing machine model 7570 and Hobbylock serger model 4870); Singer Sewing Company (model 14U555); Tacony Corporation (the baby lock Éclipse LX); VWS Inc. (model White Superlock 2000 electronic); and Husqvarna Viking Sewing Machine Co. (Huskylock model 1002LCD).

On the cover: The stunning garment by serger expert Agnes Mercik was made using a variety of serger techniques. For additional information, see page 74.

Contents

Meet the Experts

Mary Griffin

Pam Hastings

Agnes Mercik

Linda Lee Vivian

Barbara Weiland

Mary Griffin

You may recognize Mary's name because she has published ideas and tips in *Sew News, Sew Beautiful,* and *The Experts Book of Sewing Tips and Techniques.* She also presents sewing and serging seminars and classes across the country. And for the past nine years she has been a Singer Educational Consultant.

Her career path started in nursing, but a desire for change sent her back to school for an M.S. in textiles and clothing. This is where she discovered the pleasure she gets from teaching. Soon she was involved with both college and adult-education courses.

She helps sewers relax and have fun on their sergers while discovering a variety of techniques.

In her own words, "I draw on my own adventures in learning to help my students get over their fears, and I like it that they always teach me something, too."

Pam Hastings

Years ago, who would have guessed that an entire career would be launched when Pam stitched up Christmas gifts for a family pet?

She won't divulge just how many years ago that was, but suffice it to say that she's worked in the sewing industry for 18 years. The adventure started when she graduated from Keene State College in New Hampshire. After working for various companies in the industry, she switched to freelance consulting several years ago.

She's been a guest on various television programs and has written for publications. You might have read her book, *Creative Projects for Machine Embroidery*.

Agnes Mercik

Agnes has had a long and illustrious career that spans the continents. She has received awards, written numerous books, and has an active teaching schedule.

Her association with Bernina of America has taken her around the world: regularly to many parts of the United States, plus Australia and Hong Kong. In 1991, the company designated her "The Outstanding Sewing Specialist."

Agnes has contributed to several successful sewing and serging books and international sewing and craft publications. She was the main writer and technician for Bernina of America's "The Advanced Serger Guide and Supplement," and her design patterns have appeared in national ad and consumer programs. Her latest book, *Appliqué Innovations*, has opened up an exciting new world of machine-art expression.

Linda Lee Vivian

With many years of sewing experience, specializing in decoratively serged garments and embellishments on uniquely pieced clothing, Linda is fondly called the "Serger Lady" by those who know her best.

Linda worked for years in the home decorating field and has experience in pattern making. Now Linda owns her own business, Linda Lee Originals, and teaches serger techniques through shops, guilds, and national conventions. In addition, she has published a full line of patterns and educational materials on serging.

Linda has taught thousands of students to be comfortable with their sergers. Her goal is to help everyone become knowledgeable and comfortable in the exciting world of decorative serging. She has shared her knowledge on several PBS-TV shows such as "Quilting for the '90s" and "Kaye's Quilting Friends," and many of Linda's designs have appeared on other PBS shows as well. She helped organize the "Love Quilt Connection" and wrote for *Serger Update*. She also contributes to a sewing machine company's educational materials.

Linda loves the serger and helps others learn to love theirs as well.

Barbara Weiland

Barbara's lifelong passion for sewing began when she was a child. From doll clothes to dresses, she's sewn them all.

Her early hobby led to a B.S. in Textiles and Clothing from Colorado State University. She has held editorial positions at Butterick Publishing, Palmer/Pletsch, and Storey Communications. She was also the editor-in-chief of That Patchwork Place and the co-author of numerous sewing books.

Her most recent book is *Secrets for Successful Sewing*, published by Rodale Press. In this comprehensive book, Barbara explains scores of sewing machine and serger techniques.

An excellent teacher, Barbara has taught sewing workshops and contributed to other books, including the *Singer Sewing Reference Library* series. Her work also frequently appears in sewing magazines such as *Sew News*, where she was once the editor-in-chief. Now Barbara is a freelance editor, writer, and sewing consultant.

Introduction

Unlocking the Secrets of Beautiful Serging

The first time I ran a piece of fabric through a serger I was hooked. The ease. The precision. The gorgeous edge finish. What more could any garment sewer want?

It was 1983 and I'd returned to university to pursue a second career in textiles and clothing. My first sewing lab was a basic class on fitting and assembly. My professor realized that as a longtime garment sewer (ever since I could turn the handwheel on a toy sewing machine) I wasn't being challenged by her class.

One day she pointed at the sergers sitting against a wall by a window and commanded, "Learn."

I was terrified. Fortunately, my fear of flunking was overpowering. I approached the machines with trepidation. All those threads...the multiple tension dials, the threading paths...what if a thread broke?

Completing the first line of stitching was an epiphany. In the end, all I did was edge-finish the seam allowances with a 3-thread overlock before constructing my garment. I passed the course.

For years all I did was overlock edges. Never one for embellishing a garment, my poor little serger stagnated in the corner of the studio, loved but underutilized.

That was before this book. Actually, the discovery that a serger can do so much more than finish an edge started a bit sooner, with another Rodale Press book called *Secrets for Successful Sewing.* Author Barbara Weiland showed me many wonderful ways that I could use my serger. She continues to educate us in the pages of *Serger Secrets*, sharing the pages with Mary Griffin, Pam Hastings, Agnes Mercik, and Linda Lee Vivian.

You're learning from the best serger experts in North America. These women have logged thousands of hours on their many sergers, working out innovative techniques and clear instructions.

This collection of ideas, tips, and techniques is their offering to you. Any one of the subjects in "Tips and Techniques" will give you the information you need to create a stylish, one-of-a-kind garment.

The heart of the book consists of techniques listed in an A-through-Z format. It's written so that you can dip in and out of the information. You don't have to read the book from front to back, and you won't find yourself flipping between pages to get the complete instructions. Just open the book and head for your serger.

The information applies to any machine. In some cases the stitch width and length information isn't specific because the numbers aren't crucial and settings can vary between brands.

Most of the authors have affiliations with particular machine companies: Bernina, Pfaff, Singer, Husqvarna Viking, and White. You'll see all of these brands in the step-by-step photographs. (What an education this was for seamstress Sue Nester and me! Just when we were familiar with the location of the presser foot lifter on one machine, it was time to switch to another.)

If, like me, you sometimes want to explore the creative possibilities of a specific stitch, go to the index. There's an entry for every stitch, with a list of all the techniques that you can make with that stitch.

Another source of inspiration is "The Garment Gallery." This is a showcase of beautiful items created by the *Serger Secrets*

contributors. There are some great ideas that you can apply to your serging.

The part of the book that I'm most intrigued by is "Beyond the Basics." Often in sewing books this front section simply reviews general information. I wanted more, and the *Serger Secrets* authors agreed. As the name suggests, "Beyond the Basics" offers information that excites and informs both a beginner and a more skilled serger operator.

Throughout the creation of this book, the book team's primary goal has been your satisfaction. With every technique and every photograph we asked, "Does this give the reader information or inspiration?"

My personal goal is to continue the work that my professor started by shaking loose any of your residual serger fear.

My hope is that *Serger Secrets* will enable you to approach your serger with joy and satisfaction.

Susan Huxley

Susan Huxley
Editor

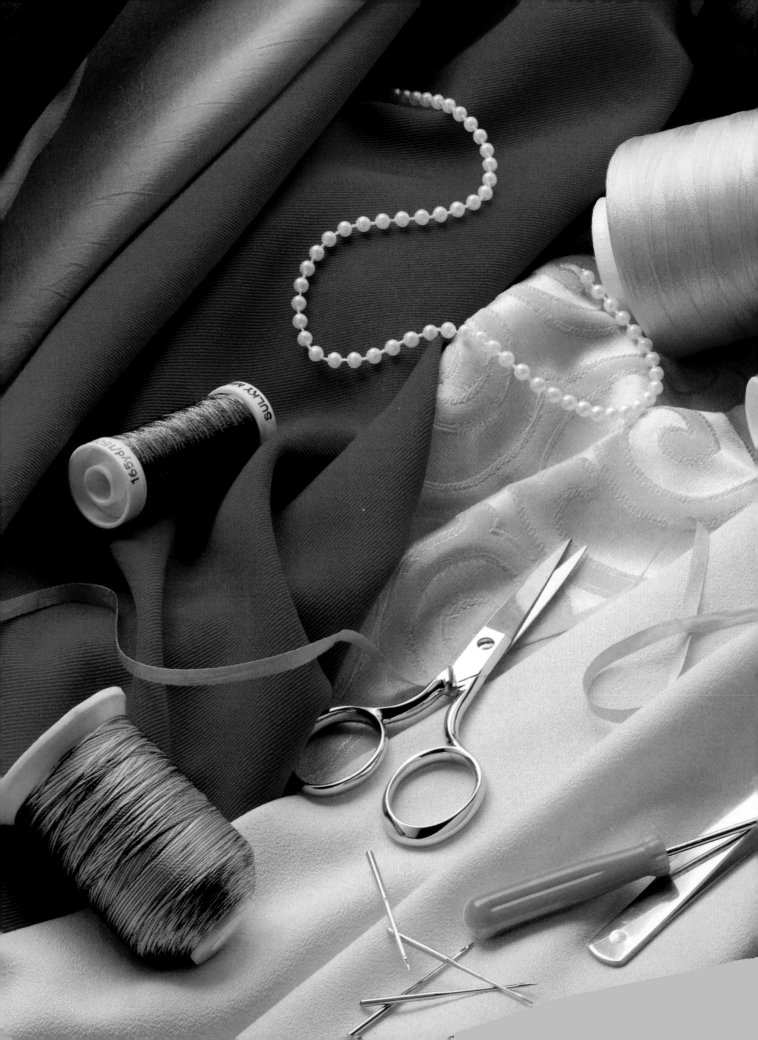

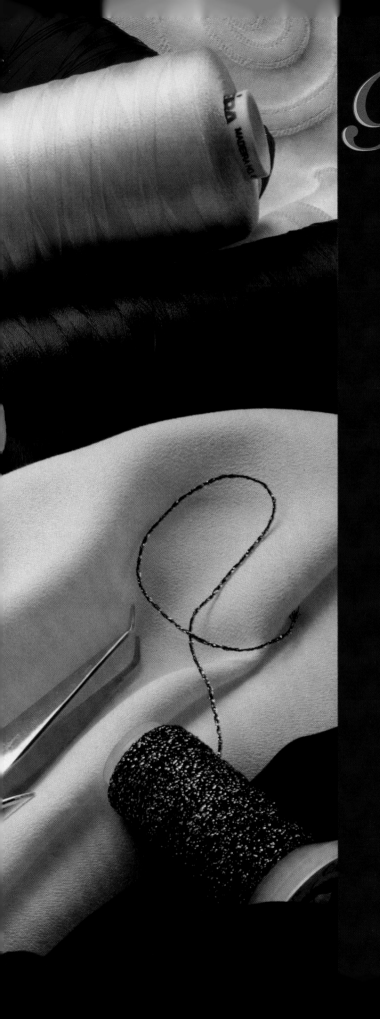

Beyond the Basics

What could be as simple—and yet as complex—as a serger? Remember how easy it was to make your first line of overlocking when you test-drove your serger at the dealership? The ease, speed, and accuracy of seaming and finishing the raw edge were delightful.

Yet things can start going very wrong very fast. Thread and needle selection, threading paths, tension settings, upper knife position, stitch fingers, throat plates, loopers…there are just so many variables.

To truly get the most from your serger, "Cutting Widths," "Feeding the Dogs," "Exploring Stitches and Tension," and "Skill Building" will help you gain an understanding of how the parts of this complex machine work and how all of the elements can be combined.

This wonderful machine can do so much more than finish a raw edge. "Beyond the Basics" gives you the knowledge to explore all of your serger's options.

Nuts and Bolts

The quality of your serger stitching depends on the smooth operation of many parts of this complex machine. The combination of anything from the cutting width and stitch finger to the differential feed and knives can greatly affect your results. In this chapter our serger experts explain some of the fine points.

CUTTING WIDTHS

The distance between the upper knife and the left or right needle is the cutting width. At the same time that you cut and serge your fabric, you create this width. Sewers use the term "seam allowance" for sewing machine work but apply "cutting width" to serger stitching. In many cases you're trimming off part of the seam allowance to obtain the cutting width, and the cutting width is usually encased in upper and lower looper threads, depending on the stitch.

It's best to fine-tune the cutting width using the two tests explained on page 5. Both these tests are applicable and important when using decorative threads and yarns. Since decorative threads come in a variety of textures, thicknesses, and "personalities," it's important for stitch density to be appropriate for the final appearance.

But as a general rule for average fabrics, if the edges curl when sewn, reduce the cutting width. On the other hand, if the loops on the fabric edge are too loose, increase the cutting width.

To set up the cutting width, there are several features that you use alone or in combination: the knives, needle position, and stitch finger.

Understanding the Knives

The two knives (also called blades) cut the fabric. (The upper knife is most visible, but there's also a lower knife, which actually moves the upper one.) On some machines

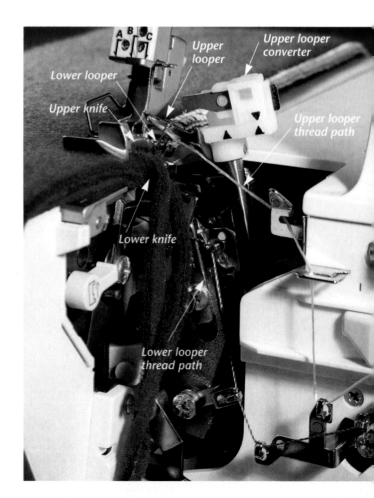

Several factors influence the quality of even a simple, balanced 3-thread overlock stitch: The thread paths of the upper and lower loopers, the distance between the upper and lower knives and line of needle stitching, and the position of the upper looper converter (disengaged) are all equally important. For Polarfleece (shown here), setting the differential feed to slightly gather is helpful, particularly when serging a single layer. Don't worry if the serger mechanisms intimidate you. This is like riding a bicycle—one day everything suddenly makes sense, and you never forget the lessons you've learned.

you can shift the position of the upper knife to the right or left, so that it cuts off more or less fabric to the right of the needle stitching.

When edge finishing, seaming, or making a rolled edge hem, it's always wise to trim some of the fabric slightly to ensure a good balanced stitch width or a well-rolled edge.

Positioning the Needles

Serger needles can't be moved, but you can use the right needle only or the left needle only, thus affecting the stitch width. On a 3/4-thread serger, for example, when you use both needles or the left needle alone, the seam allowance is wider. If you stitch with only the right needle, then the line of straight stitching is closer to the cut edge of the fabric.

Using the Stitch Finger

There is one more way of adjusting stitch width, and that's by changing the stitch finger. On some sergers, the stitch finger is adjusted as soon as you set up the width or the stitch selection. In other cases, you pull out and replace the stitch finger—or even switch the throat plate.

Most of us are familiar with the narrow and wide stitch fingers. But there's a third that's commonly overlooked, although you use it whenever you make a rolled hem. This narrowest stitch finger is commonly referred to as the rolled-hem stitch finger. It looks like a pin.

Try using it for stitches other than the rolled hem. You can set your stitch for overlock when you use this very narrow stitch finger. It works nicely for stitching seams on fine fabrics and for decorative applications, and it is good for the first step of a serger French seam (see page 144).

Sighting with the Foot

Needle placement and the exact cutting width are important when working on fabrics that take more care or a technique that involves accurate stitching lines. Marking your presser foot is one of the easiest ways to see where the stitching and cutting lines

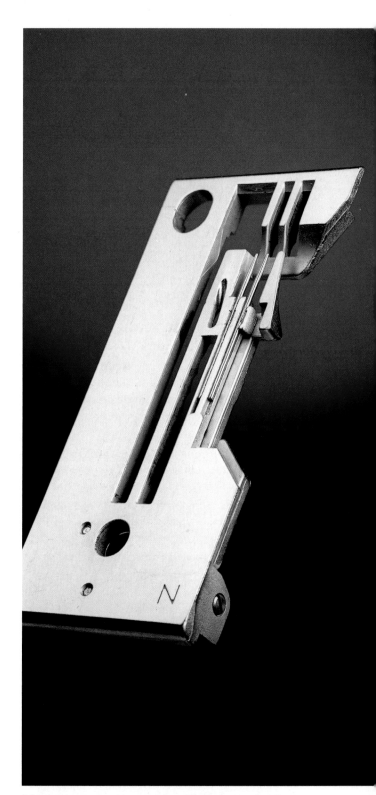

Most sergers are now made with the narrowest stitch finger built into the machine. A lever or knob engages the device. Some older models require that you replace the standard throat plate and presser foot. This plate has two narrow stitch fingers (the thin pins) plus an additional wider stitch finger to the right.

Usually, two center bumps on the presser foot indicate the needle positions, so all you need to do is make the bumps easier to see. The easiest way is to highlight the needle positions with a black permanent marking pen. Professional seamstresses find the red line on the far right quite useful. It's mainly for edge-finishing seams after the garment has been fitted.

will end up on your fabric. Then, all you have to do is guide the edge of your fabric by following the clearly visible marks on your presser foot.

Fine-Tuning the Cutting Width

If your machine has a knob or lever, the cutting width change takes just an instant.

The adjustment actually moves the lower knife. For instance, to include more fabric within the seam or rolled hem, move the dial to a higher number. The upper knife automatically moves out to the right as the lower knife pushes it out. To encourage a smoother movement, place your left finger on the upper knife screw, and push it slowly to the right.

Moving the upper knife to a lower number is easier because the pressure of the upper knife affects the movement of the lower knife.

Depending on your fabric or technique, you may be able to avoid tension adjustments by changing the cutting width. When roll-edge hemming, some stubborn fabric problems can be avoided by increasing the amount of fabric that's rolled into the seam. For loosely woven or thick fabrics, use the widest cutting width for greater protection.

The red line to the right on this presser foot indicates the cutting line. Place fabric slightly to the right of this line to cut off a sliver—enough for a good stitch. For greater visibility, continue this red line over the top of the presser foot with a red pen.

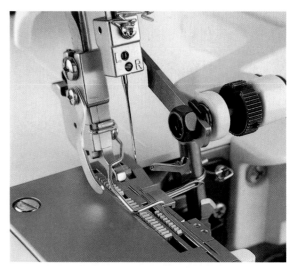

The upper knife on the machine in the photos above and to the left disengages by swinging up, rather than down. Two of the sergers shown throughout this book feature this option: the Bernina 2000DE and the Singer 14U555.

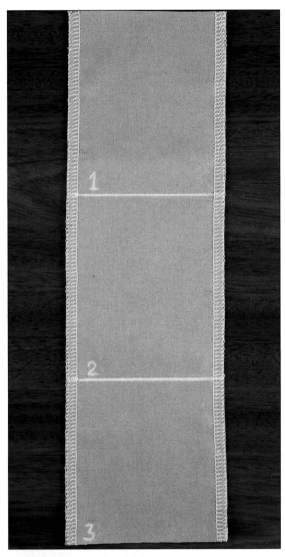

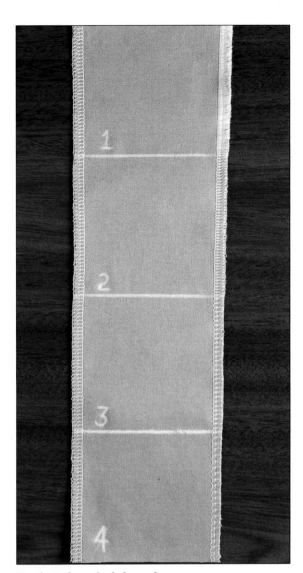

Testing the stitch width:

1. Cut two pieces of fabric measuring 3 × 12 inches (7.5 × 30 cm). Divide one piece of fabric into thirds, and place it on top of the other. Number each third to correspond with the numbers on the cutting dial. Set your machine for a 2.5-mm stitch length, 1.5- to 2-mm stitch width, and a balanced 4-thread stitch.

2. Adjust the cutting width to 1 mm, and stitch through both layers of fabric until you reach the first line. Turn the cutting width dial to 2 mm, and stitch to the next line. Turn the dial to 3 mm and serge off the fabric.

3. Look for the best section of stitching on the fabric. If the stitch needs more or less fabric to create a good seam, then fine-tune both looper tensions so that you end up with a well-balanced seam.

Testing the stitch length:

1. Cut two pieces of fabric measuring 3 × 12 inches (7.5 × 30 cm). Divide one piece of fabric into quarters, and place it on top of the other. Number each section. Set your machine for a 1-mm stitch length, 1.5- to 2-mm cutting width, and a balanced 4-thread stitch.

2. Serge to the first line. Change to a 2-mm stitch length and stitch to the next line. Continue until you have serged off the fabric.

3. Examine your sample, and review the fabric and stitch adjustments required for your project. If the cutting width is adequate, then you need to fine-tune the looper tensions.

FEEDING THE DOGS

Once you've used a serger that has differential feed, you won't want to do without it again. Although the fabric feeding system on any serger does have more "oomph" than its counterpart on a sewing machine, there are still times when you'll want even more from your serger.

Just turning a knob will make it easier to stitch a smooth hem on a knit dress or gather ruffles for a sleeve cuff. Serger expert Pam Hastings even finds it helpful when she's easing the cap of a set-in sleeve. These are quite a few functions from a single option! Essentially, you use the differential

feed system to gather or stretch fabric or to prevent puckers and ripples along your seams. So its job is both decorative and functional.

Sergers with differential feed capability actually have two sets of feed dogs, one directly in front of the other. The front feed moves forward or backward when you turn a dial on your serger.

The dial is adjusted to gather fabric at its highest setting or to stretch fabric at the lowest setting. It can also be set at various increments along this range.

The two sets of feed dogs on differential feed serger machines each have a unique function. The front set adjusts with the

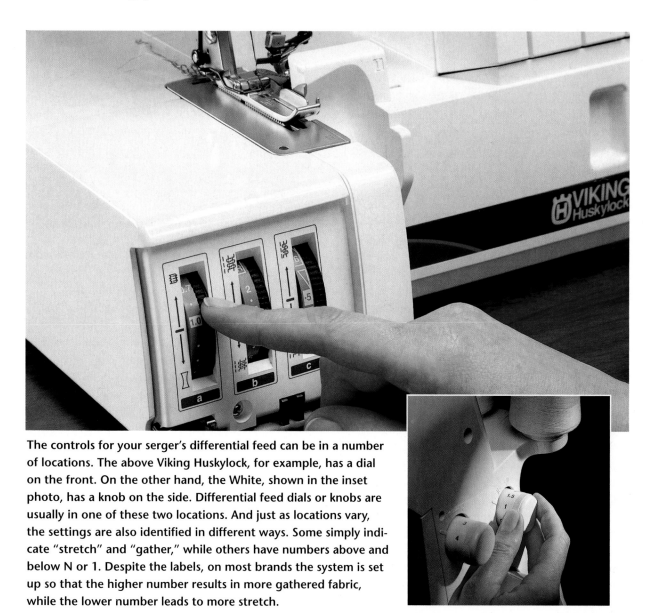

The controls for your serger's differential feed can be in a number of locations. The above Viking Huskylock, for example, has a dial on the front. On the other hand, the White, shown in the inset photo, has a knob on the side. Differential feed dials or knobs are usually in one of these two locations. And just as locations vary, the settings are also identified in different ways. Some simply indicate "stretch" and "gather," while others have numbers above and below N or 1. Despite the labels, on most brands the system is set up so that the higher number results in more gathered fabric, while the lower number leads to more stretch.

differential feed controls and actually pushes the fabric under the foot. The back set of feed dogs feeds the fabric out of the serger. The adjustment knob, or dial, sets the front feed dogs to take longer or shorter "strokes," thus feeding more—or less—fabric through the serger.

Get in the habit of using the differential settings in all areas of garment construction, from hems to sleeves. For example, a hem on an A-line skirt can be eased in no time with the gathering setting. This setting also works well on the curves of a shirttail hem. Likewise, differential feed can eliminate the frustration of puckering in lightweight fabrics by using a stretch setting. To become more familiar with the differential feed function on your serger, test a variety of fabric types and weights with the differential feed set at normal and then adjusted up or down. It's surprising to see how a seam that appears just adequate with the feed set at normal becomes perfect with a slight turn of a knob.

When set for gathering, the feed dogs actually move forward so that they're grabbing the fabric as it enters the machine. The feed dogs then force the fabric under the presser foot and through the serger. Adjust the setting to the highest number for gathers. If you want even more, or tighter, gathering, then tighten the needle tension.

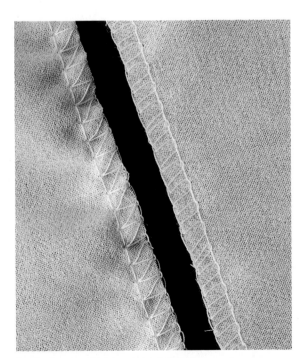

Puckering on lightweight fabric is a real nuisance. Yet a simple adjustment is enough to improve the appearance of stitching on this fabric. Turn the differential feed toward stretch. It doesn't take much, so test by adjusting the setting in small increments.

Stretching is desirable for a lettuce-leaf edging, but not for some other serging procedures. To prevent stretched or rippled seams when sewing on knits, set the differential feed in the gathering range. This draws in the fabric a bit, so it's completely flat.

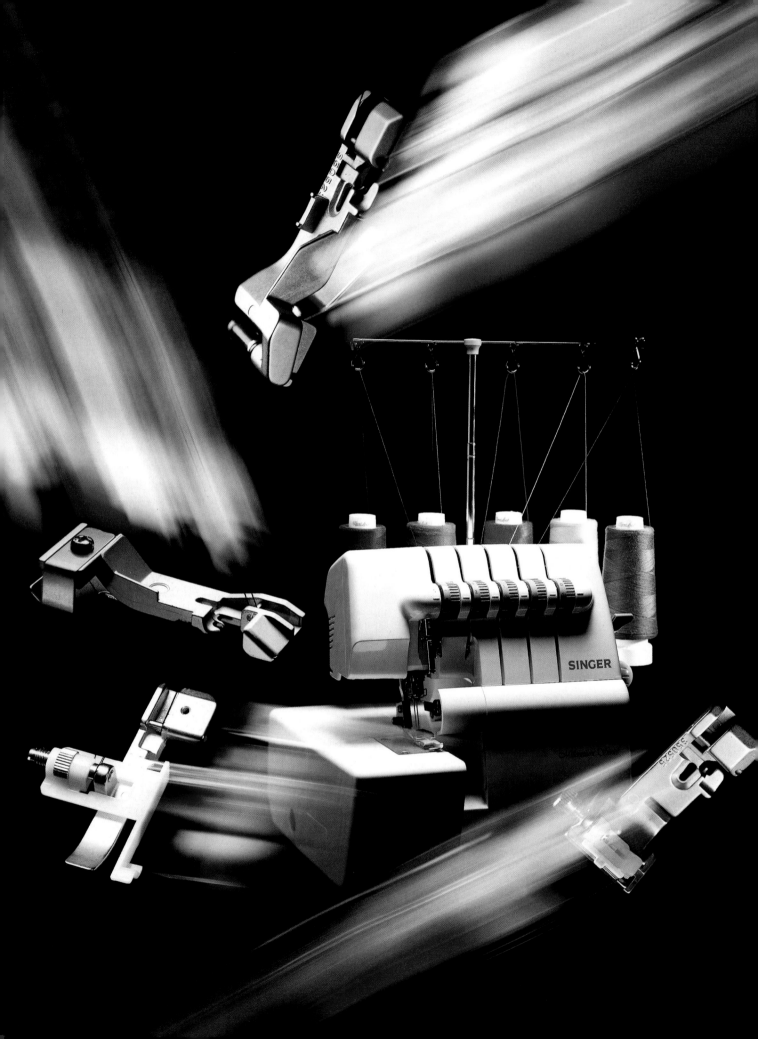

At the Improv

It isn't always necessary to to buy a special presser foot when you want to try your hand at a new serger technique. In this chapter, serger expert Mary Griffin gives you the lowdown. Equipped with her instructions, you'll find you can often improvise with a presser foot that's already on hand.

USING PRESSER FEET IN NEW WAYS

In the world of sergers, just like that of sewing machines, there's an overwhelming array of presser feet on which you can spend your precious dollars.

Just flip open the operator's guide that came with your serger, and look at the section on optional presser feet. There are probably at least five types of feet, including shirring, elastic tape, cording, blind-stitch, beading, and—just maybe—lace. This is the tip of the iceberg.

You'll find an even greater selection at your local sewing machine and serger dealer's store. Another good source is your favorite mail-order catalog of sewing notions and supplies.

Depending on the type of serging that you do, you may decide that some of these presser feet are very worthwhile. On the other hand, if you think that you may do a certain procedure or technique infrequently, then buying a specialized presser foot just isn't a good idea.

Imagine, for example, that you prefer to sew and wear clothes that have clean design lines—a tailored effect with nary a ruffle in sight. But your niece really, really wants you to make her a "fairy princess" dress for an upcoming family event. The fastest and easiest way to make such a garment is on your serger, with a gathering foot.

But if you don't have this foot, do you go out and buy one? No way! Do you refuse to make the outfit? Not a chance! Instead, turn to page 130 for instructions on how to gather fabric with a standard (or multipurpose) presser foot, then select your fabric, and head for your serger.

For quite a few techniques there are ways you can improvise by using the presser feet you have on hand. In other words, there's a good possibility that you can simply use the presser foot that was mounted on your serger when you first took it out of the box after you bought it.

In this chapter, you'll find instructions on how to bead and make a blind hem, plus how to apply lace, wire, or stay tape. The ideas on these pages are intended as launching points to get you thinking about

There are two fast and easy ways that you can gather fabric, even if you don't own a gathering foot. In the procedure shown here, the needle tension is tightened in order to draw up the fabric that's being serged. For complete instructions, see "No-Frills Easing" on page 130.

To use a blind-hem foot for applying lace, the foot needs to adjust far enough to the right for the needle to catch the lace when it sits in the groove of the foot.

other ways to improvise, have fun, and even save money.

The beauty of using the blind hemmer to overlock lace to fabric is the anatomy of this presser foot. There's a groove on the underside of the foot that helps you make the best possible stitching. The edge of the lace sits in this groove, thus protected from the knives that slice off the fabric as you stitch.

Serger expert Mary Griffin prefers a flat hem rather than a rolled one for this type of seaming. She says it's the best option because this seam presses flat. In a flat hem, the upper and lower looper threads balance on the edge of the fabric.

To try this out for yourself, serge with a narrow flat hem. Set up the machine to serge with an average or short (2-mm) stitch length. Remember to adjust the screw on the presser foot so that the guide moves to the right, and let the knives trim off some of the fabric as you serge along the lace.

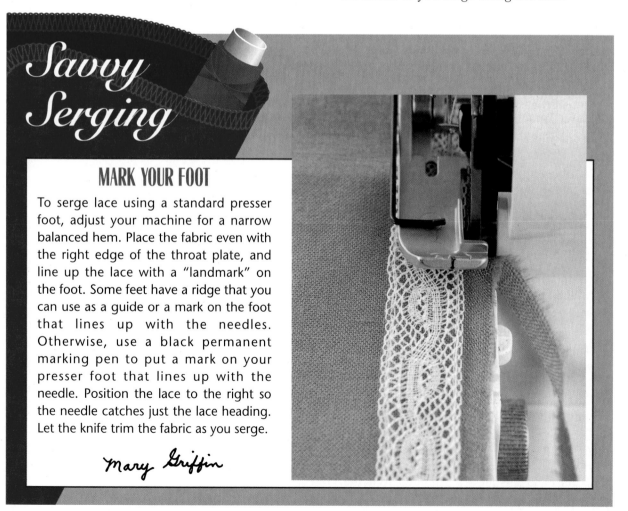

Savvy Serging

MARK YOUR FOOT

To serge lace using a standard presser foot, adjust your machine for a narrow balanced hem. Place the fabric even with the right edge of the throat plate, and line up the lace with a "landmark" on the foot. Some feet have a ridge that you can use as a guide or a mark on the foot that lines up with the needles. Otherwise, use a black permanent marking pen to put a mark on your presser foot that lines up with the needle. Position the lace to the right so the needle catches just the lace heading. Let the knife trim the fabric as you serge.

Mary Griffin

Take a look at the toe on your standard presser foot. Is there a hole? If this is the case, then you're in luck because you can still serge wire or cord into your rolled hem while maintaining some degree of control over the "filler."

Thread some wire (or other filler) up through the opening in the toe of the presser foot. This hole is a great help for guiding the wire into the correct position, but you still need to do some handwork. Run the wire over the top of the foot and to the right of the needle. You're probably stitching with the upper knife engaged, so while you're operating the machine you need to ensure that the wire is to the left of the upper knife. Otherwise, the knife will hit the wire and both will be damaged.

If your foot is solid, without an opening in the toe, simply lay the wire over the top of the foot.

Regardless of the type of presser foot you use, stop periodically and push the wire over, against the ridge of the foot, in order to straighten out the wire. This keeps the wire in the correct position for stitching.

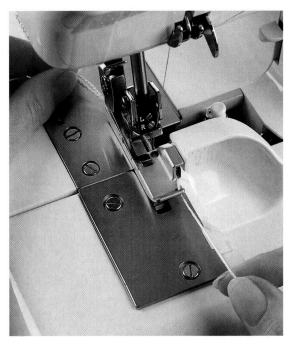

Adding cord into a rolled edge is tricky at times. For this sample, the serger expert used heavy cord and a 3-thread rolled edge stitch. In this case, she threaded the serger with texturized nylon thread (Woolly Nylon) in the upper looper and all-purpose polyester thread in the needle and lower looper.

You don't need a foot to bead! Use the left needle (if possible), monofilament thread, and a long 3-thread overlock. Serge the beads onto the fabric, to the right of the needle. Guide them with one hand and pull them through, from the back, with the other hand.

To serge a blind hem with a standard foot, fold the fabric in the usual manner. Align the fold with the right needle mark on the foot. Use a 3-thread overlock with the upper knife engaged, and just catch the very edge of the fold with the right needle.

Needles

The most important part of any serging is using the correct needle. Since most sergers now use the same needle type as household sewing machines, we now have more versatility. We can sew more easily on everything from silk to leather with the help of specialized needles.

GETTING TO THE POINT

Needles don't always receive the attention they deserve. By choosing them wisely, you'll find that fabrics and threads are easier to handle, and stitch quality will improve. In fact, simple steps, such as changing needles when they're dull, make all the difference.

To choose the right needle, you need to understand its anatomy. A needle consists of a shank, shoulder, scarf, eye, and point.

The part that's inserted into the machine is the shank. The rest of the needle is the blade. This includes the shoulder (the tapered section under the shank), scarf, eye, and point. The scarf is the indentation on the back, just above the eye. Another groove, on the front, protects the thread as it's pulled through the fabric. Next comes the eye and then the point. Eye size increases with the diameter of the needle.

The point is designed in several configurations. Gone are the days of simply deciding between a sharp or ballpoint, because needle manufacturers provide products that keep up with the rapid innovations in fabrics, threads, and yarns. We can get even better stitch quality thanks to this new technology.

Quality serger stitching depends on appropriate needle size. The needle should be large enough for good penetration without deflecting but not so large that it damages the fabric.

When serging, there's yet another reason to select carefully. To avoid hitting the loopers, stick to 70/10, 80/12, and 90/14. Needle size is pretty easy to identify, especially if you're comparing extremes—like a 60/8 to a 90/14. Differences in type, on the other hand, are subtle. For example, it's nearly impossible to see the length of a groove on the front. Nevertheless, structure does affect your stitching. The next page offers guidance on choosing the right needle.

Keep a selection of needles on hand, and make sure they meet the specifications for your machine. It's best to have several of each size and type so you're not caught in a bind when doing some last-minute stitching. Who wants to head to the store in the middle of a sewing session?

CHOOSING THE RIGHT NEEDLE

Many stitching problems, such as puckered seams, skipped stitches, and broken threads, are solved simply by changing the type or size of needles in your serger. By understanding the design of the various needle types, you'll know how to make the best choice for the task at hand. (Leather needles, which are rarely used, are not listed here.)

BALLPOINT

A rounded point makes it easier to stitch knits without dam-  aging the fibers. Rather than piercing the fibers, the rounded point slips between them. This prevents skipped stitches, snags, and holes in the fabric. There are some heavier or bulkier fabrics, such as stretch wovens and Polarfleece, that resemble knit construction and may require a 90/14 ballpoint.

EMBROIDERY

Most often used for decorative work, this needle is designed for delicate threads. The point is slightly rounded, and the eye is larger to prevent lightweight threads from shredding and breaking. The needle holds up to the higher temperatures created by the friction of decorative threads. The larger eye and groove improve thread protection and handling.

JEANS

This needle is designed to penetrate very densely woven fabrics, such as denim and home decorating and outerwear fabrics, and multilayered projects. The very sharp point creates good, straight stitches. The needle is now available in a small needle size (70/10) for lighter-weight, stubborn, woven fabrics such as silk and sandwashed rayon.

METALLIC

Fragile metallic threads fray and break very easily. It's much easier to stitch them with a needle that's specially designed to resolve this problem. The metallic needle has a slightly round point, a deeper groove along the front of the blade, and a much larger eye, which has a synthetic coating. With this needle you can use multiple threads.

MICROFIBER AND MICROTEX

By Lammertz Nadelin and Schmetz, respectively, these two brand-name needles have a sharp point similar to the Jeans needle. In addition to handling miocrofibers, which are very densely woven, these needles handle sandwashed rayons, silks, and other stubborn synthetic "silkies" quite well. The precision of this type of needle is great for penetrating delicate laces and fabrics.

QUILTING

A thin, long, tapered point prevents unexpected problems when stitching through fragile materials. The quilting needle is particularly helpful when seaming and cross-seaming because it won't damage your fabric. Be prepared to change needles more frequently because stitching through batting, particularly synthetic, dulls a needle quickly.

STRETCH

Aerobic wear, swimwear, lingerie, and braided elastic are easier to stitch with a stretch needle. The eye is higher up the shaft so there's less friction on the thread. The tiny hump between the eye and the scarf (on the back) eases the stitch formation by creating a larger loop on one side of the needle. The rounded point is somewhere between a universal and a ballpoint.

TOPSTITCH

The eye on this needle is about twice the size of a regular universal needle. This makes it possible to use heavier topstitching thread without switching to a thicker needle that would damage the fabric. The needle also has a very sharp point and a large groove to accommodate topstitching threads.

UNIVERSAL

This needle, sometimes referred to as "in between," is generically used for most basic, easy-to-sew fabrics. Designed with a slightly rounded point, it sews fairly well on both knit and woven fabrics.

Glorious Thread

Whether you're new to serging or have plenty of experience, threads offer many artistic and practical options for your stitching. The brilliance and luster of rayons, metallics, and blends enhance any garment, and quality thread increases the longevity of your garment.

SELECTING THE BEST

At times we blame our machines when something goes wrong, but the culprit can be the thread. Since the serger stitches so fast, thread strength and quality are very important. Top-quality thread breaks less and produces fewer skipped stitches, provided that the needle is also in good shape.

Though there are many types on the market today, all threads have to have certain things in common: strength, flexibility, and an appealing appearance.

For practical seaming, strength and elongation (stretchability) lead to good quality stitching. Choose thread that has a uniform diameter and a minimum of knots, weak spots, uneven twists, and slubs (clumps of overspun thread). It's these weak links that cause a thread to break. Though bargain brands may be tempting, the money saved is not worth the frustration.

Examine thread carefully. Most inferior threads are made from the linters of good threads. It's these short, leftover filaments that give the hairy appearance you see on the lesser grades. With your thumb and forefinger, run along a length of thread. You can feel the slubs and uneven twists that create the thick and thin areas.

Do the twist to test your thread quality. Unwind 2 to 4 feet (.6 to 1.2 m) of thread from the spool or cone. Grasp the two ends and bring them together. At this point a wide loop is created, and you can see if the thread winds around itself. If it does, you don't have a balanced thread.

What's the twist? Hold a length of thread between your left and right hands. Grasp each end with a thumb and forefinger. Roll your right finger and thumb to twist the thread toward you. If the thread strands wind tighter, the thread has a left twist. However if the strands loosen, the thread is a right-twist thread.

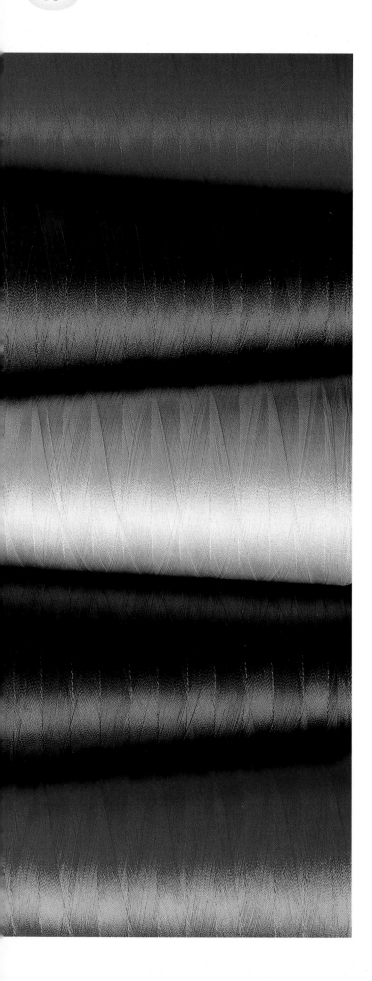

Understanding Thread

Basically, serger thread is available on either cones or tubes in large quantities. It's cross-wound to feed from the top, which is best for high-speed serging. Since typically, more thread is used in serging than in regular machine sewing, serger thread is more lightweight than all-purpose sewing machine thread. Serger seams, therefore, remain supple despite all the thread that's needed for each stitch.

Color also makes a difference. The heavily dyed threads need more of your attention; be aware that normal tension ranges need fine-tuning, most often to a slightly higher number.

Some brands of parallel-wound all-purpose thread are a heavier weight than serger thread but can be used for serger stitching. Place the notched side down and use a spool cap for even feeding. You may also want to try horizontal spool holders. And by all means, s-t-i-t-c-h s-l-o-w-e-r.

Good thread has a balanced twist. Many machines require a left-twist thread for the needle, although you can use a right-twist thread in most loopers. To be consistent, use the same twist in all positions.

The most widely available serger thread is 100 percent polyester, which has some elasticity and good strength. The best is core-spun, which has the most uniform surface finish possible.

Listing all the beautiful threads that are on the market would take an entire page of this book—or more! Rayon was a favorite in the photography studio while making this book because it catches the light and shines so beautifully. If you want your stitching to stand out without being too obvious, this is a good choice. In other situations, you may want to try a highly specialized product—something variegated (for extra color), for example. A metallic thread can be round or flat. In either case, opt for a less expensive, smaller cone or spool, and use a horizontal spool adapter or thread net to control the way it feeds into the machine.

Except in extreme situations, there is no need to purchase three to five cones of each color every time you make a garment. Unless you want a decorative effect, match thread that's visible on the right side of the garment.

Think of blending thread colors to match your fabrics. For example, gray blends nicely with a lot of medium-tone fabrics, and off-white or ivory blends well with lighter shades of thread.

Experiment with different weights and textures of decorative threads and fabrics, including pearl rayon, rayon thread, metallic thread, ribbon floss, and tinsel thread. Metallic threads look wonderful on dark backgrounds. Bronze Glamour on black is very striking. Another great look is tone on tone—for example, white Designer 6 on white linen. Even if decorative stitching isn't your "thing," try this tonal look; when it is stitched on the edge of a patch pocket, it really adds just the right touch.

Savvy Serging

MAKE A MATCH

I love using Candlelight, Glamour, Pearl Crown Rayon, Burmilana, Jeans Stitch, and Silk Stitch #30 thread in the chain-stitch looper. Opt for a longer stitch and decrease the chain-stitch looper tension. To avoid skipped stitches, I use an ELx705 Schmetz needle (for sergers). It's slightly longer and has deep grooves in the front and back of the scarf. For this colorful vest I randomly quilted with a variety of Burmilana threads that complement the colors in the fabric.

Linda Lee Vivian

DECORATIVE THREADS

These are the threads with "personality-plus." Even a simple stitch will sing when worked in one of the beautiful choices shown on these four pages. Whenever you want to make a special stitch, just review the options in this table.

THREAD TYPE	DESCRIPTION AND APPLICATIONS	HANDLING TIPS
Acrylic embroidery	• Shown in the upper looper • High-sheen • Tightly twisted • Fine • Beautiful for rolled edges, heirloom serging, and other decorative applications	Use this thread in the needles and loopers as desired. Shorten the stitch length for better coverage.
Acrylic/wool, such as Burmilana	• Shown in the lower looper • Fine • Wool-like texture • Perfect for flatlocking and edge finishing on woolens and similar fabrics	Use in the loopers with normal tension adjustments for the stitch you're using.
Cotton embroidery	• Shown in the upper looper • Soft, fine • High luster • Particularly appropriate for heirloom serger techniques	Use in the needle and the loopers and adjust tensions for the desired stitch.
Crochet	• Shown in the upper looper • Strong • High-twist cotton or acrylic • Challenging to use, but great for decorative finishes, particularly 3-thread overlocked edges and flatlocking	Use only in the loopers. Loosen the tension considerably; lengthen and widen the stitch. You may need to remove the thread from one or more thread guides. Rewind the ball onto an empty serger thread cone.

THREAD TYPE	DESCRIPTION AND APPLICATIONS	HANDLING TIPS
Elastic	• Shown in the chain-stitch looper • Stretchy • Great for serger shirring and smocking • Use it on the lower looper with a decorative thread on the upper looper to create rolled edge chain for wonderful button loops and decorative trim	Experiment with tensions for the desired technique and effect. Generally, you need to loosen the tension somewhat.
Fusible	• Shown in the lower looper, this sample is wrong side up • Heat-sensitive nylon filament melts when steam heat is applied • Great for fuse-basting braid • Edge a patch pocket, then steam baste and topstitch • Use it in the lower looper with a decorative thread in the upper looper to create rolled edge chain	Use with a 3-thread overlock stitch, and adjust tensions and stitch for the desired effect with decorative thread in the looper. The closer the stitches, the more fusible thread on the underside, which leads to firmer fusing.
Hologram	• Shown in the upper looper • Ribbonlike film with pinpoints of dazzling reflective color • Adds exciting sheen to decoratively serged edges, trims, and flat-locked seams	Place on a horizontal spool feeder, and use it in the upper looper. Loosen the tension considerably, or try Woolly Nylon or monofilament thread in the lower looper. Don't use it in the needle. This thread is heat sensitive, so take care when pressing.
Lamé and tinsel	• Shown in the needle for a chain stitch • Flat, Mylar, ribbonlike • Metallized with aluminum for high reflection • Perfect for decorative applications	Place on a horizontal spool feeder and use it in the upper looper. Loosen the tension considerably, or try Woolly Nylon or monofilament thread in the lower looper. Don't use it in the needle. This thread is heat sensitive, so take care when pressing.
Machine needlepunch and machine knitting yarns	• Shown in the upper looper • Very fine yarns • Great for decorative applications, especially on woolens, Polarfleece, sweatshirting, and other textured fabrics, including handwovens and knits made from acrylic, cotton, or wool	Only use in the loopers. Thicker yarns aren't suitable for the lower looper. Loosen the tension considerably. If necessary, remove the yarn from one or more thread guides and the tension discs, and try a wider, longer stitch.

(continued)

DECORATIVE THREADS—CONTINUED

THREAD TYPE	DESCRIPTION AND APPLICATIONS	HANDLING TIPS
Metallic embroidery	• Shown in the upper looper • Metallic foil twisted with polyester or nylon for added strength • Use it in both loopers and in the needle for decorative edges and seams • For a rolled edge, place it only in the upper looper	Loosen the tension quite a bit. Apply a lubricant such as Sewer's Aid to prevent friction and static electricity. If the needle thread shreds, switch to a larger needle. Use a shorter stitch length for even better coverage.
Metallic (heavy)	• Shown in the upper looper • Fuller, loftier metallic • Gives good edge coverage and lots of shine • Appropriate for many decorative serger applications	Position it in loopers only, and loosen the tension slightly. Use a longer, wider stitch.
Monofilament nylon or polyester	• Shown in the needle • Wiry • Transparent • Use in the needle or the loopers when you don't want the thread to show, when doing flatlock couching, for example	Start with normal tension and fine-tune as needed. Use the clear color for light- to medium-color fabrics, and use the smoke color on darker fabrics.
Pearl cotton embroidery	• Shown in the upper looper • Shiny, soft • Lovely luster • Great for flatlocking, edge finishing, and making braid trims • Most commonly used weights are #5 and #8	Use in the upper looper only with matching cotton or rayon thread in the needle. Loosen the looper tension, and use a longer, wider stitch. Serge slowly for smooth stitching. If necessary, remove thread from one or more thread guides to achieve perfect tension.
Pearl rayon	• Shown in the upper looper • Twisted threads • Very flexible • Easy to serge for decorative over-locked and rolled edges • Makes beautiful serger braid • Flatlocks nicely • Try it in both loopers for a reversible edge	Don't use it in the needle. When overlocking, slightly loosen the tension, and use a short stitch length. For a rolled edge, use it in the upper looper only, and thread the lower looper with Woolly Nylon or monofilament for a tight roll. For flatlocking, tighten the needle tension slightly.

THREAD TYPE	DESCRIPTION AND APPLICATIONS	HANDLING TIPS
Rayon embroidery	• Shown in the upper looper • Fine, shiny thread • Lovely for decorative rolled edges and delicate flatlocking • The heavier 30-weight provides more coverage • Particularly nice for heirloom serging • A less expensive alternative to silk thread	May break in the needle. If this happens, substitute a matching color all-purpose or acrylic thread. For a rolled edge, use it only in the upper looper. Cover the spool with netting to keep the thread from pooling.
Rayon (heavy), like Decor 6	• Shown in the upper looper • Multistrand • High luster • Perfect for decorative rolled edges, decorative flatlocking, and 3-thread overlock edge finishes	Only use it in the loopers. Loosen the tension and use a wider, slightly longer stitch for flatlocking and overlocking. For a rolled edge finish only, place it in the upper looper.
Ribbon and ribbon floss, 1/16- to 1/4-inch (1.5-mm to 6-mm) widths	• Ribbon floss shown in the upper looper • This category includes soft silk, rayon, acrylic, and cotton ribbons and ribbon floss • Lustrous • Good for decorative serging • Nylon and polyester ribbons are too stiff	Use in the upper looper with the tension loosened considerably. Possibly remove the ribbon from one or more thread guides and the tension discs. Try a longer, wider stitch.
Topstitching, buttonhole twist, cordonnet	• Shown in the upper looper • Made of polyester • Heavy thread • Strong, lustrous, and heavier than regular sewing thread • Ideal for many decorative serging techniques	This thicker thread requires a larger needle size to avoid shredding. It's one of the easiest threads to use. If not packaged on a cone, use a spool cap to help this thread feed evenly.
Woolly Nylon	• Shown in the upper looper • Suitable for soft, stretchy seams in lingerie, knits, and active sportswear • Blend with weaker threads to improve their strength • Because it isn't twisted, it fans out for excellent coverage • Available in a heavier version for even better coverage	Can be used in all positions. To insert this crimped, untwisted thread through the needle, use a dental-floss threader. You may need to loosen the tension somewhat. In the lower looper, it helps form a rolled edge.

Exploring Stitches and Tension

Many owners do only the basics with their machines and never learn to experiment with the numerous, exciting abilities of the serger. That's what this book is all about, and we hope you'll go beyond the basics and learn everything your serger can do.

UNDERSTANDING STITCHES

You may be surprised at the number of stitches your serger makes. For example, many people have 2-thread capability on their machine and don't even realize it.

Because we want a machine that can do a variety of stitches, there are ways to manipu-late a serger to achieve many different stitches. Two-thread serging is a good example. A "spreader" (sometimes called a "converter") blocks the eye of the upper looper and tricks the lower looper into thinking it's the upper looper. The right needle thread acts as the lower looper thread. Look for a small device that blocks the hole in the upper looper. A spreader can be a separate item or can be attached to or near the upper looper.

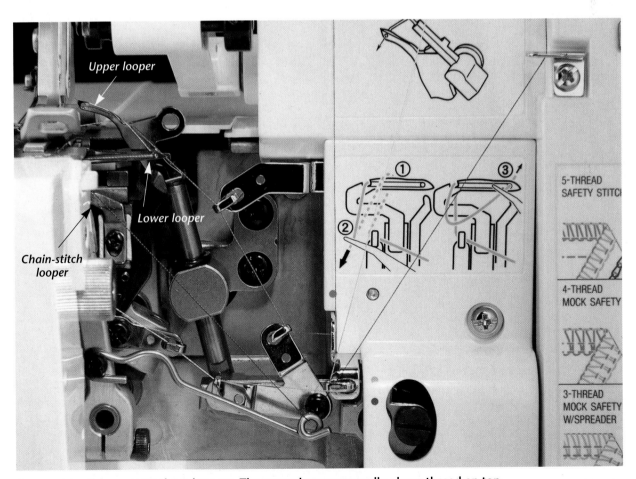

Sergers have from one to three loopers. The upper looper normally places thread on top of the fabric. The lower looper places thread on the bottom. The chain-stitch (and/or) cover-stitch looper creates the underside of the appropriate stitch. To show the thread paths, all loopers are threaded in this photo, but no stitch uses all the loopers at once.

TAMING TENSION

After threading, working with the tensions on a serger is one of the most anxiety-inducing activities that a serger owner masters. To their credit, serger manufacturers are addressing both of these situations head-on by introducing machines that offer self-threading or easy access to the lower looper and automatic tension adjustments.

Take heart if you don't have a top-of-the-line machine and want to make your stitching perfect. It's like riding a bicycle—tough at first, but soon it's second nature. There will come a day when you find yourself having fun coming up with neat new stitches by playing with the tension adjustments on your serger.

Sergers are interesting because a slight change in one setting can affect another

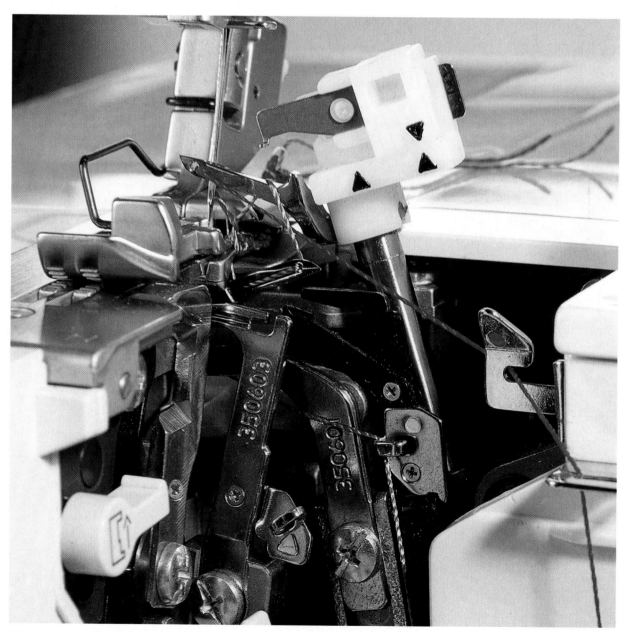

The serger certainly forms stitches differently from a sewing machine. One or two needles are used at a time, along with one or two of the three loopers. (The needle-and-looper combination depends on the stitch you select.) The needles move up and down, while the loopers move from side to side. The stitches are formed by a knitting of threads. Two knives cut the fabric as scissors would.

setting. For example, tightening a needle tension may make the lower looper tighter. Increasing the stitch length and width can also change the tensions.

Getting Started

Serge a sample of each stitch, and watch where the threads go on the fabric. Once you've made a stitch, compare it to the proper formation in the table "Easing the Tension" on pages 28–31.

Look for the thread or threads that are too loose, and begin to tighten them by about a half-turn at a time until you achieve a good stitch. Tightening the tension means less thread is released onto the fabric. Loosening the tension means more thread will be available to go onto the fabric. Loosen by turning the dial to a lower number.

Cross Correctly

Most sergers recommend you thread the upper looper first. If not, when you do thread the upper looper, it's important to turn your handwheel toward you until you can't see the lower looper.

After threading, make sure that the upper looper thread is behind (or underneath) the lower looper thread. If they're crossed the other way, the thread will break. If you need to rethread after a jam, make sure your looper threads are crossed correctly before you start again. And don't forget to place the threads underneath the back of the foot before starting to serge.

It's also a good idea to hold the loose threads behind the foot when you're starting to serge to prevent threads from curling forward into the stitches that are being formed.

Savvy Serging

GO IN ORDER

Check your serger threading chart for the proper threading order. If you're having stitching problems, the culprit could be the way that your threads cross each other as they wind their way through the thread paths. A good way to understand stitches and tension is to thread your serger with colors that match your tension discs. Begin by labeling each tension disc or dial with its proper name. Your machine may not have a chain-stitch looper (shown here at far right), depending on the stitch options that your brand and model offer.

Mary Griffin

Left needle   Right needle   Upper looper   Lower looper   Chain-stitch looper

SING

EASING THE TENSION

You're not alone if you are having tension trouble, because this is the number one problem for many serger owners. To ease the pain, start with the recommended settings. If your test doesn't look quite right, compare it to the photos. Chances are the solution may be right on these pages.

2-THREAD CHAIN STITCH

Needle tension correct

Needle tension too loose

The raw edges aren't clean-finished; nevertheless, if you're buying a serger consider one with a chain-stitch option. This stitch creates strong, straight seams, elasticized shirring (see page 192), decorative tucks (page 197), and topstitching (page 32). To stitch, you need to "block" the upper looper. See page 25 for instructions.

2-THREAD OVEREDGE

Needle tension correct

Needle tension too tight or looper tension too loose

Needle tension too loose or looper tension too tight

Also called a flatlock stitch, it isn't appropriate for regular seaming because the stitch locks at the edge rather than at the needle line. It's effective for seam and edge finishes on lightweight fabrics and for decorative seams and edges.

3-THREAD FLATLOCK

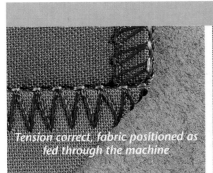
Tension correct, fabric positioned as fed through the machine

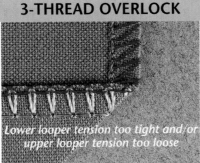
Tension correct, fabric stitched, then opened

Lower looper tension too loose and/or needle tension too tight

The next time you go clothes shopping take a look at the seaming, topstitching, and hems on the casual garments. There's a very good chance you'll see examples of 2- and 3-thread flatlocking. It's also suitable for other decorative uses, such as fagoting (see page 123), shirring (see page 192), and smocking, plus lace applications (see pages 142 and 146).

3-THREAD OVERLOCK

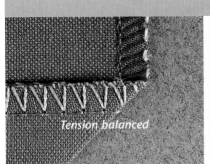
Tension balanced

Lower looper tension too tight and/or upper looper tension too loose

Upper looper tension too tight and/or lower looper tension too loose

Without a 3-thread overlock, most sewers would still be pinking or binding the raw edges of the seam allowances on their garments. So it's no surprise that most sewers buy sergers primarily for overlocking. The stitch is used to seam wovens and knits as well as to create both decorative seams and edges.

4-THREAD OVERLOCK

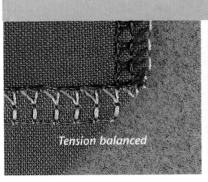
Tension balanced

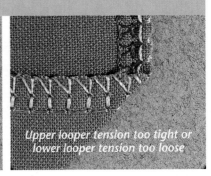
Upper looper tension too loose or lower looper tension too tight

Upper looper tension too tight or lower looper tension too loose

Knits and wovens benefit from the strong, elastic seam that's made with a 4-thread overlock. However, it can also be used for decorative purposes on both edges and seams. You can easily convert to 3-thread overlocking by removing one of the two needles: Serge with only the right needle for a narrow stitch, but use just the left needle for a wider version. Tension adjustments are the same as shown for the 3-thread overlock stitch (above). Watch that the tension on the right needle thread isn't too loose.

(continued)

EASING THE TENSION—CONTINUED

COVER STITCH

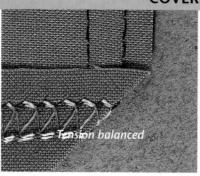
Tension balanced

Needle tension too loose

In the garment industry there's a specialized machine for the cover stitch. Home sewers don't want to buy a single-feature item, but since sergers became readily available in the 1970s, they've asked for this stitch. Twenty-odd years later the technical glitches were resolved and it became available on some sergers. The technology quickly expanded. Within a few short years, a cover stitch with a third line of needle stitching was added to some sergers. It's relatively easy to balance the tension on this stitch because you may need only to adjust the needles. When the needle tension is too tight (not shown), a tunnel forms between each set of stitching lines, as you sometimes see with twin needle work. The cover stitch is used for hemming knits, attaching ribbing, binding, and applying lace and elastic.

ROLLED EDGE STITCH

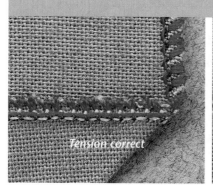
Tension correct

Lower looper tension too loose or upper looper tension too tight

Needle tension too loose

This is the second most popular stitch. You see the rolled edge stitch on the edge of garments, accessories, and home decor items like napkins, bows, and some lightweight tablecloths. Worked with either two or three threads, you can reinforce the edge with cord (see page 109), fishing line (see page 113), and even wire (see page 121).

After you've mastered the tension adjustments for the rolled edge, you could still be searching for that elusive perfect stitch. Fabric type and grainline, thread selection, needle position, and cutting width all can conspire against you. The "Problem Solver," which starts on page 220, has solutions. For a thicker fabric, it's best to abandon the rolled edge for the wider wrapped stitch.

SAFETY STITCH

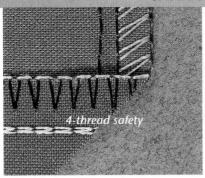

4-thread safety

5-thread safety

A chained seam running parallel to an overlocked edge is the distinguishing feature of a safety stitch. It's used for sturdy seams on wovens, particularly on fabrics that tend to stretch, like sweater knits, or pucker. Four- or five-thread combinations are available. If you're unhappy with the amount of thread that's visible at the seamline on the right side of the garment, a safety stitch is a good option. As well as being sturdy, the line of chain stitching holds the fabric together more than other serger stitches. The 4-thread mock safety stitch (not shown) doesn't have a chain stitch. From the right (needle) side, the mock safety looks like the real thing, but the underside reveals its true nature. There isn't a row of interlocking loops at the seamline. Instead, the stitching looks like a standard 4-thread overlock stitch.

WRAPPED STITCH

Try the wrapped stitch for a reversible edge on your jacket, sweater, or blanket. The appearance varies, depending on the type and number of threads. It's best to use a 2-thread version for lighter fabrics. Tension adjustments are the same as the rolled edge stitch. Note, however, that the fabric edge doesn't roll under when you make the wrapped stitch.

Tension correct

Decorative Stitching

Beautiful threads and a rapidly increasing repertoire of serger stitches make it possible for you to explore many dynamic uses for your machine. From the humble tail chain to the more involved cover stitch, you can duplicate the decorative looks that you see on designer garments. In this chapter serger experts offer ideas for placement and tips for applying your embellishments.

CHAIN STITCHING

Do you think of the chain stitch as purely functional? Most people do. After all, for years serger owners have used it alone, for basting, or else combined it with over-locking to make a very strong seam. Yet this safety stitch is really rather pretty when stitched with decorative threads.

If you have a 5-thread, or a "true" 4-thread serger, then setting up the chain stitch is rather simple. (A true 4-thread serger was an older serger model that did a chain stitch on the left and a 2-thread finish along the cut edge. By using only the chain

Decorative chain stitching is a favorite embellishment for serger expert Linda Lee Vivian. On this wool car coat she used two different colors of Burmilana thread in the chain-stitch looper to create the special color effects on the lapels. Because there were two threads through the same looper, she loosened the tension to ac-commodate the extra bulk. She then stitched ran-domly to create the wavy lines. To continue the color blending theme, contrasting threads were used in the upper and lower loopers to overlock the edges of the coat with a balanced 3-thread stitch. As the lapel rolls back at the break point, you begin to see the contrast color—a unique designer touch.

needle and the chain looper, this older model does a nice chain stitch.) The chain stitch can also be made on some cover stitch sergers by dropping one of the two needles.

The chain stitch is created with the fabric wrong side up in the machine so you don't see the decorative chain stitching until you turn the fabric over.

The chain stitch is formed with two threads: one in the chain-stitch needle and one in the chain-stitch looper. Your serger manual shows the location of this special looper and needle on your specific machine. The threads form the chain when they meet under the presser foot.

The "chain" doesn't start until the two threads actually meet on the fabric, so you always insert fabric under the needle before stitching. The loops in the chain stitch are made by the looper threads, so you insert your fabric wrong side up and don't see the decorative chain stitch while it's forming.

For more successful chain stitching, start your work by first stitching onto a small piece of stabilizer or a fabric scrap. Serge across the stabilizer and then move onto your fabric.

It's also a good idea to get into a habit of serging off your garment fabric and onto another piece of stabilizer or scrap fabric at the end of the chain stitching. Some decorative threads continue to "chain," and others refuse to stitch without fabric.

Your stitch length depends on the type of thread you use. Start with a 3.5- to 4-mm setting, and adjust from there.

Quilting with a chain stitch is exciting, but stick to garments. Since there's a space problem on serger beds, it's difficult, if not impossible, to chain stitch a large quilt. Keep the fabric bulk at a minimum by choosing a lightweight batting like Thermore by Hobbs or Quilters Cotton.

Hold the fabric and batting layers together with Quilt Basting Spray so you don't have to use pins. If you use a thin cotton batting, layer the face fabric and thin cotton batting. You can omit the lining and stitch directly onto the back of Thermore or Quilters Cotton batting.

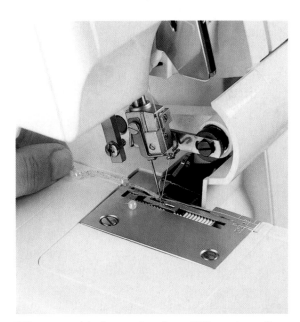

Stitch style and panache into your fabric with Burmilana, Candelight, Glamour, Jeans Stitch, Pearl Crown Rayon, or 30-weight Silk Stitch threads. So that you can see the stitches better, chain stitching was used on this fabric. But any one of these threads is suitable for cover stitching.

Why stop with decorative thread? You can easily secure beads in your chain by couching beads on rolled edge chain with a fishing line filler. It's not as tough as you think; you only need to familiarize yourself with the process or practice a bit. Step-by-step instructions for this technique are featured on pages 90–92.

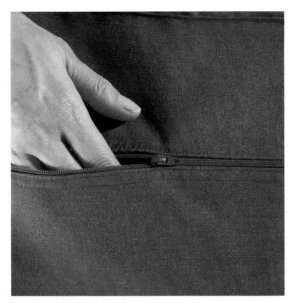

Converting this zippered pocket from functional to decorative would be as simple as switching the thread. Although it looks like topstitching, the lines of thread on either side of the zipper are cover stitched. See "Cover-Stitched Zipper" on page 209.

ROLLED EDGE CHAIN

A thread tail chain made without fabric has many decorative possibilities. The secret to creating really good quality chain is the settings. In some cases a chain made with an overlock stitch is acceptable, when stabilizing a seam, for example. (See page 39.) But the best chain is made with a 3-thread rolled edge stitch and tight tensions.

Select the right needle, remove your presser foot, and remember to change your throat plate, presser foot, or stitch finger (if required). Use decorative thread in all positions or just in the loopers. All-purpose serger thread works well in the needle.

Lower the presser foot lever and begin stitching, holding the thread tail behind the presser foot. As you stitch, continue holding onto the thread tail. Be very careful that you don't pull the stitches off the pin while the stitches are being formed.

COVER STITCHING

The cover stitch is a great decorative accent for any garment. The "right" side of the cover stitch provides a wonderful ready-to-wear finish, while the reverse (looper) side can also be the focal point of a garment.

The secret to a beautiful cover stitch is simply changing threads. For a "shiny" braid-like effect, try Decor, Designer 6, Pearl Crown Rayon, or ribbon floss. Glamour and Candlelight are thicker, metallic yarns that add a festive touch. For an elegant metallic accent, try Sliver.

Parallel rows of stitching are a great first project for learning to embellish with the decorative cover stitch. After you master the basics, don't be afraid to move on to stitching curved lines and other pretty shapes. On garments, try using decorative threads for accents at necklines and hems, or create your own free-form designs on pockets and cuffs. Or try making rows with various decorative threads to create a unique fabric for a vest or belt.

Adjusting Settings

The machine settings for a decorative cover stitch are essentially the same as the standard cover stitch.

You use the cover-stitch looper and two cover-stitch needles. Many sergers offer two needle positions. The wider position is best for heavier decorative threads. If you're using metallic thread, either position is appropriate.

The upper looper on your serger is either dropped or blocked when setting the cover stitch. Refer to your instruction manual for the exact settings. It's a good idea to follow the manual, step by step, to ensure that your cover stitch is set up correctly.

When making a decorative cover stitch, the decorative thread is placed in the cover-stitch looper, and matching all-purpose thread is used in the needles. Begin with a 4-mm stitch length, and then decrease as necessary.

Serger expert Pam Hastings's favorite stitch length is a setting that allows the stitches to just meet so little fabric shows through the loops. This creates a braidlike look rather than looking as if you used the "wrong" side of the stitch.

Practice Helps

If you're just familiarizing yourself with the cover-stitch option on your serger, it's best to practice on a few fabric scraps. This will make you comfortable with the stitch before switching to decorative thread for work on a garment.

Also experiment by adjusting the tension dials, since you'll probably need to make some adjustments to accommodate the "personality" of the decorative thread you selected. For example, a fine metallic thread may require a tighter tension than one of the heavier decorative rayon threads.

If you're using ribbon floss on a tube, try using a horizontal spool feeder so the thread feeds into the serger evenly. Or you can place a small juice glass or mug behind your serger and place the tube in the container.

When first trying this technique, embellish the fabric pattern pieces before constructing your garment. Smaller pieces are easier to manage than a completed project. If you're using a lightweight or soft fabric, place a tear-away stabilizer under the fabric for more body when sewing.

Decorative cover stitching is a two-step process. Start by marking your placement lines on the wrong side. You can mark your fabric with whatever is suitable: chalk, pencil, or air-erasable pen. If your lines are parallel and closely spaced, you need only to mark the first.

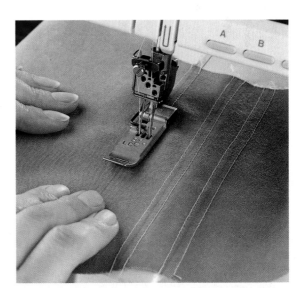

The last step of decorative cover stitching is also simple. Serge with the right side of the fabric face down. Position the placement line between the two needles. After the first row of stitching is complete, simply align the edge of the presser foot along the edge of the previous row of stitching.

FLATLOCKING

The grande dame of decorative serger stitching, flatlocking has been around since home sewers started using sergers. Through the years we've used the stitch to seam garments, add interesting detailing to a surface, and couch trim.

To flatlock, you serge along a fold or two edges, and then open the fabric so that it's flat. If worked on a fold, the fabric is usually flat under the stitching, unless you want a tiny tuck for a decorative effect. With two pieces of fabric, the edges should butt underneath the stitching. Make the stitch with either two or three threads. A 2-thread version is easier to open.

Successful flatlocking depends on proper tension settings. For 2-thread flatlocking use a balanced setting. A 3-thread flatlock takes a bit more work. Really loosen the needle tension, and tighten the lower looper tension. This makes it possible to open the fabric flat. If you can't get the lower looper tension tight enough, switch to Woolly Nylon because this thread increases tension to the equivalent of two to three settings.

Flatlocking is a great way to join fabrics like Polarfleece because bulky seam allowances are eliminated, and the fabric edges won't ravel.

The "Tips and Techniques" section includes seven interesting ways to use the stitch. While some of these ideas are tried and true, like "Fagoting" (see page 123), others are very innovative. Why not piece curved fabric strips or insert a zipper with flatlocking? To give these ideas a whirl, check out the instructions on pages 183 and 215, respectively. Both techniques are easy.

The looper side of flatlocking is used most often. But don't ignore the needle side. Just stitch with the right sides together. You can run ribbon through the needle thread "ladders," or leave it plain. On this garment it looks like evenly spaced hand stitching. The larger edge stitches are done by hand on this collar.

If your woven or knit fabric has a tendency to fray or unravel, straight stitch your seam, then flatlock. Another option is to finish the raw edges, fold along the seamlines, and then flatlock the two folds together.

Serger expert Agnes Mercik reinforces the back of a flatlocked seam with a strip of fusible interfacing. Since she plans to use the ladders (needle stitching) on the right side, the looper threads are covered by the interfacing.

PLAYING WITH STITCHES

Once you've learned to adjust the tension for the basic serger stitches—overlock, flatlock, and rolled edge—you can throw caution to the wind and play with the settings to create other interesting stitched effects along garment edges.

Unbalanced tensions often result in interesting stitch variations that add an unexpected decorative touch. For example, you can create the look of blanket stitching by loosening the needle thread and excessively tightening the lower looper thread in a 3-thread flatlock stitch. This forces the lower looper thread to lie along the garment edge. When you serge with the underside face up, the right side results look like a blanket stitch. (This technique looks great along the collar and front raw edges of a jacket made from Polarfleece fabric.)

When you want the appearance of a rolled edge but your fabric won't cooperate, consider using the wrapped stitch instead. It's a super finish when you want or need the same stitch appearance on the top and underside of a garment edge—along the front edge of a jacket with a notched collar, for example. A simple adjustment draws the upper looper thread all the way to the needle stitching on the underside so that both sides look the same. This is a truly reversible serger stitch.

To get you started, the stitch variations mentioned above plus a few others are presented on the next four pages, in "Using Rolled Edge Chain" and the table called "Stitching Creatively." Begin with the serger set up for the basic stitch in the left-hand column of the table, then adjust as directed.

It's easy to work with the stitches on your serger. Just adjust the standard settings for some of the common serger stitches for dynamic results.

A classy tone-on-tone color scheme pulls together the diagonal lines of stitching and lace on this vest. Using off-white cotton fabric, lace, and thread, serger expert Agnes Mercik embellished the fabric, cut out the Fronts, and then joined and lined the garment.

She varied the width of the flatlocking on the Left Front. Note, however, that the spacing between the diagonal lines is consistent.

Agnes was more adventurous on the Right Front, shown in the photo at left. She added lace to the flatlocking. This makes it harder—but not impossible—to open the stitching so that it's completely flat. Lace rosettes on the Left Front add balance.

USING ROLLED EDGE CHAIN

Since you can stitch without fabric on a serger, you can make yards and yards of thread chain. It's fun, it's easy, and there's lots that you can do with it. This is a great way to use up bits and pieces of decorative thread. Use the rolled edge settings, appropriate throat plate and stitch finger, and adjust the tension for the thread you're using.

BUTTON LOOP
Use decorative thread in the upper looper, elastic thread in the lower looper, and all-purpose thread in the needle to make delicate, lacy, rolled edge chain. Experiment with a slightly wider than normal stitch to create a wider trim.

DECORATIVE BOW
Use a 3-thread rolled edge setting and your favorite decorative thread in the upper looper. Metallic thread is nice for rolled chain bows to dress up a plain sweater for festive occasions. Tie the chain into a bow, and machine bartack it in place.

DECORATIVE TRIM
Couch the chain to the surface of a garment. Begin and end your design lines at garment edges so the chain is caught in the garment construction seams. Otherwise, thread the chain tails into a tapestry needle, and pull each one to the wrong side, tying it off in an overhand knot.

MONK'S CORD
Fold a length of chain in half. Thread the loop through a hole on your sewing machine bobbin, bring the free ends through the loop, and tighten. Using the machine's bobbin winder, spin to twist the strands. Hold the twisted cord at the center, and let the cord twist back on itself. Tie a knot in the twisted cord. Cut the cord from the bobbin.

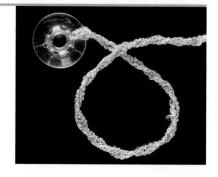

ROLLED HEM ENHANCER

Add definition and crispness to a rolled edge finish by catching serger chain under the rolled edge stitching. Feed the chain through a beading or cording foot for extra control while you stitch over it. You may need to use a slightly wider stitch to cover the chain smoothly and evenly.

SEAM STRENGTHENER

Catch a rolled edge chain under regular serger stitching to reinforce a seam so that it doesn't stretch out of shape. This is a particularly good strategy for the shoulder seams in knit garments. If available, use a beading or cording foot to help guide the chain under the stitching.

SPAGHETTI STRAPS

Braid three lengths of decorative chain together to make thin yet strong straps. For extra strength, use Woolly Nylon thread in the needle and lower looper with decorative thread in the upper looper to make the rolled edge chain. For thicker straps use two or more chains as one, then braid them together.

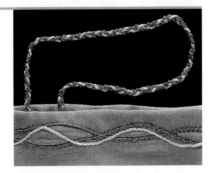

SWING TACK

A 2-inch (5-cm)-long chain at each side seam prevents the lining from twisting by linking it to the hem. To make one, on the inside of a garment, hand- or machine-bartack one end of the chain to the top of the hem allowance. Stitch the remaining end of the chain to an adjacent spot on the lining. (The chain on the hem allowance helps it hang evenly.)

TASSEL

Wrap the serger chain around a cardboard template to make a tassel of the desired length. Slip the wraps off the cardboard after tying the loops together at one end, then wrap more chain around the loops to create the tassel head. Cut the remaining loops and knot or treat the cut ends with seam sealant.

STITCHING CREATIVELY

Consider this small offering a menu, a place to turn when you'd like to sample something new. And before you throw away any of your serger tension-testing samples, examine them. The stitch variations in this table are the results of creative sewers discovering the decorative possibilities in unbalanced tensions.

BASIC STITCH	STITCH VARIATION	THREAD, TENSION, AND STITCH ADJUSTMENTS	TECHNIQUE TIPS
Flatlock, 2-thread	Blanket	• Use decorative thread in the needle • Stitch with the wrong side of the garment facing up • Disengage the upper knife (if possible)	Stitch over a folded or finished edge so the needle thread shows on the right side.
Flatlock, 2-thread	Wrapped	• Use decorative thread in the looper only • Use matching color serger thread or transparent thread in the needle • Disengage the upper knife (if possible)	Tighten the needle tension until it pulls the looper thread from the front to the underside, completely wrapping the folded or finished edge. Remember to block your upper looper.
Flatlock, 3-thread	Blanket	• Use decorative thread in the needle and both loopers • Loosen the needle tension • Tighten the lower looper so the looper thread lies along the folded or finish-ed edge (like a 3-thread flatlock) • Disengage the upper knife (if possible)	You may need to adjust the upper looper tension a little. Stitch from the under-side so the needle thread shows on the right side.

BASIC STITCH	STITCH VARIATION	THREAD, TENSION, AND STITCH ADJUSTMENTS	TECHNIQUE TIPS
Overlock, 3-thread	**Blanket**	• Place decorative thread in the needle and loopers • Loosen the needle tension (usually to 0) and tighten the looper tensions until the threads interlock at the edge and the needle thread shows on both sides • Use the longest possible stitch length • Stitch over a fold or a finished edge • Disengage the upper knife (if possible)	The decorative thread must fit through the needle. For a fine stitch use a decorative thread like 40-weight rayon. Try topstitching thread for more pronounced stitches.
Overlock, 3-thread	**Wrapped**	• Use decorative thread in the upper looper • Tighten the lower looper tension until the thread disappears and the upper looper thread wraps all the way to the needle stitching on the underside • Place this stitch on a folded or finished edge • Disengage the upper knife (if possible)	Use Woolly Nylon or monofilament thread in the lower looper if you need more tension in order to pull a heavier decorative thread to the underside.
Rolled edge	**Fine blanket**	• Use lightweight decorative thread in the needle and the loopers • Select the longest stitch length • Loosen the needle tension • Tighten both looper tensions so the needle thread shows on both sides and the looper threads meet at the rolled or folded edge	Use a stretch differential feed setting, if necessary, to prevent puckering.
Rolled edge, narrow	**Tuck and roll**	• Use a short 4-thread overlock stitch with the narrow rolled edge setting • Tighten the lower looper tension until a tuck forms between the two rows of needle stitching • Use this stitch to finish a raw edge	If you can't use the left needle on your serger with a narrow rolled edge setting, substitute a wider 4-thread overlock stitch, and tighten the lower looper until a tuck forms.

Seams Incredible

It's easy to assume that the seam repertoire of a serger is limited because there are so few stitches in comparison to all the choices on the fancier sewing machines. But this isn't the case. Here serger experts Agnes Mercik and Pam Hastings guide you through the options and possible applications.

MAKING CHOICES

We all want our garments to look like ready-to-wear—only better. So we count on our sergers to professionally trim, seam, and complete a garment in a single step.

Most sergers feature a wide range of stitches, though a few may only have one or two types available. (It's common to own two machines to cover all of the applications.)

Older sergers, for example, don't have a cover-stitch option. But it's such a valuable stitch that more than a few experts have bought another machine just for this function. The cover stitch, shown on the opposite page, resembles a favorite seam on ready-to-wear garments. The most common version uses two needles and one looper. There are two choices for space between the needles. Both are used for wovens, knits, and elastic. You can also simulate stripes and plaids, and you can even smock using elastic thread in the looper.

With a choice of two to five threads from which to make stitches, there are some interesting combinations. Pick through the available seams to ensure you're choosing the best ones for the garment you're making.

While the serger certainly has improved garment construction, with its speed and professional finishing ability, it has also left many sewers in a quandary about how and when to use different seaming techniques and stitches. The dress at right shows the selections made by serger expert Pam Hastings.

When constructing a garment, it's tempting to use the same serger stitch again and again. While a 3-thread overlock will do in most situations, there are times when other stitches are more appropriate.

To serge the side seams in a loose-fitting garment, choose the 3-thread overlock or 4-thread safety stitch because both are equally appropriate. If desired, you can also try using a 5-thread stitch.

Appearances can hide the truth. In this case, the French seams weren't stitched entirely at the sewing machine. Rather, the first step, joining the fabric with wrong sides together, was done on a serger. To make a narrow version, use a balanced stitch and the stitch finger that you use for making a rolled edge stitch.

USING THE RIGHT SEAM

Edge finishing is great with 3-thread overlocking. But if your serger converts to a 2-thread overlock this stitch is the best choice. The 2-thread stitch has fewer threads, so the seam allowances won't be as bulky or imprint on the right side of the fabric.

Stress areas in woven fabrics are good candidates for a sturdy seam with little stretch, like the 5-thread safety. It combines a chain-stitch seam with an overedge stitch. (See page 30.) You can also use the stitch for side seams in a close-fitting garment.

For a smooth look with a tight fit, try 2- or 3-thread overlocking before seaming on your sewing machine. Then press the seam allowances open.

Savvy Serging

FINISH FIRST

When constructing an unlined garment where the seams are sewn with a sewing machine and then pressed open, it's best to serge the raw edges prior to construction. This is a real time-saver. It's also easier than overlocking the seam allowances after sewing the seam. This garment is made from the jacket pattern sold with Sandra Betzina's book No Time to Sew. (For information see page 244.) Hem lace was topstitched to the edges of the 2-thread overlocked seam allowances after seaming.

Susan Huxley

You can also use a 5-thread stitch, or straight stitch the seams and then serge the seams allowances together.

Deciding which stitch to use for sleeve insertion is a bit tougher. The selection for sewing and inserting your sleeve depends on the fabric. For knit fabrics, simply serge with a 4-thread safety stitch or 3-thread overlock.

On wovens, use a two-step process. First insert the sleeve at your sewing machine, then finish the seam allowances with a 2- or 3-thread overlock stitch.

For best results with stretch fabrics, serge the seams and attach ribbing using a 4-thread mock safety stitch. The extra row of stitching adds strength that this stretchy seam requires. The 4-thread safety stitch works particularly well with two-way stretch fabrics, such as spandex, and is the perfect seam for bathing suits and leotards.

The 3-thread overlock and 4-thread mock safety are suitable for virtually any seam. Just bear in mind that you're trimming away the seam allowances, so it won't be as easy to make alterations. Serger expert Pam Hastings's loose-fitting dress is a good choice for overlocking. Since the garment has a considerable amount of ease, alterations aren't an issue.

SEAMING WITH EASE

The majority of sergers are capable of doing more than creating a rolled edge and overlocking raw seam allowances. The key to using the decorative and functional seams in the same manner that you see them used in ready-to-wear is to ensure that you choose the right one for the fabric and function.

COVER STITCH

The needle threads stitch parallel lines on the right side, while a looper thread covers the seam on the wrong side. The needle spacing determines the width between the two parallel lines of stitching. The widest distance is usually 5 mm. The narrower setting is either 2.5 or 3.5 mm. Use it for hems, topstitching, flat joining seams, and edging with elastic and bindings. It's ideal for all stretch and woven fabrics. Using only one needle, you get a single chain-stitch seam.

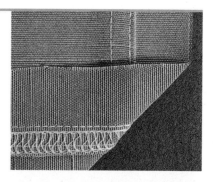

4-THREAD COVER STITCH

New on the market, this example was stitched on a Bernina prototype before this new machine was available to the public. The 5-mm, 3-needle version cover stitch is sewn with one looper thread and three needle threads. Apply this stitch anywhere the 3-thread version is used. It's another variation. Great for highlighting seams, hems, or places that need more strength.

COVER-STITCHED HEM

Suitable for just about any fabric, this stitch adds weight to a hem. It's a nice decorative touch, especially if you select your needle threads carefully. You may even want to try using the looper thread on the right side of the garment. The stitch starts and ends anywhere on the fabric.

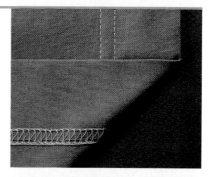

COVER STITCH, LAPPED

Intended to reduce bulk, the raw edges are simply overlapped and stitched in place. This is a great time-saver for Ultrasuede, leather, and other fibers that don't fray. You can use it for woven and nonwoven fabrics, as well. With knits, ensure that the cut edge doesn't curl.

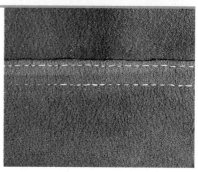

ROLLED

Known more as an edge finish, it can also be a seam. On fine fabrics use the 2-thread to reduce weight. The best threads are Metrolene and Madeira Tanne #80 or Mettler fine heirloom cotton. Use Woolly Nylon for impact, curvature, or a piped look. Switch to 3-threads for other fabric.

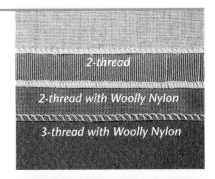

FRENCH

This serger version is ideal for fine and sheer fabrics. Join, wrong sides together, using a narrow 2- or 3-thread overlock. For the second step, fold the fabric around the seam allowances, and straight stitch, encasing the previous seam allowances. (Also see "Serged French Seam" on pages 144–145.)

FRENCH ROLLED, EXTRA-NARROW

On batiste, organdy, and very fine silks, use the narrow stitch finger (the "pin") to make a French seam using a rolled stitch. Since the thread wraps the fabric roll, it's no longer necessary to complete the seam on your sewing machine. You can't ask for a finer couturier's finish.

SINGLE CHAIN

Sometimes called simply a chain-stitch seam, serger expert Agnes Mercik prefers a single chain stitch so that it isn't confused with the more traditional 3/4-thread (mock safety) seam. Dressmakers baste with this seam because it can be quickly pulled out. The needle side shows only straight stitching, but the looper side has a chainlike appearance.

SUPER STRETCH

This is a 3-thread seam that stretches and recovers without snapping stitches. It's a good choice for bathing suits, leotards, and aerobic wear. Use Woolly Nylon in the lower looper. (The upper looper is blocked.) For extra stretch add Woolly Nylon to both needles as well. In the needles, Woolly Nylon looks the same as all-purpose serger thread.

(continued)

SEAMING WITH EASE—CONTINUED

MOCK FLAT-FELLED

Serger versions aren't as bulky. For heavy fabrics, make the seam with 4- or 5-thread stitch. Press to one side and cover stitch. Another version (not shown) starts at the sewing machine. Straight stitch first, slightly trim the bottom layer, then overlock the upper layer. Press the wider seam allowance over the narrower one, and topstitch.

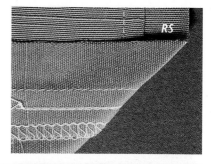

MOCK SAFETY

A simultaneously stitched 4-thread overlock and safety seam, this is the best choice for general seaming. It offers the strength of a two-needle seam, which is needed for wovens and knits. The standard width is ¼ inch (6 mm). For a narrower seam, as often seen in ready-to-wear, use the narrower (rolled hem) stitch finger.

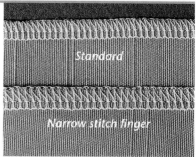

REINFORCED

Control the stretch of knit, loosely woven, and bias-cut fabrics by reinforcing seams with twill tape, Seams Great (a fine, sheer tricot), clear elastic, or a serger tail chain. Feed it through the slot of a standard presser foot (if it has a slot through which to feed the tape—you may need a specialized tape foot) while serging the seam.

2-THREAD FLATLOCK VARIATION

This is stitched with the garment pieces together, then they're opened. If you serge with the fabric right sides together, the needle thread is visible upon opening. The looper thread is visible when the garment pieces are serged with the wrong sides together. For a very flat seam, fold back one seam allowance, cut the seam allowance off the adjacent garment piece, butt the fold against the raw edge, and serge.

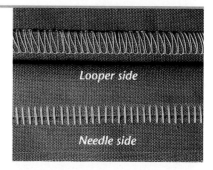

2-THREAD NARROW FLATLOCK

Used mostly for applying lace and elastic to lingerie, this is the best version of flatlocking. It's flatter and more lightweight. Don't use it when a sturdy seam is essential. Fold both seam allowances to one side for additional strength, particularly with woven fabrics. You may or may not want the decorative "pleat" visible down the center of the needle thread.

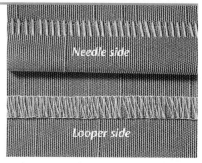

3-THREAD FLATLOCK

So you can't quite justify buying a new serger, but you want to flatlock? It's more difficult, but you can make a flatlock even if you don't have the option of blocking the upper looper. Loosen your needle tension, and select the left or right needle, depending on the stitch width that you prefer. The looper side is shown in both examples.

3-THREAD OVERLOCK

Try seaming and edging with the left needle. It's a good choice for fabrics that ravel. Most people use only the right needle, even though you get the widest, cleanest finish and better thread coverage with the left. Use balanced tension and the rolled hem stitch finger for finer fabrics and narrower seams because there's less bulk.

4-THREAD SEAM, SEPARATE CHAIN, AND 2-THREAD OVERLOCK

Not too many people think about using this stitch. Since there's one less looper thread, this stitch eliminates bulk in the seam while still offering the stability of the single chain stitch. Remember that if you have a 5-thread serger, you can block the upper looper.

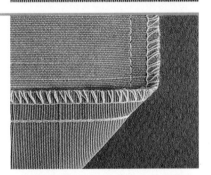

5-THREAD OVERLOCK

A straight, sturdy seam, it's a favorite among weavers. For fabrics that ravel, use the left needle position. General wovens are joined with the right needle position. To stabilize a loosely knitted fabric, use either.

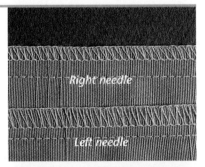

2-THREAD EDGE-FINISHED

Combine the edge finish with straight-stitch seaming wherever you need a flat seam allowance. This is a good choice for woolens, because the impression of a 3-thread overlock is visible from the outside of the garment. It's excellent for lined, tailored garments made from fabrics that ravel easily. Apply the edge finish before seaming.

Skill Building

Seaming and serging curves, corners, and circular areas require just a bit of know-how and skill. Serger expert Pam Hastings shares the tips and techniques that helped her master these problem areas. She guarantees that with this new knowledge you'll soon be tackling tough—but exciting—projects.

MASTERING THE TOUGH STUFF WITH PRACTICE

The first seam that you stitched on a serger was probably a straight edge. How clean. How easy. Then you tried circles, corners, and curves. Not so easy. Yet they can be if you know the right tricks.

As you've already discovered, sewing on a serger is a real time-saver, not to mention all those beautiful seam finishes that you end up with. You've also learned, no doubt, that what makes this machine so wonderful, the trimming and the nice clean edges, can also create challenges. For example, the presser foot is a bit longer than a sewing machine foot, so curves must be stitched with care. Gradually moving your fabric to the left or right—just the right amount—results in beautifully finished edges and perfectly sewn seams.

When it comes to corners, the upper knife and the way the stitch is formed (wrapping around the stitch finger and fabric) rule out the pivoting movement you use at your sewing machine. The good news is that once you learn how to stitch a corner on your serger, you'll find it quicker and easier than pivoting.

Practice, practice, practice. That's the best way to master any serger challenge. Before applying Pam's techniques to your garment project, she strongly suggests that you cut remnants of fabric into squares, curves, and circles, and follow the steps on pages 52–55. You may even want to cut out pattern pieces like square and round necklines and facings in muslin so you can practice actual garment sewing. You'll perfect the skills in no time, and incorporating them into your sewing will be a pleasure.

Why not overlock the outside edge of a facing with decorative thread, and then attach the facing so that it's on the outside of the garment? With fusible thread in the lower looper, overlock the raw edge, then straight stitch the right side of the facing to the wrong side of the garment. Turn the facing to the right side and press. Fuse-baste, then topstitch the outer edge of the facing to the garment.

When sewing inside corners where the seam allowance will be trimmed away, diagonally clip into the corner to the same depth as your seam allowance. For example, for a ⅝-inch (1.5-cm) seam allowance, the clip depth is ⅝ inch (1.5 cm). Begin serging your fabric, position the left needle stitching ⅝ inch (1.5 cm) from the fabric edge. As you approach the clip, simply straighten out the corner. The needle enters the deepest point of the clip just next to, or barely touching, the fabric.

CUTTING CORNERS

Inside and outside corner techniques are used in a variety of ways when constructing a garment.

You use inside corners to construct square necklines and kick pleats. These corners also appear on garments that have a side or back slit. When sewing an inside corner, as a general rule, think of your corner as a straight line. (This makes the entire process less intimidating.) When you enter the corner you're moving the fabric to form a straight edge.

Collar points and decorative edges on scarves and pocket hankies are all outside corners. These edges are finished by stitching off one edge of the corner and then bringing the other edge into the serger. Serging is a great way to stitch outside corner seams, like those found in collars and cuffs, because the seam is trimmed as you sew, thus eliminating the need to trim the collar seam allowances.

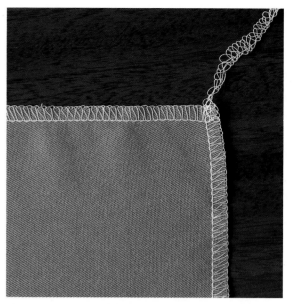

For an outside corner, sew off the edge of the fabric when serging the first side of the corner. Turn your fabric, and serge the next raw edge. As you begin to serge the second side of the corner, the upper knife cuts off the tail chain at the corner. Dab the corners with a liquid seam sealant, and trim off any remaining thread tails.

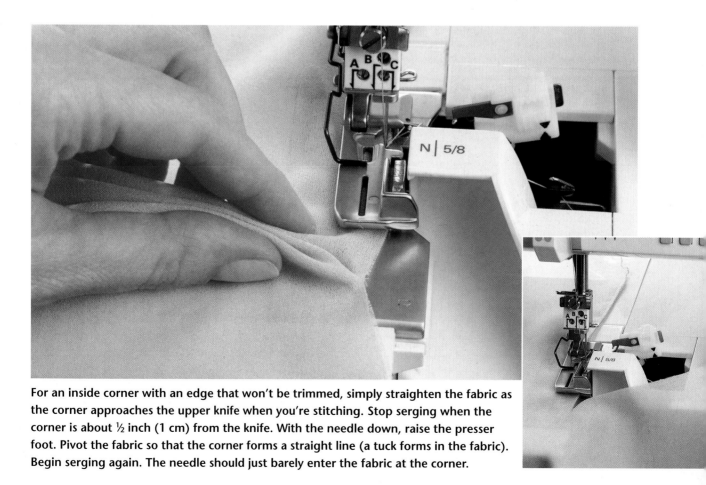

For an inside corner with an edge that won't be trimmed, simply straighten the fabric as the corner approaches the upper knife when you're stitching. Stop serging when the corner is about ½ inch (1 cm) from the knife. With the needle down, raise the presser foot. Pivot the fabric so that the corner forms a straight line (a tuck forms in the fabric). Begin serging again. The needle should just barely enter the fabric at the corner.

THROWING A CURVE

If you look carefully at your pattern pieces you'll notice that they're made up of many inside and outside curves. Facings have both inside and outside curves, while sleeve caps, shirttail hems, and inseam pockets all have outside curves. Armholes and neck edges are inside curves.

Curves can be sewn when finishing edges or constructing a garment. In both cases, using a serger is beneficial. Overlocking the outer edge of a facing, for example, not only gives a professional finish but also results in a smoother line on the outside of the garment after pressing.

Finishing the edges of a shirttail hem with a serger actually makes it easier to turn up and press the hem before topstitching. The additional benefit gained by using a serger is that for curved seams, serger stitching reduces bulk and trims away the excess seam allowance, thus saving time ordinarily spent clipping and trimming.

You won't hesitate to add interesting serger details to the edges of the garment, whether it's to a sleeve or a collar. Knowledge of outside curves and corners were needed to apply the metallic thread blanket stitch on the shawl collar and hem. This serging also utilized pivoting for two outside corners, while the rolled edge hem on the sleeve was perfected with the notch-out method for circular stitching.

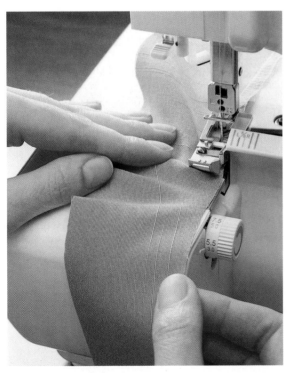

Inside curves are easy. Serge along the edge until you start to enter the curve. At this point, simply straighten the curve of the fabric while you continue to serge. As the fabric approaches the presser foot, move the curve toward the left.

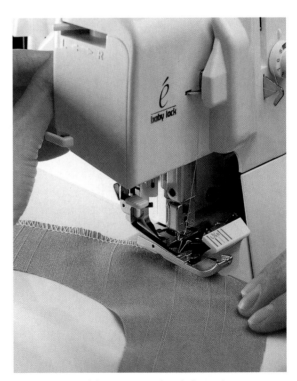

Move an outside curve to the right as it approaches the presser foot. If you're serging a tight curve, stop serging, shift the fabric, and then resume stitching for another short length. Repeat around the curve.

Going in Circles

Serging in a circle isn't always sewing a piece of fabric shaped like a circle. Any time you begin and end a seam at the same point you can use the techniques explained on this page.

Ribbing at a neckline, cuff, or bottom of a sweatshirt or pants are all circular seams. You can also include garment edges like hems on skirts, sleeves, and trousers. Necklines in pullover tops without a back slit incorporate sewing a circular seam and sewing the edges of a circle (the facing pieces form a circle when sewn together.)

There are two common methods for sewing circles. The stop-and-fold method is most appropriate when sewing a seam. The fabric is folded away from the needle at the end of the seam. The notch-out method is generally used for sewing the outside edge of circles or for edge finishing. A small section of fabric is trimmed away prior to sewing the seam.

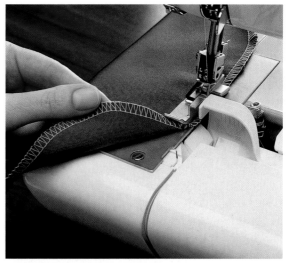

The fast-fold method for stitching a circle is simple. Serge two stitches past your starting point without cutting the original stitching. Raise the presser foot. Fold the fabric to the left and behind the needle. Drop the presser foot and chain off (stitch with your serger, without any fabric, to create a "chain" of continuous stitching). Trim the chain after securing it with liquid seam sealant.

Savvy Serging

EXPOSE THE EDGE

For a really clean finish on an exposed circular edge, I use a notch. Before serging, cut a 2-inch (5-cm)-long rectangle from the fabric edge. Only go as deep as the cutting line that the knife will make when you serge. Start serging at the closest end of the notch. Serge around the circle, until you're back at the starting point and the remainder of the notch is cut off. Now raise the needle and presser foot, pull fabric toward the needle, lower the presser foot, and chain off. Hide the chain in the stitching.

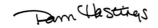

Complete serging to cut off the notch

APPLYING YOUR SERGER SMARTS

When constructing a garment, you use your serger in various ways, sometimes employing it to construct a seam and sometimes for simply finishing an edge. The garment below shows how a variety of applications can be easily and elegantly combined.

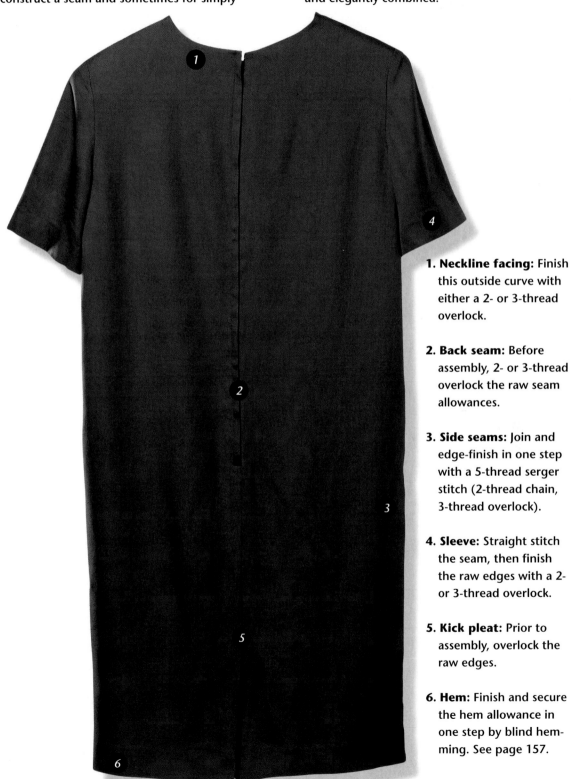

1. **Neckline facing:** Finish this outside curve with either a 2- or 3-thread overlock.

2. **Back seam:** Before assembly, 2- or 3-thread overlock the raw seam allowances.

3. **Side seams:** Join and edge-finish in one step with a 5-thread serger stitch (2-thread chain, 3-thread overlock).

4. **Sleeve:** Straight stitch the seam, then finish the raw edges with a 2- or 3-thread overlock.

5. **Kick pleat:** Prior to assembly, overlock the raw edges.

6. **Hem:** Finish and secure the hem allowance in one step by blind hemming. See page 157.

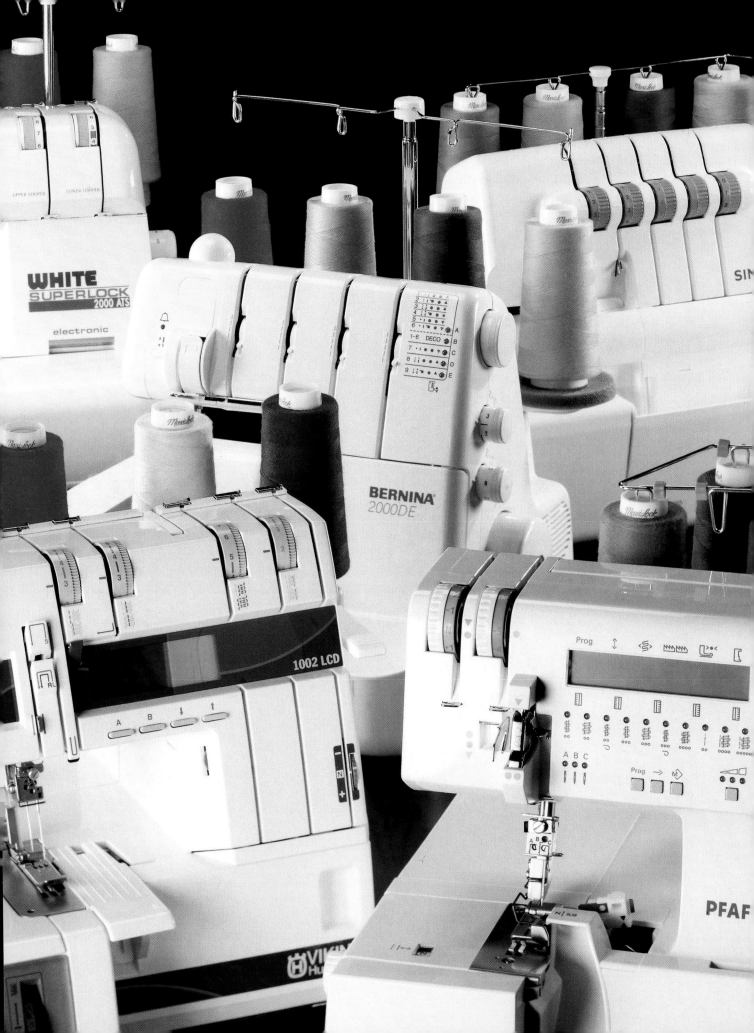

Buyers' Guide

A serger is a great addition to a sewing room, and you certainly wouldn't want to give yours up…or would you? Now that sergers have been available to home sewers for some time, improvements and upgrades have really changed the machines, making the newer ones easier to operate than the first models that were available.

MAKING THE DECISION

How do you know when it's time to upgrade to a new machine?

The "when" and "why" of buying a fancier machine are always a dilemma. If you use your serger regularly, but you're always seeing new techniques that can't be done with your serger, then you may want to take a serious look at what's out there. If you use a serger for seam finishing and little else, your current machine probably suits all of your needs.

When you decide it's time to make the move to a new serger, really go for it—purchase the best machine that you can afford, and make sure that it's one that offers the features you're likely to use.

Pick a feature that gives you headaches—tensions, for example—and see if there is a serger available that solves your problem, like automatic tensions or built-in adjustment guidelines.

What stitches do you frequently use? If you sew delicate fabrics, look for a machine with a built-in rolled hem so the stitch adjustment is as simple as flipping a switch or moving a stitch finger rather than changing plates. Likewise, if you've been eyeing the cover stitch for months and can think of all the times you've wanted to use that stitch *if only*, then it's time for a high-end serger.

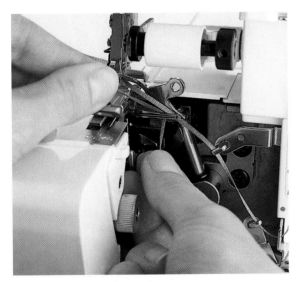

If you're a fan of decorative threads, bring along a variety you're likely to work with. After the demonstration, try rethreading the serger (yourself) with your threads. See if changing threads is an easy process, and find out if your favorite decorative threads work well on a particular machine.

Bring scraps of fabric from recent projects so you can test "real" fabric that you love and use frequently. Be sure the serger you're considering performs well on your fabric. If you're not happy with the results, it's time to move on and test-drive another serger manufactured by a different company.

COMPARING FEATURES

The number one rule is to test-drive the machine. Let the salesperson show you what the machine can do, but then get behind the machine and see for yourself.

All sergers perform the same operation: one-step fabric trimming and finishing, in half the time it takes on a sewing machine. As you move up the product line, you'll find that some sergers make this process easier than others.

All or most sergers offer color-coded threading, numbered tension dials, rolled hem capabilities, and 3- or 4-thread stitches.

Upgraded models usually offer all of the basics plus lay-in threading; built-in rolled hemming; differential feed; a self-threading lower looper; and 2-, 3-, or 4-thread stitching.

Top-of-the-line models offer all of the above plus automatic tensions and LCD screens that give you tension settings and other set-up details at the push of a button. In addition, high-end machines offer a complete stitch package—from rolled hem to cover stitch. Most top-of-the-line sergers offer a wide range of optional presser feet to make some sewing tasks, like elastic insertion or attaching pearls, easier.

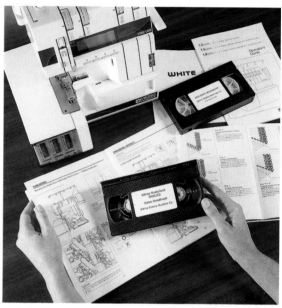

Take a look at the kind of materials that are available to help you become comfortable with your new serger. Videos and workbooks are great tools for additional information and guidance.

Savvy Serging

INSPECT CLOSELY

Little things can become big deals when you get your new serger home. If you've sewed on a particular brand for the past few years, you're probably used to finding the switches, dials, and levers in certain locations. All dials are not equal! Depending on the brand, they can have a completely different look and feel. Even the presser foot lifter is located in different areas from brand to brand. Pay close attention when you test-drive a serger. If something feels uncomfortable or odd, move on to the next machine.

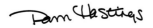

CHOOSING ACCESSORIES

As with the serger itself, accessories do improve and become more abundant as you move up a product line. Most sergers come with oil, needles, and an extra upper knife, but the remaining accessories vary. A complete package can include hexagonal wrenches for removing needles, extra needles, lint brushes, looper threaders (if the looper is not self-threading), small and large screwdrivers, thread caps, nets, tweezers, and even videotapes.

When deciding which accessories to purchase for your serger, there are some general rules that you can follow. The demo looked great, but do you ever use the technique? Is it as easy as it looks? Is the tool easy to use? Will you use it?

Above all else, shop for a dealer as well. Buy from a dealer who is willing to teach you about your machine and help you when you're stuck.

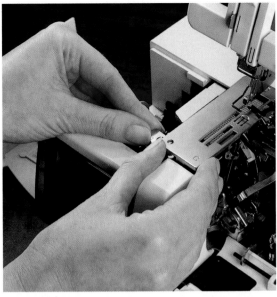

Setting up a cover stitch takes a bit of fussing. Try to make the conversion on your own. If the setup seems a bit complicated, ask yourself if this is something that will be a breeze with a bit of practice. Or is it something that you'll shy away from doing on your own?

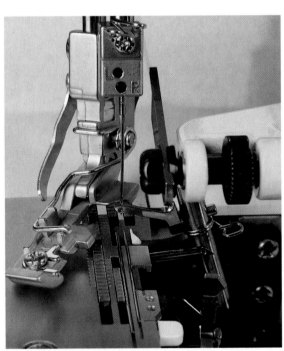

Some machine owners insist that there's little worse than trying to insert one or more needles into a serger that has the upper knife mounted on the top of the machine. Bernina's solution is a swing-out presser foot that offers easier access. Other brands can make needle insertion easier by including a well-designed tool.

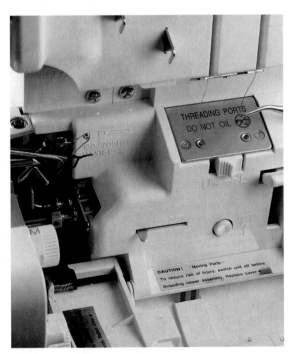

Frustrated with threading the lower looper? There are sergers that don't even give you access to the lower looper. Instead, you insert your thread into a hole and use air to pump it through. It's so easy! For heavier, decorative threads, there's a gizmo to help move the thread through the machine.

The Garment Gallery

Inspiration. That's what this section is all about—how to choose the right techniques for your garments and how to combine them tastefully and with style.

Just as painters finesse their craft by reviewing the works of Leonardo da Vinci, Michelangelo, and Pablo Picasso, so, too, can you learn from the masters.

In this section, the talented Serger Secrets contributors share their work and explain how they achieved the results. All of the serger techniques they used to make the garments are explained either on the following pages or elsewhere in the book.

Chiffon Confection

Who says the hem of a delicate garment has to be subtle? Clothing designer Kimberly Kukkola-Muñoz overlocks the edges of her chiffon gowns with a decorative thread. Here she explains how and why.

The first impulse of almost every serger owner is to roll edge–finish the hem on fine fabric. Think again, because there are options.

I was looking for something with flair, an edge that would give my garments, well, an edge in the competitive world of fashion. The featured hem gives me that advantage because no one else is doing it.

Besides, the old-fashioned way to finish the edge is a hand-stitched rolled hem. I'm a designer first and foremost, but I'm also a businesswoman. Hand stitching just isn't cost-effective.

The edge is finished with a pearl stitch. That's what it's called in the industry. It's pretty much the same as the 3-thread over-lock on your machine. Use pearl rayon decorative thread in the upper looper and cotton thread in the other positions. I modify the color selection to suit the fabric and the design. The color of the upper looper thread matches or contrasts with the fabric, but the needle and lower looper threads always match the fabric.

For this gown I wanted the stitching to draw attention to the double-layer skirt.

I think it's the prettiest hem, and it doesn't look bulky. The fuschia gown, far right, has the same pearl-stitch (3-thread overlock) hem. To attach the sheer fabric to the satin, I opted for a stitch that you may know as a 3-thread flatlock. Your serger may offer a 2-thread flatlock stitch, which is worth trying. I prefer the pronounced effect of the additional thread.

You might have seen this garment or another one like it that I have made. During my 15 years of sewing, designing, and manufacturing, my pieces have appeared in several top fashion magazines.

Kimberly Kukkola-Muñoz

Elegant fabrics and pretty threads translate into eye-catching garments. Rather than hiding the serger stitching, it's a focal point for both of these pieces of lingerie. The sheen of rayon thread adds a subtle but decorative touch. For guidance on thread selection, see "Decorative Threads" on pages 20 and 21.

Safari Tucks

"It's time for a trek. Explore and capture a garment that features cover-stitch tucks," we said. With nothing but the instructions for the technique, seamstress Sue Nester hunted down fabric and then serged this wonderful blouse. Here she explains her techniques.

A relatively simple garment can capture your heart. In this case, the combination of complementary fabrics and some well-placed tucks make all the difference.

As you can probably guess, I like dramatic, trendy clothes. Animal prints were popular the season that I made this, so it was easy to find several fabrics to carry the theme. It was important to select prints with maximum impact and contrast but that still shared commonalities, like color.

The plain fabric is a strong color, so it isn't overpowered by the prints. It also offers the eye some relief from the activity happening elsewhere. Nevertheless, I knew that the plain fabric could be very boring in contrast to the prints.

This is why I added the cover-stitched tucks to the right front. I followed the same instructions that are featured on pages 194–196. In her directions, Agnes Mercik broke the vertical lines of her tucks by stitching across them horizontally, but I stopped before that step.

Sue Nester

Sue Nester

The adventure begins! Track down another neat way to use your cover stitch with these simple tucks. On top, it looks as if you invested a considerable amount of time and effort to topstitch each tuck close to the fold. Yet it's a simple one-stitch, one-pass procedure.

Marching to a Different Drummer

If there's such a thing as faux flatlocking, then this is it. Technically speaking, the serging on this jacket really is flatlocking, of the decorative variety. But that isn't how seamstress Sue Nester seamed the garment.

This garment is inspired by a fashion research trip that I took with book editor Susan Huxley. We were looking for inspiration (there were no plans to steal ideas, honest) for the application of flatlocking. Surely, we thought, there is some way to apply this wonderful stitch to a garment without making it look like activewear.

Among the few pieces that we found, we discovered that the key is selecting a quality fabric that doesn't say "sports."

On some garments, flatlocking was used in a purely ornamental fashion, such as horizontal and vertical rows stitched to a pocket before it's topstitched to a jacket.

One garment intrigued us: a simple pullover top made in cotton fabric. Very casual, but interesting, because the Front was joined to the Side Front panels along straight-stitched princess seams, and then flatlocking was applied as topstitching.

What a neat way to add detail! (To say nothing about how it's a good way to ensure nice, flat seam allowances.) Princess lines are perfect because the garment patterns draw the eye to the vertical seamlines.

I applied the idea to a jacket pattern, and this is the result. Vertical flatlocking alone is pretty boring, so I added additional stitching along the cuffs, pockets, and dropped-waist seamline.

If you want to add detail to a plain garment, start by examining the structural and design lines on the pattern illustration. Your eye will be drawn to certain areas. The next step is to enhance these with flatlocking or couched braid. You could do the same thing with decorative cover stitching.

Sue Nester

Sue Nester

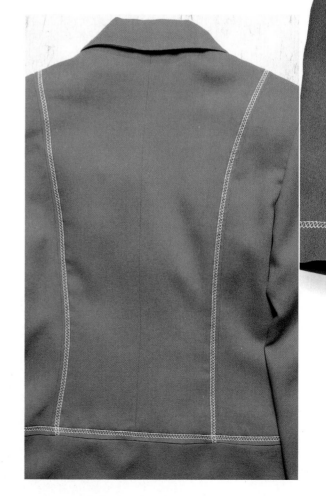

Ensure beautifully straight, even flatlocking by seaming a garment at your sewing machine, then applying the overlock. This "topstitching" approach gives you more control. Keep fabric weight in mind when selecting your stitch. A 2-thread version opens the flattest, while you may end up with a tiny tuck under the 3-thread stitch.

Transition in Silk

The romance of ribbon and lace calls for a delicate touch. The designer Linda Lee Vivian knows it's possible to achieve this look with a serger because that's how she and a friend did everything from joining the lace to making wire-edged roses.

I call this Transition in Silk because it's my way of creating a transition between traditional techniques and the updated look achieved with today's easy sewing and serging. For several years before tackling this top and skirt, I envisioned using elegant laces and fancy fabrics to make my Around the Block top pattern. (I love to create "new" fabric with the heirloom serger techniques explained on pages 133–153.)

The entire top was pieced in a "log cabin" style, adding strips all the way around the yoke. I started with a lace combination strip for my first trip around the block, then alternated subsequent trips with fabric and lace strips. I finished the "new" fabric by adding a very wide strip of silk. After creating the fabric, I cut the garment from the "new" patchwork fabric, then assembled it with a 4-thread overlock stitch.

The beautiful wide lace along the edges of the top and skirt was attached with the sewing machine. I love the elegant effect of ribbon, so I wove it into the ladder stitch of the wide 2-thread flatlock (see page 142) and into the beading on some of the laces.

I knew I had to create a very special skirt to go with the top. I decoratively flatlocked with silk threads as I serged together fabric with lace overlays and several wide strips of fabric. To continue the bias effect in the top, I cut the skirt gores on an angle. Silk ribbon enhances the ladder stitch of each row of flatlock. I alternated ribbon colors to add to the effect.

Linda Lee Vivian

Linda Lee Vivian

My dear friend Marilyn Adams helped create the matching hat (above) by making roses and leaves from wire-edged ribbon. (You can purchase the ribbon ready-made or add your own wire. See page 121.) These decorative accents are attached to a hatband that I made by serging embroideries and laces together.

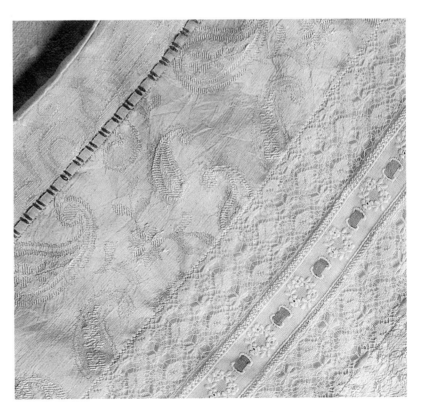

For much of the top (above), hand-dyed silks and elegant laces were pieced together with either a narrow or wide 2-thread flatlock. All of the serger stitching was done with 30- and 50-weight silk threads from YLI, alternating thread colors for added interest.

Trompe l'Oeil

Fabric, says educator Agnes Mercik, is the launching point for many creative garments. Her projects often start with ideas that pop into her head while she's looking at yardage.

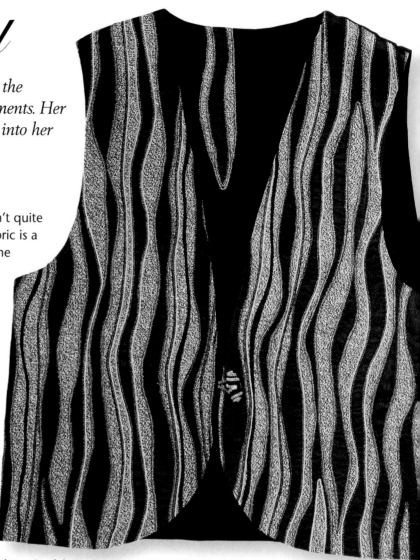

As the French phrase suggests, this vest isn't quite what it appears to be. The background fabric is a simple black, white, and silver print, and the seemingly intricate appliqués are just couched trims. In addition, the trim and the fabric aren't really woven together.

I like to enhance interesting lines by adding stitch texture. Furthermore, an entire fabric is used as the base, without cutting separate pieces. This project is a good way to use leftover thread or learn to handle a variety of new textures and thicknesses.

I chose a variety of silver, gray, and black metallic and Woolly Nylon metallic threads that enhance the fabric. These threads are serged into trims of varying textures. Then, at my sewing machine, I couched the trims with monofilament thread along the predominant wavy lines that separate most of the main sections of the print fabric. Even upon closer examination, these sections appear to be intricately appliquéd. It's a simple but effective process.

You can create trims by serging a narrow balanced overlock or rolled hem setting over knitting yarn or soft cord. Use a 2- or 3-thread stitch with decorative thread in a looper. The stitches are close together but don't overlap. The thicker the looper thread, the longer you need to make the stitch length. If you try another braid technique, take a look at the step-by-step instructions on page 93.

The couching stitches are zigzag, straight, or decorative to enhance the trim. The sewing machine needle thread I most frequently use for this technique is a monofilament, since it conceals and disguises the sewing machine stitch. The object here is to minimize the appearance of too many stitches, which takes away from the concept.

Agnes Mercik

Agnes Mercik

A fabric toggle button is a subtle and attractive closure for many embellished garments. To visually link the button to the vest, the same threads were used on both the button and the couching. See pages 95 and 111 for complete instructions.

Curves Ahead

Natural suedes and skins won't hold a satin stitch, so Agnes Mercik (a.k.a. the Serge-On General) serger-appliqués snakeskin motifs to deerskin. We've all struggled trying to make curved serger stitches, so you'll love Agnes's solution to the challenge of stitching around the shapes.

One of my other favorite areas of fabric embellishment (I do have many) is appliqué. Traditional appliqué uses a sewing machine's fine satin stitch to cover the raw edges of motifs. But the needle perforates and separates natural suedes and skins. By examining commercially made garments, I found that even the expensive high-fashion garments use a wide-open zigzag for attaching motifs. This stitch doesn't appeal to me, so I take an alternate approach.

I cut motifs from a variety of reptile skins and temporarily glue-baste them into position on the deerskin vest pieces. I then individually stitch the edges of the motifs with a long straight stitch to hold them in place permanently.

Monofilament thread works well, and it doesn't have to be removed.

Similar to the black, white, and silver Trompe l'Oeil vest (see the opposite page), this vest has serger trim. It's made with a fine variegated copper thread (Madeira FS #2/2) in the looper and fine knitting yarn as the filler. I prefer yarn filler, for the most part, as it's more forgiving and easier to mold around tight corners and curves. (I often confuse knitting store sales clerks when I tell them I'm looking for yarns to use on my sewing machines and sergers.)

Using the same metallic thread in the needle of my sewing machine, I couched the trims along my design curves and along all edges of the snakeskin motifs. The serger trim now takes on the look of a close zigzag stitch. I found the metallic needle most helpful on both machines.

Agnes Mercik

Agnes Mercik

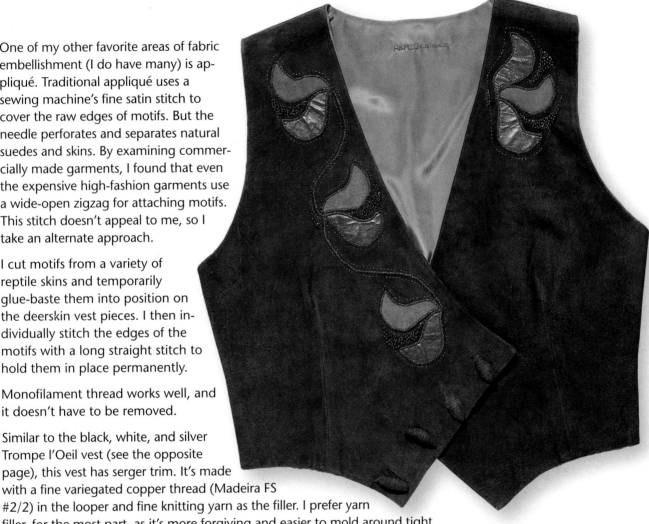

To be sure that the serger trim totally covered the raw edges of the motifs, I used a leather roller presser foot. It increases visibility, and it's easier to manipulate on the skins since you don't lift the presser foot nearly as often as you would a standard foot.

Pipe Dream

Serger expert Agnes Mercik loves the reaction she gets when she tells students that they can puff and pipe at the same time on their sergers. This vest has two neat techniques.

The amazing thing with sergers and their related accessories is that you can combine functions that normally take two or more steps to perform on a sewing machine. For instance, on this vest I piped a seam and gathered a narrow strip of fabric into the seam in the same operation. It sounds complicated (impossible?), but attachments make this super quick and easy.

A gathering attachment that joins to the front side of the presser foot area gathers a strip of fabric onto the main fabric. This method eliminates the procedure of pregathering the strip. In addition, a multipurpose (Bernina) presser foot used together with the gathering attachment holds piping in place while it's stitched onto the gathered piece. The grooved-out tunnel under the multipurpose foot also holds the zipper coil in place.

Medium-weight fabrics with minimal sizing gather at a 2:1 ratio when the stitch length is set on 4 mm and the differential is set on maximum gather. If there is some resistance to the fabric's gathering satisfactorily, increase both needle tensions to a higher number. There have been occasions where I maxed out on needle tensions. Once I used Woolly Nylon in both needles since it increases tensions by two to three numbers.

I explain zipper coil seaming, a favorite among my students, on page 178.

Agnes Mercik

Agnes Mercik

The notions-motif fabric is the inspiration for this fun vest. An assortment of compatible fabrics pull the unusual techniques together. The puffed strips are created using traditional piping on one side and zipper coil piping on the other.

Serger Treasures

Even a 6-inch (15-cm) patchwork square can tastefully feature more than one serger technique. The photograph below shows a section of a bomber jacket that serger expert Agnes Mercik made of embellished patches and fabric strips.

What a wonderful way to learn a variety of techniques—practice new techniques on fabric squares, and use the most successful ones to make the fabric for a garment.

Lay the stitched squares side by side on one piece of preshrunk fusible lining. This is the fun part. It's like putting a puzzle together.

Once satisfied with the arrangement, lightly fuse the two fronts to the lining and put it aside. Then roll edge–finish the strips of fabric following Step 2 on page 207. These are applied, lattice-like, between the squares. The decorative thread, an untwisted rayon, blends with the fabric. It's just enough to highlight the edge but not steal the thunder from the squares.

I laid the serged strips over the butted square sections and stitched alongside the overlock stitching with monofilament on the sewing machine once again, thus concealing the sewing machine stitch.

Agnes Mercik

Agnes Mercik

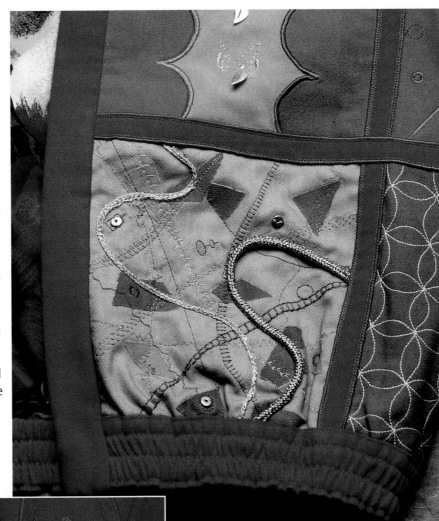

Embroidered motifs on the sleeves and back of this jacket reinforce the decorative work on the front panels. Serger expert Agnes Mercik stitched the geometric tone-on-tone shapes using lightweight rayon embroidery thread.

Texture and form give life to yards of complementary fabrics that make up this exceptional jacket. Creator Agnes Mercik tastefully combined many serger techniques to give the garment both body and texture. Shirring, rolled edging, faux piping, and decorative machine embroidery all add to the stunning effect.

Sew Many Circles

S–t–r–e–t–c–h your imagination with coach Agnes Mercik. She loved making this jacket because she was challenged by trying a new way of gathering fabric and by adding several interesting serger embellishments.

This was a fun jacket to work on since it more than stretched my imagination. In addition to the serger shirring and piping, trim and prairie points pick up the metallic threads used in the printed fabric at the shoulders.

You can gather fabric by serging with elastic thread in the looper and using chain-stitch settings. Fine to medium-weight fabrics will automatically gather during the process. (See "Shirring" on pages 192–193.)

I created elasticized yardage by stitching row after row using the presser foot as a general guide for spacing. (Closer spacing is used for the circle motifs on separate pieces of midnight and royal blue sandwashed rayon fabrics.)

The shrinking process continues when the yardage is steamed. Place the iron just above the fabric, so that it's barely touching, on the elastic side of the garment. It'll shrink right before your eyes. The threads in fabrics and elastics react and shrink in differing ratios, so I strongly advise

testing a piece to avoid disappointment. You'll need three to four times the amount of fabric yardage that the pattern recommends.

To stabilize the elasticized areas, gently press a lightweight fusible interfacing to the back of the entire piece of fabric before cutting out the pieces.

I found a stitch on my sewing machine that will make circles, so to enhance the circle theme, I stitched a combination of sashiko stitch designs onto the lining. I also finished the lining's edges with a rolled edge stitch, then topstitched it to the garment.

I love finding new ways to use techniques. This lining application is a fun way to try Mock Piping, explained on page 174 by Barbara Weiland.

Agnes Mercik

Agnes Mercik

Linda's Fabrication

Pattern maker Linda Lee Vivian not only serged this car coat but also "made" the fabric and customized the color of both the fabric and the looper thread.

This coat is very special because it's assembled from wool mohair fabric that I felted and dyed myself. It took many hours, so I wanted the stitching and pattern to be just perfect.

The garment is made from my Serger Coat pattern (for ordering information, see the "Shopping Guide" on page 234), assembled with a 4-thread overlock (with Woolly Nylon in the loopers), and edge-finished with a 2-thread wrap stitch. This stitch is very reversible, and it's stronger than a 3-thread version—perfect for the outer edges of the coat. The instructions for the stitch are on pages 117–118.

My "new" fabric is a very unusual color, so it was tough finding thread to match. Blending was the obvious choice. There are actually three colors in the stitching: Burmilana in gray and blue, plus turquoise Kreinik #8 Fine Braid.

All were mounted on a Thread Palette and then fed through the lower looper. If you want to try this, test the combination by feeding all the threads through the thread guides and tension disc to see if they pass through easily.

The fabric for this coat was created using a unique boiled wool process. There's considerable shrinkage, so I bought twice as much yardage as necessary and chose a pattern layout for narrower fabric. To duplicate my process, machine wash the fabric (with agitation) in hot water and detergent. Reposition the fabric frequently to ensure that all areas shrink evenly. I discovered that stitching the fabric into a tube prior to washing will help it retain its shape. Rinse with cold water and repeat the above process until you're happy with the results. Spin until damp, then block, shape, and air dry.

By the way, I found that differential feed in the gather range was necessary when I serged this fabric because it gave me added control.

Linda Lee Vivian

Linda Lee Vivian

A reversible stitch is your best choice for serging the raw fabric edges of a shawl-collar garment. This ensures a pretty continuous-edge finish at the break points, where the front starts to roll out to form the bottom of the collar. Linda's choice, a 2-thread stitch, is ideal. You can also have fun with a 3-thread overlock stitch. Use two contrasting colors, one in each of the loopers, and a needle thread that matches the fabric. When the collar rolls out, you'll see a different color.

Dinner at Tiffany's

Serger expert Linda Lee Vivian collects many beautiful fabrics to keep in her "stash" until the appropriate moment—when she has what she wants to create a masterpiece. It may take years before she has enough to flatlock shapes into a pieced garment.

I love luxurious fabrics and threads, and I was able to combine my love for these in this color-blocked vest. It's one of my simple patterns, called Linda's Easy Vest. (For ordering information, see the "Shopping Guide" on page 234.) The pieces of burgundy velvet and lamé offer a good variety of contrasting textures, and the decorative serger stitching adds enough elegance to make this a nice part of an evening ensemble. In the same manner that you create heirloom fabric by playing with the arrangement of laces and fabric, I arranged and rearranged the fabrics until the design "spoke" to me. With the

serger set for a 2-thread flatlock stitch and with antique gold Glamour thread in the lower looper, the decorative piecing began.

I always use a 2-thread flatlock because a 3-thread isn't strong enough for piecing. Since the fabric pieces are on the bias, a plus setting on the differential feed helped keep the seams flat. This also helped control the velvet's nap so seaming was easier.

Linda Lee Vivian

Linda Lee Vivian

If my selection of lamé doesn't quite fit my color scheme, I often use the reverse side for an additional effect. A lightweight lamé can be combined with heavier velvets by attaching a fusible knit interfacing to the wrong side. This gives the lamé the additional body it needs.

It's All in the Details

Students mob Agnes Mercik when she brings a new garment to class. They like to check out the linings in her garments just as thoroughly as the outside—they're always curious about the additional details that she has added, often at the last minute.

The beautiful blue-and-purple dyed tussah silk used in this jacket not only gathered nicely but also was a super foundation for some unplanned decorative stitches.

I'm intrigued with elastic thread and use it extensively because it stretches my imagination. Luckily, this is a growing trend because the ready-to-wear industry is using elasticized fabric. I make my own shirred fabric, thank goodness, because I'm not willing to pay $300 to $500 a yard. Instructions for shirring start on page 192.

In researching this technique further, I found that colored elastic threads add an unexpected texture either to sections of a garment or appliqué motifs, such as the circles on the Sew Many Circles jacket on pages 74–75.

While the outer fabric is very beautiful, the really dynamic effects are on the interior. The "piping" along the edge of the lining is actually a faux version, which you can duplicate on your serger by following the instructions on pages 174–175. I used a very glitzy purple serger thread to roll edge–finish the lining, and then I stitched it to the facing. It's an unexpected detail that really pops out when I open the jacket.

The sleeves and lining are further embellished with geometric lines of decorative machine stitching.

Agnes Mercik

Agnes Mercik

Serger shirring, a rolled edge finish, and decorative sewing machine stitching sizzle on base and lining fabrics. If you want to duplicate this look, you can also apply the cuff and waistband elastic, using one of two methods that are explained on pages 104–108.

Sweet Dreams

Heirloom sewing is usually done on fine cottons and linens. But serger expert Mary Griffin wanted to create a sample with a nontraditional fabric, like satin, using her serger and sewing machine.

I fell in love with heirloom sewing in the early 1980s, when we first started seeing these garments in some of the sewing magazines. I had not yet begun my new career in the sewing industry and was still busy helping to bring new babies into the world as a registered nurse. I was thrilled to find a shop that held lessons and faithfully took my well-loved Singer there once a week to learn delicious techniques such as lace-to-lace and entre-deux insertion. It was fun, amazingly easy, and so addictive!

My first project was a party dress for my niece—a pink confection with a wide fancy band and entre-deux galore. I innocently went to the shop and purchased whatever they told me, having no clue how much French laces can cost. Eighty-two dollars later I walked out of the store trying to pretend I was not about to faint! The dress turned out perfectly.

In making the camisole set, I wanted to experiment with a nontraditional fabric. Because the fabric isn't cotton, and the lace at the top isn't French, this isn't a "true" heirloom garment. But I wanted you to see that you can try these techniques without having to spend a fortune, as I did when I made my niece's dress. Besides, satin also has a more contemporary and luxurious look and feel.

Originally, heirloom work was done by hand. Then we discovered that many of the techniques look just as good when stitched on the sewing machine. It was only a matter of time before creative serger owners found ways to replicate the look with their machines. The overall impression is the same, but there are differences when you inspect the work.

Serged pintucks, for example, rely on a narrow hem with balanced looper threads. The two looper threads lock on the folded

I used the expensive French lace on the hems of the tap pants. Joining lace to fabric is a breeze with a blind hem or lace foot. These feet protect the lace from the knife, and you can comfortably serge the lace in place without worrying about ruining your investment. I love the neat rolled hem because the inside edges look just as beautiful as the outside.

edge of the pintuck. (Sewing machine pintucks are either folded and sewn with a straight stitch or made with a twin needle.) Using the serger to create pintucks, as I did on this camisole, is just downright fun and fast.

One of the things I like about heirloom sewing is that you create the "fabric" and then you cut out your garment pieces. There's no need to estimate the extra fabric that your technique will consume on every garment piece (which sometimes has disastrous consequences).

Instead, you join narrow strips of fabric, lace, and entredeux. By "creating" the fabric, then cutting out the pattern, the fabric won't "shrink" and "grow" as you add tucks and lace.

For this garment set I worked from the center out, beginning with the lace insertion. I used rayon thread for an elegant look, then added decorative stitches and cut out the camisole. The finishing touch is a rolled hem for the lower edge of the camisole.

Serged tucks and rolled hem finishes save time and let you create beautiful heirloom garments that look as if they took days to make!

Heirloom serging isn't as complicated as it sounds. This book walks you through the entire process, starting on page 133.

Mary Griffin

Mary Griffin

Touch 'n Go Trim

Take off into the exciting world of serger trim with seamstress Sue Nester as your co-pilot. Here is Sue's guided tour of the technique. Two-tone customized piping is the ideal way to make your garments soar to new heights of creativity.

You're at the controls of your serger as you make the overlocked trim on this knit-fabric sweater. Like an airplane pilot doing touch-and-gos (practicing landing and taking off on a runway), you command the trim by touching the needle thread.

I made this black-and-white trim by stitching on the folded edge of a bias fabric strip, and then inserting the finished piping into a seamline. The stitching is simple enough for people who are just starting to spread their wings with a serger.

Start with a basic 3-thread overlock stitch. Test-fly the stitch on a strip of folded fabric until it's balanced. Also play with the width of the stitch until you achieve a nice look. It's best to keep the stitching dense, so keep the stitch length on the short side.

Now you're ready to go solo. Disengage the knife, and insert your bias strip under a standard presser foot that's mounted on the machine. Serge several stitches with the balanced stitch settings. Stop, and use your finger to press the needle thread against the machine below the tension disk. Continue serging, counting out the same number of stitches that you made with the balanced tension. What you've done, in effect, is temporarily tighten the tension. By so doing, you pull the lower looper (white) thread around to the front of the bias strip.

Release the tension, count out the same number of stitches, and then re-vert to the tighter tension. Continue in this fashion until the piping is as long as needed for the garment.

Sue Nester

The starting point of this piping—a sturdy bias strip— adds stability to the seams of the knit fabric used for this casual jacket. If you doubt that your garment fabric will stretch until it's out of shape, you can substitute another material for your piping. A strip of tricot, like Seams Great, is more suitable for lightweight fabrics. And if you're ready for a challenge, use clear elastic to make piping for a fabric with lots of stretch.

A–Z Tips & Techniques

Excited by all the ideas you saw in "The Garment Gallery"? Then you're ready to learn all about them. "A–Z Tips and Techniques" will give you the nitty-gritty: step-by-step information that you can use to do some dynamic serging.

All five of the Serger Secrets authors—top experts in America—pull out all the stops. They share techniques they've developed, methods that their students love to learn, and innovative solutions to problems that you may encounter.

Beading

You can bead any garment with very elegant results. Try creating a chain of beads that you can couch or weave or flatlocking a string of beads to fabric.

FLATLOCKED PEARLS

Who wants to hand stitch yards and yards of cross-locked beads on a string to a fabric surface? It's time-consuming work, and you can achieve the same effect at your machine with "invisible" monofilament thread. The most common method is at your sewing machine, using a zigzag or blind-hem stitch. For more security and faster attachment, why not try flatlocking the beads to fabric with your serger?

Pearl beads are usually serged along the edge of a fabric. Yet this isn't your only option for their application. For a different effect, flatlock the beads with monofilament nylon thread so they "float" on top of the fabric.

Experiment with pearl placement to create a variety of exciting effects. If your serger has a 2-thread capability, choose a 2-thread flatlock stitch so that one less thread crosses over the pearls. Follow the steps on this page and the opposite page. The instructions also explain how to serge a seam that would normally cross over the beads.

Stitching is hardly visible when you use monofilament thread—the strands of beads float across the surface of the fabric.

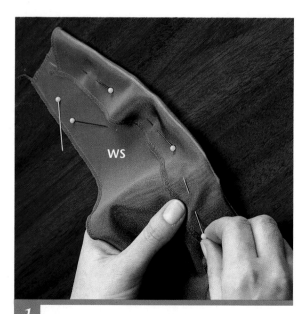

1 Mark straight or gently curved placement lines for the string of pearls. When creating the design lines for your beads, it's important to keep in mind that angles and bias lines are more challenging. Fold the garment fabric, wrong sides together, along one of the lines. Pin the fold, but don't press it. Keep the pins well away from the fold.

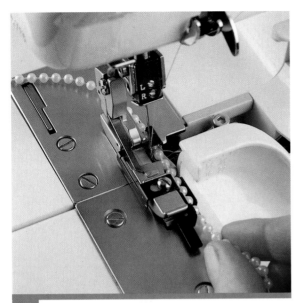

2 Place the start of the string of pearls into the groove of the presser foot, pulling 1 to 2 inches (2.5 to 5 cm) out behind the foot. Turn the handwheel toward you to take a few stitches around the beads by hand. This will secure the start of the pearls in the stitching chain.

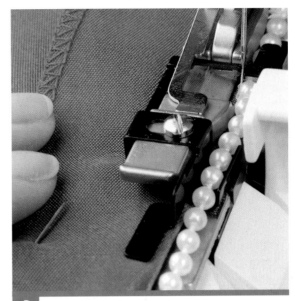

3 Place the folded fabric under the presser foot. Find a mark on the foot with which you can sight and align the fold to guide it so that the stitches hang slightly off the fold. If you can't disengage the knife, make sure that the fold is not cut off while you're stitching.

4 Flatlock along the fold, catching the pearls in the stitching. Sew slowly to ensure that the looper threads wrap around the sides of the pearls. Serge off the fabric and pull the stitching flat. Don't worry if you can't pull the stitches perfectly flat. This makes a pretty tuck that can become a part of your design. Serge all the rows in the same direction.

5 Remove the marking pencil lines. Dot liquid seam sealant about 1/4 inch (6 mm) inside the seamline, or pull out the threads around the pearls and tie them off by hand. Clip out the excess pearls. Now a side seam can be serged without crossing over the pearls. This keeps your stitching line straight and prevents needle breakage.

Free-Motion Beading

There are times when applying an entire string of beads to a garment is a bit over the top. If you're faced with this situation, a chain of decorative thread interspersed with beads is the solution.

Stitch a tight rolled hem over fishing line, occasionally slipping a bead up to the needle. (Each bead is secured by looper threads during the stitching.) The work goes relatively quickly once you have a feel for stitching without fabric. The most difficult part is guiding the thread chain without pulling it off the stitch finger.

If you've done any free-motion beading by sewing machine, you'll notice similarities because the serger presser foot and shank are often removed before you start stitching.

Author Agnes Mercik often weaves her finished beaded chain in and out of fabric strips. In this situation she needs to remove some beads. (See "Hit or Miss" on page 92.)

Breaking the string of beads is easier than figuring out the exact length to make each beaded chain. If your beads are precious, then by all means take the time to measure the exact distances. Allow 2 to 3 extra inches (5 to 7.5 cm) of chain without beads at the end of each length, to eliminate the possibility of beads ending up in the seamlines. You don't want to stitch over pearls because they can break your needle and cause unsightly lumps.

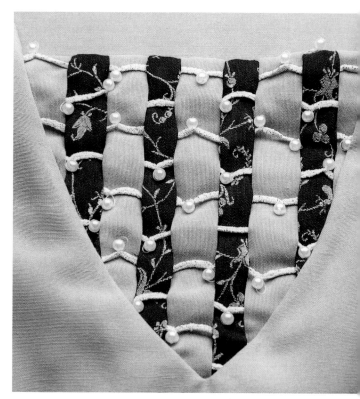

Free-motion beading fascinates serger expert Agnes Mercik. She adds the finished chain to woven fabric. (See page 206.)

SETTINGS & MATERIALS

Stitch: 3-thread rolled
Stitch length: 1 to 1.5 mm
Needle position: Right
Presser foot: None
Throat plate or stitch finger: Rolled (if necessary)
Needle thread: All-purpose or decorative
Looper threads: 30- or 40-weight rayon in solid or variegated colors, Woolly Nylon, or Woolly Metallic
Upper knife: Disengaged
Notions: Beading needle, fine fishing line, loose beads

Fast Fix

THINK LIGHT

Is your finished beaded chain too stiff? Most fabric drapes and moves, so your beaded chain also needs to be just as flexible.

When your chain isn't as soft as you'd like it to be, it's more than likely that the culprit is the fishing line. Eight-pound test weight is the best choice.

Don't select line that's heavier than 10-pound test weight because this is just too thick.

If you're unsure about the line weight you've selected, stitch a 6-inch (15-cm)-long test chain.

Agnes Mercik

1 Using the hand beading needle, string the beads on to the fishing line. To avoid losing the beads while serging, don't cut the fishing line off the reel. Instead, let it rest in your lap as you add the beads. In fact, it can remain in your lap during the entire stitching process.

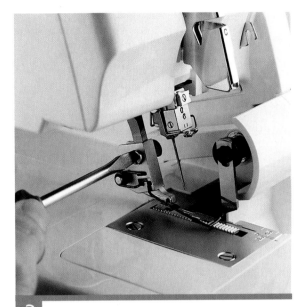

2 Remove the presser foot and the shank from your serger. Disengaging the knife is optional for free-motion beading. Lower the presser foot bar. Even though you don't use a foot for this technique, the lever must be down. This ensures that the thread tensions are properly engaged.

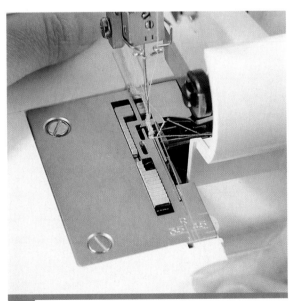

3 Stitch a few inches of rolled hem chain. Guide the serged chain with your left hand, taking care not to pull it off the stitch finger. Keep an even tension during this process. This procedure takes practice to get the correct tension. You may want to stitch more than a few inches of thread chain until you are comfortable with this process.

Fast Fix

PUSH 'N PULL

It's tempting to pull on the stitches as they're forming. By doing this, the more fragile threads, such as rayon embroidery, will break. On the other hand, if the chain of stitches isn't encouraged along, then the chain will pile up and look unsightly. Try to be consistent. If you stop periodically, lower the needle to hold your place.

If the thread accidentally breaks, stop and remove the loose pieces. Serge over the broken area with two or three stitches, and immediately place a small dab of liquid seam sealant on the spot. Let it dry before continuing, then trim the excess threads.

Agnes Mercik

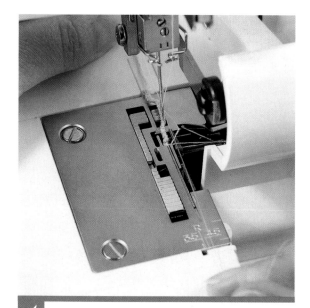

4 Place the fishing line just slightly to the right of the needle so that it's on top of the very narrow stitch finger. This position ensures that the upper looper will wrap over the fishing line. Serge over the fishing line for at least a few inches. Again, guide the thread chain with your left hand.

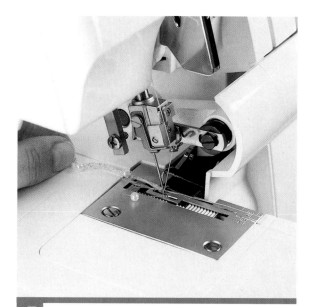

5 To add a bead, stop serging, and then lower the serger needle. Pull out a small loop of unstitched fishing line to the left of the needle. From the collection of beads on the fishing line, slide a single bead up the fishing line to the center of the loop that's near the needle.

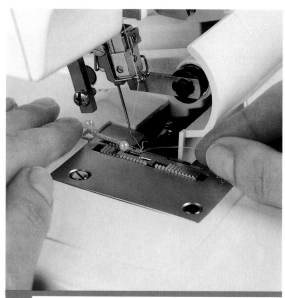

6 Serge two or three stitches in place, catching the fishing line past the loop in the stitching. Hold the thread chain behind the presser foot, and then very gently pull the unstitched fishing line in a straight line toward you until the loop to the left of the needle disappears. Repeat wherever you want a bead.

Fast Fix

HIT OR MISS

Beads can break a needle or damage your fabric or iron.

If beads intersect a seamline, a needle can hit one and snap off when you're stitching. So break the pearls off the stitched chain with small hand pliers to eliminate any lumpy areas. Shake the fabric to get rid of all of the broken pieces.

If the beads are plastic, take care when pressing because the iron can melt them into the fabric. I use a Teflon pressing sheet whenever I have any doubts about the fabric, fragile decorative threads, or embellishments like the beads.

Agnes Mercik

Braid

The wonderful selection of decorative threads on the market enables you to create made-to-order braid for any garment.

CUSTOMIZED TRIM

Create a Chanel-inspired garment by embellishing it with braid. In many cases the key, as a close inspection of the genuine designer garments will attest, is a trim that combines fabric and threads from the fashion fabric.

You can choose the color you want and quickly serge your own beautiful trims. The starting point is Seams Great, or you can cut your own ⅝-inch (1.5-cm)-wide strips of tricot. To create the braid, you encase the tricot in the decorative thread as you serge.

There's a real bonus to making your own trim: If you place fusible thread in the lower looper, your finished braid can then be fused to the right side of the fabric. This makes it easy to form the flexible trim into various shapes, including curves. If you plan to wash your finished garment, topstitch the braid after fusing it to the fabric.

Customize by blending different 40-weight rayons or metallics as one through the upper looper. Variegated threads are fun to serge with, and Coats Color Twist works quite well. Heavy metallics, such as Madeira's Glamour and YLI's Candlelight, reflect light beautifully. Pearl rayon, pearl cotton, and even baby yarn create interesting effects. There aren't too many rules here; just make sure the thread fits easily into your upper looper and flows smoothly. On some sergers you need to loosen the upper looper tension or remove the thread from one of the many guides.

SETTINGS & MATERIALS

Stitch: 3-thread overlock
Stitch length: 1 to 1.5 mm
Stitch width: 3 to 4 mm
Needle position: Left (if possible)
Presser foot: Taping, elastic, or standard
Needle thread: All-purpose
Upper looper thread: Decorative
Lower looper thread: Fusible
Upper knife: Engaged
Notions: Clear press cloth, Seams Great or ⅝-inch (1.5-cm)-wide strips of bias-cut tricot

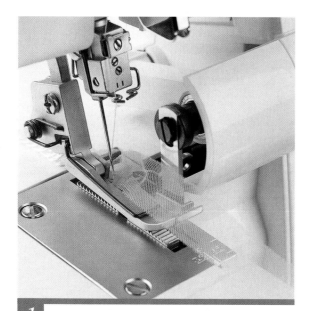

1 Fold the tricot in half, and feed it into the guide on the taping or elastic presser foot. (With a standard foot, guide the tricot as shown, using the knife edge as a guide.) The tricot should ride between the knife and the needle. Pull 2 inches (5 cm) of tricot out behind the back of the foot.

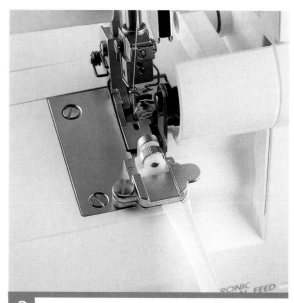

2 Grasp both ends of the tricot, and pull it taut so that it curls along the length, forming a tube. Begin serging, allowing the serger to feed the tricot under the needle and stitch on it to form the braid. Hold the tricot taut. Be sure to hold both ends so the thread flows evenly.

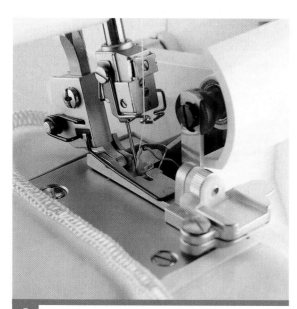

3 The stitches form around the tube with the upper and lower loopers evenly balanced. Increase the stitch width if the tube isn't covered, or pull the tricot to make it narrower. Decrease the stitch length if the stitches aren't close enough together. Serge the desired length.

4 Mark placement lines on the fabric, and press the fabric to heat it. Position the braid, and press firmly, using a press cloth and a temperature appropriate for the thread. Press the back of the fabric. Topstitch the braid with monofilament thread and a straight stitch.

Buttons and Bows

Whether your taste is tailored or ruffled, you can use your serger to add fabric buttons to any garment, make a decorative version of a bound buttonhole, or stitch the perfect bow.

BUTTON TOGGLE

A novel idea, fabric buttons are sure to draw attention. The concept is the same as making paper beads from magazine pages. Instead of using the colorful printed paper, you finish the edges of a fabric triangle with decorative serging, then roll it up. To design your button, experiment with thread choices and the triangle shape and size. If the base of your triangle is 1¼ inches (3 cm) wide and 6 inches (15 cm) long, then the finished button width is the same. To beef up a light fabric, you can fuse two triangles together.

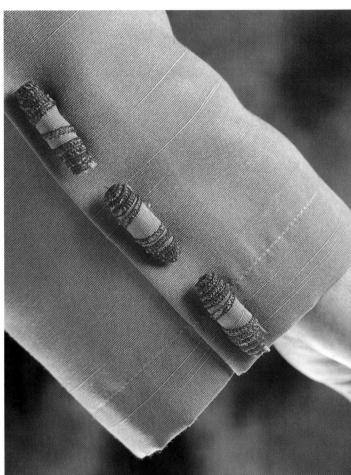

Decorative thread sparkles on the stitched edge of these rolled buttons. Just stitch along the edges of a fabric triangle, roll, and secure.

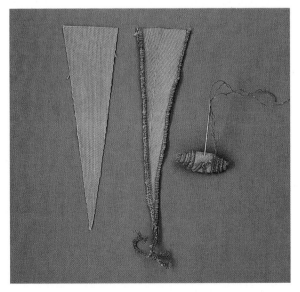

Cut a long, narrow triangle. Serge the long edges, using differential feed on a gather setting to control wavy edges. End your serging with a chain. Don't cut it off. Starting at the wide end, roll the triangle into a snug tube, and secure it with the chain threaded on a needle.

SETTINGS & MATERIALS

Stitch: 3-thread overlock
Presser foot: Standard
Needle thread: Decorative or all-purpose
Looper threads: Decorative
Notions: Hand sewing needle, liquid seam sealant (optional)
Recommended fabric: Medium- to heavy-weight fabrics with body

DECORATIVE BOUND BUTTONHOLE

For a decorative touch on a tailored gar-ment, use a fancy thread to embellish the "lips" of a bound buttonhole.

You need your serger and sewing machine to create this glamorous version of the traditional bound buttonhole. The thread you select will have a dramatic im-pact on the garment. It's worth experi-menting with several types and colors. Consider metallic, variegated, and rayon. Matching thread for the buttonhole lips adds subtle color and texture for a more subdued and decorative effect.

Use decorative serging in other areas on the finished garment so the bound button-holes aren't distracting. For example, use the same thread to serge-finish the edges of patch pockets, sleeve bands, and the neck-line and front edge on a cardigan-style jacket to create a unified look. You can also serge-embellish the lips for a welt pocket (using the widest serger stitch possible).

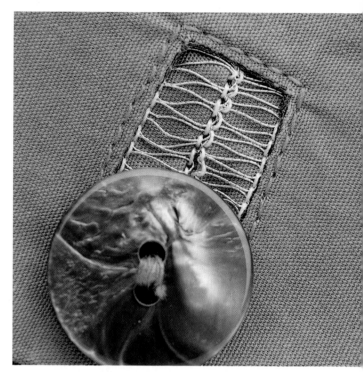

Select a contrasting color thread if you want your buttonholes to attract attention. Matching thread adds subtle color and texture.

SETTINGS & MATERIALS

Stitch: 3-thread overlock

Stitch length: Adjust for thread type and desired coverage

Stitch width: To match the width of the button "lips"

Presser foot: Standard

Needle thread: All-purpose or lightweight decorative to match upper looper thread color

Upper looper thread: Decorative

Lower looper thread: Decorative or all-purpose

Upper knife: Disengaged

Notions: Lightweight fusible, nonwoven interfacing; pencil; press cloth; strips of paper-backed fusible web, each ¼ inch (6 mm) wide

Recommended fabric: Medium- to heavy-weight fashion fabric; matching lightweight lining

Fast Fix

BREAK THE TENSION

Breaking threads. Uneven tension. Unbalanced tension. If you have these problems, your first reaction is to fiddle with the tension settings. But that may not be the cause of your woes, espe-cially if you're using metallic or ribbon thread. There's a good chance that the problems are caused by the way the thread feeds off the spool. The thread on serger cones is cross-wound so that it feeds easily from the upright spool pin on your serger. Parallel-wound thread needs to feed into the thread guides with the spool positioned hori-zontally. If you're in a bind, just place the spool in a mug behind the serger.

Agnes Mercik

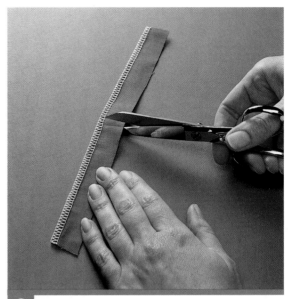

1 For each buttonhole, cut a 2-inch (5-cm)-wide strip of fabric twice the finished buttonhole length plus 2 inches (5 cm). Each strip will be the "lips" for one buttonhole. Press each strip in half lengthwise with the wrong side to the inside and the raw edges even. Repeat for all of the fabric strips.

2 With decorative thread, serge over the folded lengthwise edge of each strip. If you are unable to disengage the upper knife, be careful not to cut the fold. Cut through the middle of a strip to make two pieces of equal length. These are the "lips" of one buttonhole. Repeat with the other strips.

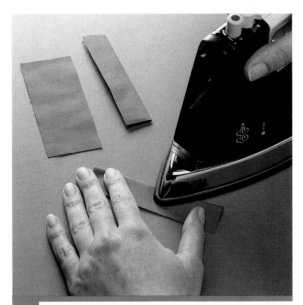

Bartack →

Bartack →

Button opening plus ⅛ inch at each end

3 Butt together the serged edges of one set of lips. Decide on the size of the opening for your buttonholes. At your sewing machine, bartack the ends together ⅛ inch (3 mm) past each end of the desired size of the buttonhole opening. This creates the "patch" for your buttonhole.

Fast Fix

CHOOSE WISELY

Decorative threads should not only enhance the garment's total look but also have a texture compatible with the fabric.

Your thread choice should enhance the fabric qualities, assuming, of course, that a reasonably good-quality fabric is used. Though contrast threads appear to be the obvious choice for this decorative bound buttonhole, examine the fabric for texture and subtle colors that perhaps can be expanded upon and emphasized with the overlock thread.

Tone-on-tone may not appear as dull if the thread color is a deeper tone or a variegated variety.

Agnes Mercik

4 Trim the buttonhole patch into an oval shape. On the right side of the patch, fuse a ¼-inch (6-mm)-wide strip of paper-backed fusible web just inside each row of serging, from bartack to bartack only. Repeat Steps 3 and 4 with the remaining sets of lips.

Patch of interfacing on garment WS

5 Measure the total width of the serger stitching across both buttonhole lips to determine the finished buttonhole width. With a pencil, draw a rectangle of the finished length and width on the wrong side of the interfaced garment front. This is the buttonhole "window opening."

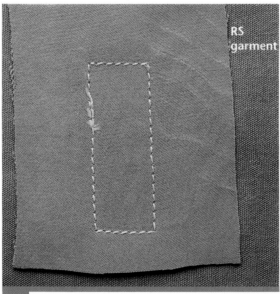

RS garment

6 Cut a lining rectangle 1 inch (2.5 cm) longer and 2 inches (5 cm) wider than the size of the buttonhole you marked in Step 5. Pin the lining rectangle face down on the right side of the garment, over the buttonhole location. On the wrong side of the garment, stitch along the marked rectangle.

7 Remove the work from the sewing machine. With small, sharp scissors, cut horizontally along the middle of the stitched rectangle, cutting through all fabric layers. Snip diagonally into the corners as far as possible. Snip close to the stitching in the corners so the buttonhole corners will be nice and sharp.

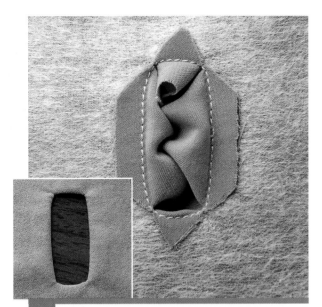

8 Turn the lining to the wrong side of the garment by pulling it through the hole you made in Step 6. Get the lining completely flat in the corners. If you can't achieve this, return the lining to the other side, and snip closer to the stitching. Turn the lining again, and press. This is the buttonhole window.

9 Remove the backing paper from the fusible strips on the patch. Center the patch under the buttonhole window opening. Fuse, using a press cloth. Edge-stitch around the opening, stitching through all layers of the garment and the buttonhole patch.

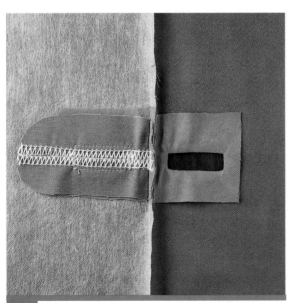

10 On your garment facing, make buttonhole windows that correspond with each set of buttonhole "lips" on the garment. To create each of the windows, again follow Steps 6 and 7. Attach the facing so that each buttonhole window is directly opposite a set of lips.

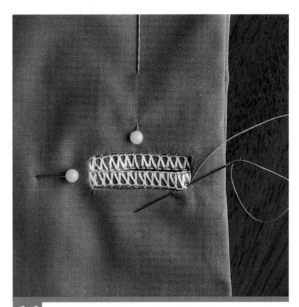

11 Fold the facing to the wrong side of the garment along the seamline. Press it in position. Now you secure the windows over the buttonhole lips by hand sewing or fusing the window in place on the wrong side of the buttonhole. With slippery fabric, you may want to both fuse and stitch.

BEAUTIFUL BOWS

The nicest bows have both body and shape. One of the most important ingredients for obtaining the correct shape is selecting a stiff fabric. A firm edge is just as important because it adds stability and definition.

Luckily, such an edge is easy to obtain by serging a filler, such as cord or crochet cotton, to the fabric strips that are then assembled into a bow. To marry the cord to the fabric, serge-finish a rolled hem or narrow balanced overlock stitch over the filler of your choice. Fabric "pokies" are less obvious when the filler and thread color match the bow fabric.

The type of filler you select depends on your fabric. For example, to add body to the rolled edges of soft fabric ruffles, it's best to serge over fishing line. (See "Fishline Edge Finish" on page 113.)

To stabilize loosely woven or stretchy fabric, crochet cotton is the best choice. In this case, the thread you select is just as important. Author Agnes Mercik recommends using Woolly Nylon Regular or Woolly Nylon Extra in the upper looper.

The instructions on pages 101–103 will help you make a double-layer bow that has the finished dimensions 11 × 7 inches (28 × 17.5 cm).

Serger expert Agnes Mercik used Woolly Metallic thread to add a hint of sparkle to the edge of this bow. It adds a beautiful finish along with providing a personal touch. Agnes creates bows and ribbons simply by choosing an interesting and exciting combination of fabrics and threads. For example, if the fabric contains a hint of metallic thread, she uses a metallic decorative thread to complement it. After trying this basic technique for bow and ribbon making, you'll find endless possibilities and variations for expanding and diversifying your own projects.

SETTINGS & MATERIALS

Stitch: 3-thread rolled
Stitch length: Short
Stitch width: Narrow to medium
Needle position: Right (if possible)
Presser foot: Cording
Needle thread: All-purpose
Upper looper thread: Decorative Woolly Nylon
Lower looper thread: All-purpose
Upper knife: Engaged
Notions: Filler cord, liquid seam sealant*

*The filler you use depends on the type of fabric and thread. You can use crochet cotton, fishing line, kite string, topstitching thread, and lightweight knitting and crochet yarns of varying weights and sizes.

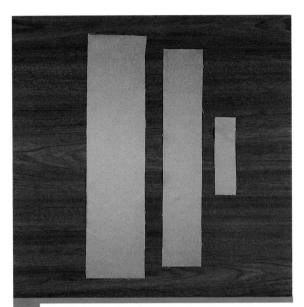

1 From your bow fabric, cut three strips. Each strip is a different length and width. The lower layer is 24 × 8 inches (61 × 20 cm). The upper layer is 22 × 5 inches (56 × 12.5 cm). The "knot," which wraps around the upper and lower layers, is 4 × 1½ inches (10 × 4 cm).

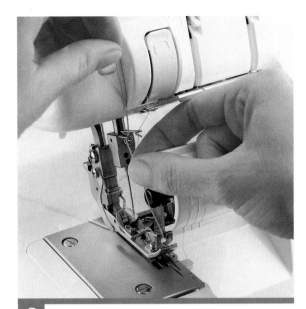

2 Place the filler cord through the hole in the front of the cording presser foot and under the groove, with a 4-inch (10-cm) tail behind the foot. Place your filler cord either on the table behind the machine or on the left needle spindle. Thread the cord through the first and last left needle guides.

Fast Fix

OVERRULE THE ROLL

If the bow fabric is stubborn and won't roll as much as you'd like, switch to a narrow, balanced (overlocked) stitch. In this case, use decorative thread in both loopers. These simple adjustments should make it easy to obtain good edge coverage and eliminate fabric "pokies."

One of the secrets to a successful corded edge is the correct thread choice. If your threads don't completely cover the cord filler, then you should change the product in your upper looper. Woolly Nylon Regular or Woolly Nylon Extra are both good choices.

Agnes Mercike

3 Place the long edge of any one of your fabric strips under the presser foot so that the knife will cut off just a bit of the fabric as the serger creates the stitch by wrapping looper threads around the cut edge. This ensures a good, firm edge when stitched. Serge the length so that the filler cord is completely hidden within the rolled hem stitching.

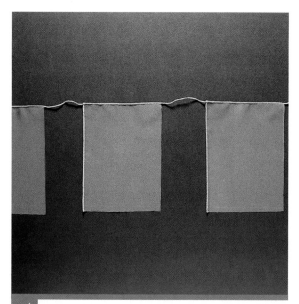

4 Run a short chain without fabric, then serge along a long edge of the next fabric strip. You'll have made a "kite tail," which is a fast and easy way to serge-finish edges on many fabric strips. Serge the remaining edges in the same manner, except for one short side of the "knot." Cut the center of each chain.

5 Place liquid seam sealant on all corner tail chains, wait for them to dry completely, and then trim them close to all of the corners. Center the upper layer strip on the lower layer, both right side up. Fold the layers in half. Straight stitch through all layers 6½ inches (16.5 cm) from the fold.

Fast Fix

USE EXTRA THREAD

If your threads don't completely cover the cord filler, then you should change the product in the upper looper. Two strands of Woolly Nylon Regular or Woolly Nylon Metallic are both good choices. Thread the looper in the usual manner, handling the two threads as one. Place the additional thread on an extra cone stand directly behind the other spool that's on the machine. Continue threading all of the guides in the usual manner. Serge slower, so that both threads are unwinding off the spools at the same rate.

Agnes Mercik

6 Refold the layers so that the loose ends of the fabric strips are split to the right and left, and the lower layer is on the bottom. Push down the center of the folded section so that it rests on top of (and covers) the straight stitching you made in Step 5. Make sure that the section on top of the stitching is evenly distributed.

7 Set up your sewing machine for a long straight stitch, and sew two rows of gathering threads down the center of the bow. Stitch through all of the layers of fabric. In this photo, the fabric strip to the right of the bow is the "knot." You'll work with the knot in the next step.

8 Draw up the gathering threads that you made on your sewing machine in Step 7. Pull them until you like the shape of the layered bow. Now wrap the "knot" strip around the gathering stitching. Place the unfinished edge at the back. Hand-tack it to the back of the bow.

9 You can use single fabric layers for a bow. The lower layer is 8 × 6 inches (20.5 × 15 cm). The middle layer is 7 × 5 inches (17.5 × 12.5 cm). The upper layer is 6 × 4 inches (15 × 10 cm). The "knot" is 4 × 1½ inches (10 × 4 cm). Follow Steps 3, 4, 5, and 6, but don't fold the layers in half. Continue with Steps 7 and 8.

Fast Fix

DELIGHT IN LIGHT

You can still make a scrumptious bow, even if your fabric is rather lightweight. Just use two layers!

To seam lightweight fabrics together (such as collars and cuffs), serge the two layers of fabric with wrong sides together. Use decorative thread such as rayon or topstitching thread in the upper looper of a 3-thread stitch or the lower looper of a 2-thread stitch.

You may want to join the fabric layers before you serge the edges together. The most common method is basting the layers around the edges. By far the fastest and easiest is joining the layers with fusible webbing.

Agnes Mercik

Casings

Do you remember making your first waistband by inserting elastic into a casing? Now, thanks to the cover stitch, you have two attractive techniques for waistbands, sleeve cuffs, and pant legs.

COVER-STITCHED CASING

Both casing techniques in this chapter are based on the same stitch and very similar procedures.

This is the faster method. All you need to do is assemble your garment side seams, set up the serger for the cover stitch, and get to work. The nicest part about these instructions is the simplicity of the process.

In fact, there's a good possibility that you can assemble the entire garment without changing the settings on your serger. Join the side seams, insert the casing, and even topstitch the hem using the same stitch. Step-by-step instructions on cover stitching a hem are on page 159.

You can use this technique whether you're working on polar fleece, cotton, or polyester. Don't worry about finishing raw edges before starting the casing. Even fabrics that are prone to fraying are kept in check by the looper threads on the underside of the fabric.

Although shown on a cuff, this casing is quite suitable for a waistband or even the legs on a pair of casual pants.

The elastic insertion method is the ultimate time-saver because it's completed in a few short steps. Plus, since the cover stitch also encases any raw fabric edges caught underneath the looper threads, it isn't necessary to overlock the raw edge before inserting the elastic.

If you're short on time, you'll also like the easy machine setup. You don't need to switch the settings on your serger because the technique requires only one stitch. You can use the cover stitch to seam the sleeve and topstitch the casing.

SETTINGS & MATERIALS

Stitch: Cover
Stitch length: 2.5 to 3 mm
Presser foot: Cover (if necessary)
Needle positions: 2.5 or 5 mm
Throat plate: Cover (if necessary)
Thread: All-purpose
Upper knife: Disengaged
Recommended elastic: Braided or sport, 1 to 1½ inches (2.5 to 4 cm) wide*

*Braided elastics with a firm stretch work best. Avoid the extremely soft and stretchy elastics commonly used in lingerie or on children's clothing.

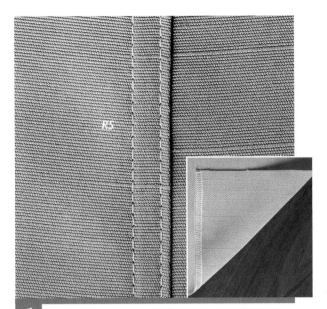

1 Don't overlock the raw fabric edge where you're inserting the elastic (the sleeve hem, in this example). With the right sides together, join the garment side seams with the cover stitch. Press the seam allowances to one side, and topstitch from the right side using the cover stitch.

2 To make a casing, press the hem to the inside. Make your casing twice the width of the elastic plus a bit extra for ease. Cut your elastic, and sew the ends together by overlapping the raw edges by ½ inch (1 cm) and zigzagging or cover stitching. Insert the elastic circle under the casing.

3 Place the casing and elastic to the right of the foot. If you prefer, they can go under the foot. Serge, stretching the elastic and fabric so that it's flat in the area you're stitching. Be careful not to pull so hard that the serger's timing is damaged. You can catch the elastic in the stitching, or else arrange the casing so both lines of stitching are to the left of the elastic.

Fast Fix

GET DOWN

The most common problem my students have is slipping elastic. While stitching, the elastic scoots away from the fold, up inside the fabric casing. I find this also happens when readjusting the fabric layers. When you use the cover-stitch function, the needles automatically stop in the down position. Place the casing under the presser foot with the elastic to the right. Serge, keeping the elastic and fabric flat in the area where you're stitching. Do this by stopping and pulling the elastic so that the casing behind the presser foot is gathered. Don't catch the elastic in the stitching.

Agnes Mercik

QUICK CASING

In a hurry? Then pick this technique to insert elastic into your waistband. Just sew it to the wrong side of your garment, and then topstitch it in place.

All you need is a 3-thread overlock and a cover stitch on your serger. The cover stitch is your best choice for topstitching because it stretches with the elastic, thus creating a smooth finished edge on the inside of the waistband. If your serger is not equipped with a cover stitch, don't despair. You can achieve the same effect using a twin needle and topstitching with your sewing machine.

While this technique is commonly found on activewear such as running shorts and sweatpants, it works equally well on both dressy and sporty skirts and slacks. It's also great for the bottom of baseball jackets, when you want to place elastic in the hem or cuffs.

When planning this project, keep in mind that the finished casing for the elastic will be slightly wider than the elastic you select. Depending on your pattern, you may need to extend the garment pieces ¼ to ½ inch (6 mm to 1 cm) at the top of the waistband. This extra fabric allows for turn-of-cloth—the amount of fabric taken up when you fold the elastic to the inside of the garment. (See Step 4.)

SETTINGS & MATERIALS

Stitch: 3-thread overlock and cover
Stitch length: 4 mm for overlocking, 3 to 4 mm for the cover stitch
Stitch width: Widest possible for overlocking
Presser foot: Standard for overlocking, as required for the cover stitch
Throat plate: Cover (if necessary)
Thread: All-purpose
Upper knife: Engaged for overlocking, disengaged for the cover stitch
Recommended elastic: Any brand or width, the 1½-inch (4-cm) width is most commonly used for waistbands

Twists and turns are great fun in the plot of your favorite book, but they're a bit of a pain in a garment's waistband.

Just think about all of the times that you've had to fiddle with the slippery elastic in a waistband casing in order to get the elastic to lie completely flat.

There is an easy way to prevent this problem in future garments, just by trying out the "Quick Casing" assembly technique featured here. You can prevent the elastic from twisting by securely anchoring one lengthwise edge to the fabric edge with overlocking.

1 With right sides together, serge or sew together the side seams on your garment. Now cut a length of elastic for the waistband. Make this elastic as long as your body's waist measurement, plus ½ inch (1 cm). Divide both the elastic and waistband into quarters and pin-mark.

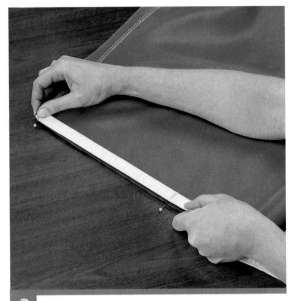

2 Place the elastic at the waist on the wrong side of the garment. Position the elastic so that one of the long edges is even with the raw edge of the waist on the garment. Pin the start of the elastic to the garment at one of the quarter-pin-marks that will end up near, or at, the side of your body.

Fast Fix

BOUNCE BACK

Sometimes students do an absolutely wonderful job serging elastic to the garment but return a few days later with broken stitches or distorted elastic. They don't understand why they're having these problems, because the very nature of serger stitching gives it more stretch.

I tell them that it's important to make the stitches and elastic in their garment as resilient as possible.

For maximum stretch when sewing elastic, be sure to use the longest stitch length possible. This allows the elastic to return to its original state more readily.

Pam Hastings

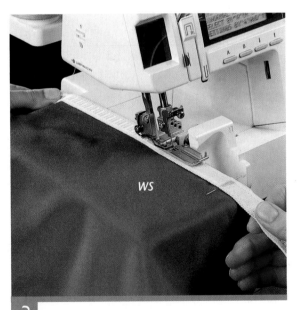

WS

3 Stretch the elastic so that the first pin-mark on the elastic matches the next pin-mark on the garment. With your 3-thread overlock set up, begin serging. As you serge, stretch the elastic to fit the waistline. Match all of the corresponding pin-marks on the garment and the elastic. Back at the starting point, butt the elastic ends.

4 The lower, unstitched, lengthwise edge of the elastic becomes the upper edge of the waistband. To make this happen, fold the stitched edge of the elastic to the wrong side of the garment. This results in the elastic being encased in the fabric. There's no need to pin the elastic in place.

5 Change your serger setup to make the cover stitch, changing the presser foot or needle plate if needed. Put the garment right side up on the serger bed. The right cover-stitch needle should enter the bottom edge of the elastic. Do not run a chain of stitching. Start cover stitching directly on the fabric.

Fast Fix

GET STEAMED

The whole purpose of inserting elastic into a garment is to give that area the ability to stretch and recover. Unfortunately, this objective is sometimes thwarted by elastic that loses its stretch during the assembly process. Take heart, because you don't have to rip out the stitching and start with a new piece of elastic.

If elastic stretches out of shape after topstitching with the cover-stitch settings on your serger, simply steam the elastic back into place with an iron. Hold your iron just above the elastic, and steam. Don't press the elastic.

Pam Hastings

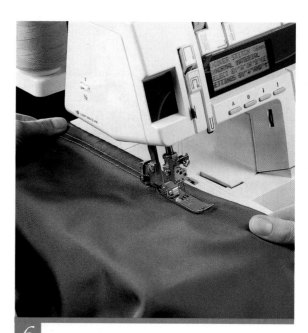

6 Secure the elastic inside the casing by serger-topstitching through all layers. As you serge, pull the front of the waistband with your right hand, and position your left hand behind the serger. Don't pull too hard on the elastic, or you'll end up with skipped stitches.

Cording

From belt carriers to button loops, the thread chain made by your serger is a valuable feature. Pages 38–39 show many interesting ways to use the chain. This feature offers yet another idea, based on a chain that's stitched over filler. Since it's a functional chain, the filler adds strength.

REINFORCED BELT CARRIERS

You can make a "crocheted" chain simply by setting your machine for a rolled hem and serging off the desired length. However, it's possible to create a stronger, more decorative version using pearl cotton thread and a gimp foot. Pearl cotton gives the loops strength and body, and the special foot eases the process because the hole in the foot guides the cord. (If you don't have a gimp foot, you can still make beautiful cord with these instructions. See "At the Improv" on page 9 for a suggested foot substitution.)

Once you've given this a whirl, you'll probably want to experiment with colored cords and threads. For novelty, try variegated thread. If you want to see the contrasting "cord," increase the stitch length.

There are as many ways to use a reinforced cord as there are types of garments. Here, a length was sewn into the side seam of a raincoat.

SETTINGS & MATERIALS

Stitch: 2- or 3-thread rolled
Stitch length: 1 to 2 mm
Stitch width: 3.5 mm
Needle position: Right
Presser foot: Gimp
Throat plate or stitch finger: Rolled (if necessary)
Needle thread: All-purpose
Upper looper thread: Decorative (rayon or Woolly Nylon)
Lower looper thread: All-purpose
Upper knife: Engaged or disengaged
Notions: Dental-floss threader (optional), filler cord such as pearl cotton, large-eye tapestry needle

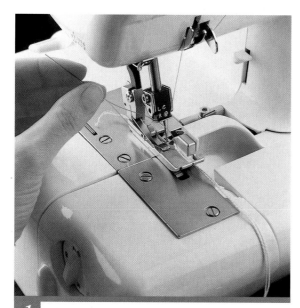

1 Thread the pearl cotton cord through the hole in the gimp presser foot. To make this easier, use a dental-floss threader. Extend about 2 inches (5 cm) of the cord out the back of the foot. The knife can remain engaged because the gimp foot protects the cord from being cut.

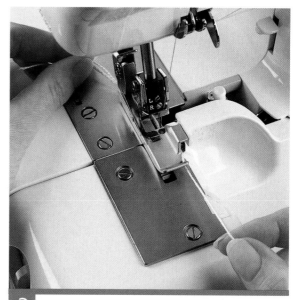

2 Serge without any fabric to make a short stitched chain. Hold the thread tails and the cord behind the foot with your left hand. Hold the cord in front of the foot in your other hand so it's taut. Stitch with the needle on the left side of the cord so the cord is caught inside the stitching.

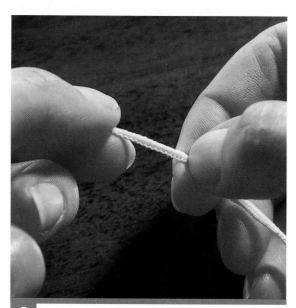

3 For consistent stitching, avoid pulling the cord through the machine. Serge out the needed length of chain. If desired, adjust the loops when you're finished stitching. If you managed to avoid stitching through the cord, you can do this by pushing the loops closer together along the length of the cord with your fingernail.

4 Thread the cord through a tapestry needle with the dental-floss threader. Pull the stitched cord through the garment side seam. You'll find this much easier to do if you pull the thick cord between the stitches. On the inside, make a knot in the end of the cord. Attach the other end of the cord in the same manner.

Couching

Decorative ribbon is traditionally attached to a fabric surface with glue or sewing machine stitches. But the serger offers a faster option.

FLATLOCK COUCHING

Ribbons, yarns, metallic braids, or even a decorative serged chain can be couched onto fabric with your serger. The only limitation you'll encounter is that the couching material must fit between the needle and the knife. You don't even need a special presser foot.

While these instructions recommend using a 2-thread flatlock stitch, couching can also be done with a 3-thread flatlock with a decorative or monofilament thread in the upper looper. Take care that the couching material is not so large that it gets caught in the upper looper.

Look at ready-to-wear for inspiration. Ribbons couched onto a blouse add a feminine touch, whereas yarns, braids, and metallic trims result in a more colorful, festive look on a garment.

Serger expert Linda Lee Vivian embellished this vest with several techniques. Flatlock couching is shown with metallic braid on the multicolor fabric at lower left.

Fast Fix

NIP 'N TUCK

The key to top-notch couching is a very flat flatlock stitch. While we can usually make the fabric almost flat, with a tiny little tuck underneath the stitches, a completely flat version is more elusive. When I have this problem, I let more of each stitch hang off the folded fabric edge.

SETTINGS & MATERIALS

Stitch: 2-thread flatlock
Stitch length: Medium to long
Stitch width: Medium
Needle position: Left (if possible)
Needle thread: All-purpose
Lower looper thread: Decorative
Presser foot: Standard
Upper looper converter: Engaged or attached
Upper knife: Disengaged
Notions: Air-erasable marking pen, liquid seam sealant
Couching material:* Length of beads, pearls, or sequins; metallic braid; ribbon; trim; or yarn

*Choose material that fits inside the seam and between the needle and the blade.

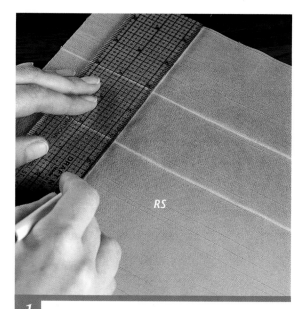

1 Draw straight or very gently curved placement lines on the right side of the fabric, for your couching material. You can also create the design as your work progresses, for a more random effect. After you have drawn the lines, fold the fabric wrong sides together along the first line.

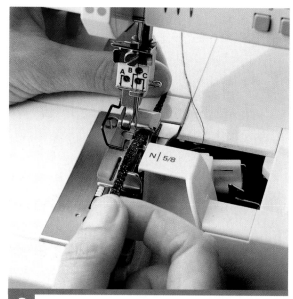

2 Lift the presser foot. Take a length of the couching material and place it under the back of the presser foot and over the front and the top of the foot. It's important to make sure that you place the material between the needle and the knife. Lower the presser foot.

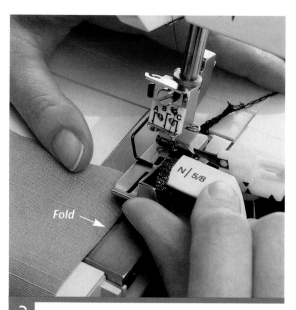

3 Hold onto the couching material in front of and behind the presser foot. Now take several stitches. Lift up the front of the foot (the toe) with your thumb. Try this with the knife guard engaged to protect your thumb. Place the folded fabric under the foot and under the couching material, moving it up so that it's just in front of the needle.

4 Stitch over the couching material so that half of every stitch hangs off the fold. Keep an even stitching line by aligning the fold with a spot on the machine. The material is captured within the stitch. Open the fabric flat before you stitch another row. Secure the ends with liquid seam sealant. Continue to fold and stitch along each design line.

Edgings

Special threads, filler, fabric handling techniques, and stitches can lead to an interesting edge for your garment. Whether you're looking for an idea for a hem or a reversible edge, this chapter has a solution.

FISHLINE EDGE FINISH

Have you ever admired the layers and layers of perfectly curved ruffles on bridal veils and trains? Accomplishing this is much easier than you think.

Unroll a spool of fishing line. See how it retains its curl? It's this curling form that shapes the fabric and hides the thread. As long as the fishing line is heavier than the fabric, the edge curls up once again after stitching. Use 10- to 15-pound fishing line for lightweight fabrics like tulle and 25-pound fishing line for heavier fabrics.

For best results, cut the ruffle on the bias. This will provide the most stretch and the prettiest look. When working with tulle, cut in the direction that you think has the most stretch.

SETTINGS & MATERIALS

Stitch: 3-thread rolled
Stitch length: 1 mm
Needle position: Right (if possible)
Presser foot: Standard or rolled
Throat plate or stitch finger: Rolled
   (if necessary)
Thread: All-purpose
Upper knife: Engaged
Notions: Fishing line*
Recommended fabric: Light- to medium-
   weight dress fabrics*

*The weight of the fishing line is determined by
   the fabric. The lighter the fabric, the finer the
   line. Finer line is used for lightweight fabrics
   and tulle. If the hem doesn't curl enough, try
   using a heavier line.

Applying a fishline hem is the ideal way to create yards and yards of ruffles or a flounced hem in just a few simple steps. The finish is also a nice edge for ruffles on a collar, cuff, or the front of a blouse. As you can see, the hem is appropriate for sheers like this georgette fabric, but you can also apply it to other materials. It's the perfect technique for ruffles on tulle, and it works equally well for beautiful flounced edges and ruffles on taffeta. This georgette garment is cut on the bias. A bias edge has more "give," which is necessary for the fishline hem because you need maximum stretch at the hem.

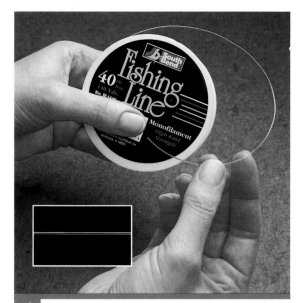

1 Fishing line is available in a wide range of weights and colors at sporting-goods stores. Use clear line and a weight that is appropriate for your fabric. This is 40-pound fishing line, used for heavier fabrics such as taffeta. You can hold your fishing line against the inset photo to compare the size.

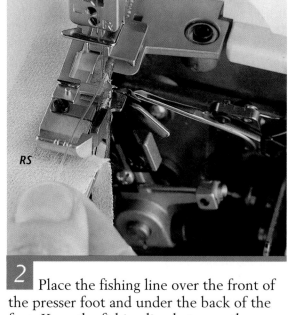

2 Place the fishing line over the front of the presser foot and under the back of the foot. Keep the fishing line between the knife and the needle. Stitch over just the fishing line, then insert the fabric right side up. Stitch with the fishing line on top, stretching the fabric as you serge.

3 After stitching the hem, continue serging off the fabric. Continue stitching over the fishing line. Trim the fishing line, leaving a 4- to 5-inch (10- to 12.5-cm) tail beyond the end of the fabric. Spread the fabric over the fishing line, stretching the fabric as much as possible. Bury the remaining thread/fishing line tail.

Fast Fix

SEPARATE THE ANXIETY

Is your beautiful fishline hem separating from the edge of your fabric? This often happens when working with fine material like organza and delicate cottons. The problem is probably a combination of two things: a needle that's too large and too many stitches to the inch. To avoid perforating very sheer, lightweight fabric such as organdy, switch to a smaller needle, and adjust your machine setup for a longer stitch length. Two additional options to consider are loosening the lower looper tension or switching to a slightly wider stitch. There's less stress on the finished edge when the stitch is a bit wider.

Pam Hastings

LETTUCE-LEAF EDGING

Lettuce-leaf edging is back in fashion, thanks to the renewed popularity of stretch fabrics. Spandex, tricot, interlock, and sweater knits are all ideal candidates for this fun edge finish. Rib knits work especially well because they have excellent stretch. Experiment with woven fabrics, too, because the effect of lettucing on bias-cut edges is lovely.

Just as there are many suitable fabrics, the types of garments that you can embellish are just as extensive. Use lettuce trim to add interest to lingerie, swimsuits, sweatshirts, jackets, and tops. Decorate the hems of a camisole and tap pants. Add designer flair to swimsuits with skirts, sashes, and blouson edges.

Making this type of edging on sweatshirts is simple: Lettuce the ribbing on necklines and sleeves, or cut off the bottom band and then serge the raw fabric edges.

Consider decorating a jacket's shawl collar, pocket edges, or sleeve hems. Create strips of curly lettuce trim to stitch on at random, in bow shapes or in perfectly placed rows.

You can also experiment with different decorative threads in the upper looper in order to create unique splashes of your favorite colors.

A fabric's curl is affected by many factors, including the type of fabric, differential feed setting, amount that you stretch it, and even the way that it's placed on the serger. Yes, the curl can vary, depending on which side of the fabric is "up" when stitching. This ribbed knit looks best when serged with the wrong side up. Another important consideration is the amount of stretch that's built in to the fabric. When laying out your pattern, identify the areas that will be lettuced, and lay those edges in the direction that gives you the amount of stretch that you prefer.

SETTINGS & MATERIALS

Stitch: 2- or 3-thread rolled
Stitch length: Short
Stitch width: Narrow
Presser foot: Standard or rolled
Throat plate or stitch finger: Rolled (if necessary)
Thread: Woolly Nylon
Upper knife: Engaged
Differential feed: Stretch*
Notions: Liquid seam sealant, washable stabilizer

*If you don't have differential feed, stretch the fabric in front and in back of the foot as you serge.

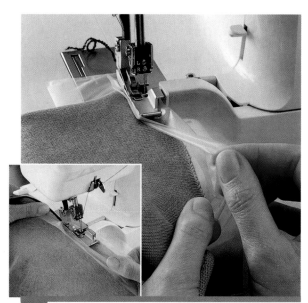

1 Cut a piece of stabilizer 3 inches (7.5 cm) wide and 6 inches (15 cm) longer than the edge to be serged. (The fabric "grows" as you stretch it.) You can use shorter strips and overlap the ends. Wrap the stabilizer around the edge to prevent thread showing through the stitching.

2 Place the fabric "wrap" under the presser foot and serge about ½ inch (1 cm). Stop and stretch the next few inches of the fabric. Hold the fabric taut, but don't pull it through the machine because this can force your serger out-of-time. Let the knife trim off just a bit of fabric.

3 Continue serging, repeating Step 2 until the fabric edge is completely covered with stitching. Carefully tear away the stabilizer. If desired, use tweezers to pick out the smaller pieces of stabilizer. Any excess will dissolve in the first washing. Dot any free ends of the stitching with liquid seam sealant, and let dry before trimming.

Fast Fix

STRETCH A POINT

Some of my students have trouble getting the right amount of lettucing along the fabric edge.

This is a pretty common problem because not all fabrics are the same (thank goodness, because that would be pretty boring). But even with your differential feed adjusted for maximum stretch, heavy knits can still require additional stretching.

Increasing the presser foot pressure will push the fabric forward and improve the stretch. To stretch the fabric more, pull the fabric in front and in back of the foot as you serge.

Mary Griffin

REVERSIBLE WRAPPED EDGE

Also called a binding stitch or reversible edge, this is an excellent technique for making edges and hems look as if they're bound with densely packed thread.

Though you can use a 3-thread stitch, the 2-thread version is more successful. In both cases, start with an overlock stitch, and then adjust the tensions so that one of the looper threads wraps completely around the fabric edge.

This sounds a lot like a rolled edge, doesn't it? The difference is that the fabric edge doesn't curl to the underside of the fabric. You prevent the curling by not switching to a rolled edge stitch finger or throat plate (depending on your machine). With the wider stitch finger, the rolled edge will also be wide. Of course, fabric selection also helps. Stick to sturdy fabric like Polarfleece or woolens that don't roll or fray easily.

If you're stitching through very thick fabrics, like quilted materials, narrow zigzag the hem first. This condenses the fabric edge so that it's easier to work with.

This simple, practical stitch is ideal for the single-layer coats and jackets you see so often these days. The fabric buttons are explained in more detail on page 95.

SETTING & MATERIALS

Stitch: 2- or 3-thread wrap*
Stitch length: 2 to 3 mm
Stitch width: 2 mm
Needle position: Left or right (use the left for thicker threads)
Presser foot: Standard
Needle thread: All-purpose
Looper threads: Decorative and/or all-purpose†
Upper knife: Engaged
Differential feed: Gather slightly on curves if your fabric tends to grow

*Convert an overlock to a wrapped stitch by adjusting the tension. See "Wrap It Up," at right.

†For a 2-thread wrap, place decorative thread in the lower looper. Decorative thread goes in the upper looper for the 3-thread stitch.

Fast Fix

WRAP IT UP

Perfect tension adjustments make a perfect wrap stitch. Since there are two threading options for this versatile stitch, the tensions are significantly different for each. For a 2-thread version, loosen the lower tension so the thread wraps the edge. (There's no upper looper.)

A 3-thread wrap is a bit different: Tighten the lower looper and loosen the upper looper. The upper looper thread is pulled over the fabric by the lower looper thread.

Agnes Mercik

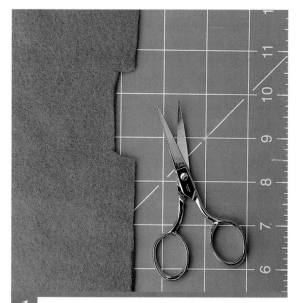

1 Join the side and shoulder seams, and insert both sleeves. At the hem, cut out a rectangular notch at least ¼ inch (6 mm) deep. (The amount you trim off as you stitch is the same as the notch's depth.) It's easier if the notch is the same length or slightly longer than the presser foot.

2 It's hard to see a curve as you're stitching, so trim the hem where it's curved before inserting the fabric under the presser foot. At the serger, place the cut-out area of the notch firmly under the presser foot. Place the end of the notch closest to you against the knife.

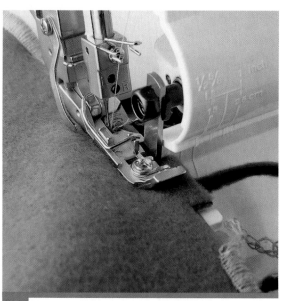

3 Serge the hem completely. On sharp outer curves, gently push the fabric at the front of the presser foot to the right, toward the cutting knives. Upon returning to the notch, let the upper knife cut off the remaining edge of the notch. Disengage the upper knife, and continue serging until you have overlapped three or four stitches.

Fast Fix

TRY A COVER-UP

It's awful when your stitching doesn't cover the entire edge of the fabric, and bits of the material are visible between the threads. A nicely covered fabric edge needs to be completely encased in fabric.

If the decorative thread doesn't wrap completely to the other side of the fabric, there are ways to fix the problem. Take the decorative thread completely out of the tension guides and use the deco guide.

Other options are to narrow the cutting width on your serger or use either Woolly Nylon or monofilament thread in the needle.

Agnes Mercik

2-THREAD ROLLED EDGE

The most beautiful scarves have one thing in common—a fine rolled hem that's often made with only two threads. This provides an edge finish that's perfect for lightweight and sheer fabrics.

You can duplicate the stitch on your serger by using a converter to block the upper looper. Only the needle and lower looper threads are needed for the stitching. When making a stitch, the lower looper thread is held up with a converter that's attached to the upper looper. The converter raises the lower looper thread so that the needle can pass through the thread loop to create a stitch.

Not all sergers are equipped with a 2-thread capability. Yours, however, may have this option without your realizing it. Look for a converter attached either somewhere on or near the upper looper. The converter can also be detachable. The shape varies, but it's always small—about the size of a fingernail—culminating in a small piece of metal that pops into the upper looper.

Careful selection of thread is the key to success. Matching lightweight monofilament or embroidery-weight thread will create a fine, nearly invisible rolled edge.

SETTINGS & MATERIALS

Stitch: 2-thread rolled
Stitch length: Short (1 mm)
Stitch width: Narrow (1.5 mm)
Needle position: Right (if possible)
Presser foot: Standard or rolled
Throat plate or stitch finger: Rolled (if necessary)
Differential feed: Normal or slightly stretched
Upper looper converter: Engaged or attached
Thread: Lightweight monofilament or embroidery-weight (Sulky, Madeira, or Coats & Clark)
Upper knife: Engaged
Recommended fabric: Lightweight silks, georgette, batiste

The next time that you make a garment from fine fabric, why not make a scarf with the leftover yardage? The entire process takes only minutes. Just cut the desired length, and then serge all of the raw edges with a 2-thread rolled hem. Whenever you need to apply an edge finish to a fine, lightweight fabric, this stitch will work. For example, consider using it on the sleeve and lower hem of a georgette blouse or at the edge of ruffles on silk. The 2-thread rolled hem is also perfect for lingerie; use it for hemming camisoles and slips made from delicate and sheer fabrics.

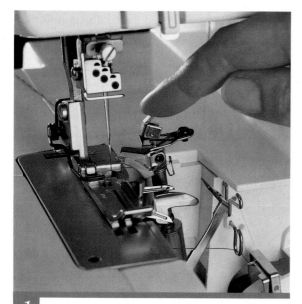

1 Set the upper looper to a 2-thread stitch by engaging the converter. Refer to your manual for the correct procedure for your serger. The name of this gizmo varies by brand. It's also called a spreader. For additional information, see "Cutting Widths" on page 2.

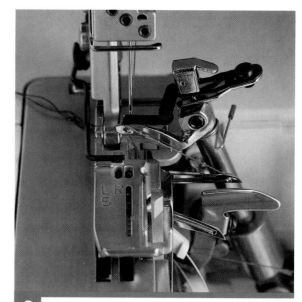

2 Thread the right needle and the lower looper. Bring the lower looper thread up and over the upper looper, under the presser foot, and out the back of the serger. Hold the thread tails, and turn the hand-wheel toward you two or three times to form the first few stitches.

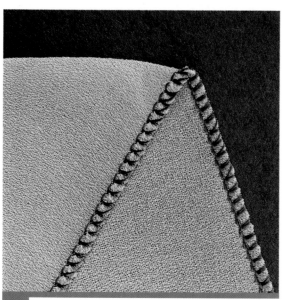

3 Place your fabric under the presser foot, and begin serging along the raw edge. If you're finishing the edge of a scarf or ruffle, align your fabric with the edge of the throat plate. The knife shaves off the fabric's raw edge, leaving a straight edge. At the end, apply a liquid seam sealant to the thread tail, let dry, then trim the tail near the fabric.

Fast Fix

STRETCH DAILY

When I'm serging a rolled edge stitch on a very lightweight fabric I've noticed that the edge tends to pucker. If you're as lucky as I am and own a machine with differential feed, your solution to this problem is quite easy. Simply turn the differential feed to the stretch setting. (As mentioned earlier in this book, differential feed settings can vary between bands, so to obtain stretch on your serger's system, the equivalent setting may be a number below 0 or else a "—" setting.) If your serger isn't equipped with a differential feed option, gently stretch the fabric as you serge along the edge of the fabric.

Pam Hastings

WIRED EDGING

You can make French wire-edged ribbon yourself for a fraction of the cost of ready-made because you get yards of ribbon from a single yard of fabric.

This method makes a continuous length of straight-grain ribbon from a fabric tube—just like cutting continuous bias, only you cut and sew in one step.

Fine wire is stitched into a rolled edge, which you can then turn into lush roses. Without making a fabric tube, you can use the same process to edge an evening or wedding gown.

To shape a hem, simply press the hem allowance to the wrong side, insert the wire in the hem fold, fold the fabric tightly around the wire, and serge over the fabric-encased wire.

You can also serge beaded wire to the outside of a fabric. (You may need to lengthen the stitch so that the thread settles between the beads.) For a festive garment, skip the fabric, and serge over wire to make curlicues. After stitching, wrap the wire around a pencil to shape it into curlicues.

Wire-edged roses make lovely accents on the front of a garment. You can also add them to a bow at center back on a fancy dress.

SETTINGS & MATERIALS

Stitch: 2- or 3-thread rolled
Stitch length: Short (up to 2 mm)
Stitch width: Narrow (1.5 mm)
Presser foot: Beading or cording, rolled, or standard*
Throat plate or stitch finger: Rolled (if necessary)
Upper looper converter: Engaged or attached (if using the 2-thread stitch)
Needle thread: All-purpose
Upper looper thread: Decorative
Lower looper thread: All-purpose
Upper knife: Engaged
Notions: 24- to 30-gauge rust-proof craft wire on a spool; paper scissors; ruler; water-soluble marker or tailor's chalk

* If you don't have one of the specialty presser feet, use the standard foot. Guide the wire between the needle and the knives, then under the back of the presser foot.

1 Test your stitch and fabric by serging along both the fabric's crosswise and lengthwise grains. This helps you determine which edge rolls the best. Testing your stitching is very important because you may discover that the stitching pulls off one of the edges of your fabric.

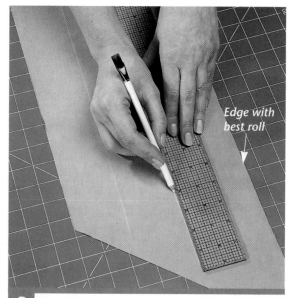

Edge with best roll

2 Decide on the width of your ribbon. This width is the distance between the lines on your fabric. Draw lines on your fabric parallel to the edge that rolled the best. Perpendicular to these lines, cut each end of the fabric at a 45-degree angle, making sure that the two cuts are parallel.

3 Set your sewing machine for a medium-length straight stitch. Join the angled ends of your fabric strip, with right sides facing, and offset the top and bottom of the seam by one ribbon width. This will form a fabric tube with a single, continuous, spiraling line.

4 Insert the top of the fabric tube under the presser foot so that the knife will cut off a bit of fabric as you serge. Insert your wire through the tunnel on the right side of the toe, then over the fabric and under the back of the foot. To avoid equipment and needle damage, it's important to position the wire so it's between the needle and the knife.

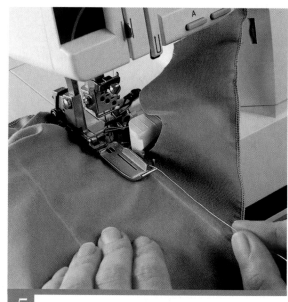

5 Serge along the marked line, catching the wire under the stitches and cutting along the line as you serge. Because the lines are offset, the resulting "ribbon" is one continuous piece. If desired, serge the remaining raw edge of the ribbon, and catch another length of wire in this second row of the stitching.

Fagoting

A version of flatlocking, this is simply a method of seaming fabrics with an open row of stitches that look like ladders.

DECORATIVE WIDE FAGOTING

Traditionally, fagoting is a hand-stitching technique that involves pulling horizontal threads out of a fabric. The remaining vertical threads are either left open or tied together in groups.

Serger fagoting is easier, but the result is slightly different since flatlocking is the starting point. The stitched "ladders" can be left open or filled with ribbons, metallic thread, or embroidery floss. You can make both wide or narrow versions.

These instructions recommend a 2-thread flatlock, although you can also serge with three threads. If you have a choice, select two threads because the stitching pulls flatter and isn't as bulky.

The wide fagoting on this vest is used for heavier, metallic, decorative threads because the stitching has more visible open space.

SETTINGS & MATERIALS

Stitch: 2-thread flatlock
Stitch width: 2 to 3 mm
Needle: 80/12 or 90/14 embroidery
Needle position: Left (if possible)
Presser foot: Standard
Upper looper converter: Engaged or attached
Needle thread: Heavy decorative*
Looper thread: All-purpose
Upper knife: Disengaged
Notions: Filler for weaving: decorative ribbon or yarn; tapestry needle

*Try Decor 6, Designers 6, Success, Burmilana, Pearl Crown Rayon, Glamour, Candlelight, Jeans Stitch, multiple finer rayons, or hand embroidery flosses.

Fast Fix

AVOID TENSION

I own a high-end Bernina serger, so it's easy to obtain nice stitching—even with heavy decorative threads. My machine has a deco guide that keeps the thread from falling back into the tension slots, thus ensuring that I have the correct tension. If you don't have this, take the thread completely out of the tension dial, and stitch slowly.

Agnes Mercik

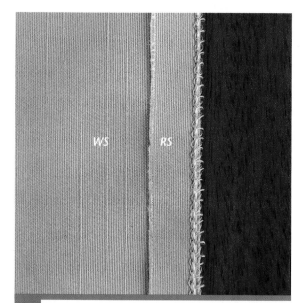

1 Edge-finish the raw seam allowances of the fabric pieces that you're joining. Press the seam allowances to the wrong side along the seamline. Place the fabric pieces right sides together (seams facing each other). Serge the folds together, letting the stitches hang halfway off the folded edges.

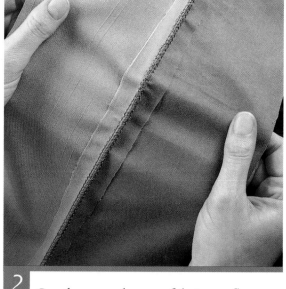

2 Gently open the two fabrics to flatten the seam. The needle (ladder) stitches will be visible on the right side of the fabric. The folds on the two fabric pieces will either butt together or have a slight gap at the seamline. If they overlap, your needle thread tension is too tight. Press the seam.

3 Thread the tapestry needle with the filler you plan to use for weaving. On the right side of the fabric, weave the interesting yarns or ribbons under and over the ladder stitches. In this example, serger expert Agnes Mercik decided to make two separate rows of weaving, each with a double strand of filler.

4 To reinforce the seam, apply a strip of ⅝-inch (1.5-cm)-wide fusible tricot interfacing that's the same length as the seamline. Place your work wrong side up on an ironing surface, and lay the interfacing, resin side down, on top of the seamline. Fuse the two together in place. This strip of interfacing stabilizes and reinforces the seam.

NARROW FAGOTING

This technique is a nice way to join lace to a delicate fabric. Best applied to areas that aren't stressed, the application controls stubborn fabrics that won't lie flat.

Narrow fagoting is created in much the same way as the wider, decorative version on pages 123–124. However, in this case, you use the right needle (if possible) and the narrowest possible stitch width. Serger expert Agnes Mercik prefers to make this type of fagoting with the needle-like rolled hem stitch finger.

Of course, because the stitch is narrow, when the fabric pieces (or fabric and lace) are pulled apart, there's a much smaller gap at the seamline. Consequently, you can't weave thick filler through the "ladders" made by the needle thread. Instead, try weaving several layers of a lustrous embroidery floss through the ladders.

SETTINGS & MATERIALS

Stitch: 2-thread flatlock
Stitch length: 3 mm
Stitch width: Narrow (1 to 2 mm)*
Needle: 80/12 or 90/14 embroidery
Needle position: Right (if possible)
Presser foot: Standard
Upper looper converter: Engaged or attached
Needle thread: Heavy decorative or 30-weight rayon[†]
Looper thread: All-purpose serger
Upper knife: Disengaged
Notions: Deco guide; filler for weaving: rayon or silk embroidery floss; tapestry needle[‡]

*Use a narrow (rolled hem) stitch finger, or engage the regular stitch finger for a slightly wider stitch.

[†]Try Decor 6, Designers 6, Success, Burmilana, Pearl Crown Rayon, Glamour, Candlelight, Jeans Stitch or multiple finer rayons.

[‡]A deco guide keeps thread out of the tension slot. If your machine doesn't have this accessory, just remove the thread from the tension guide, and stitch slowly.

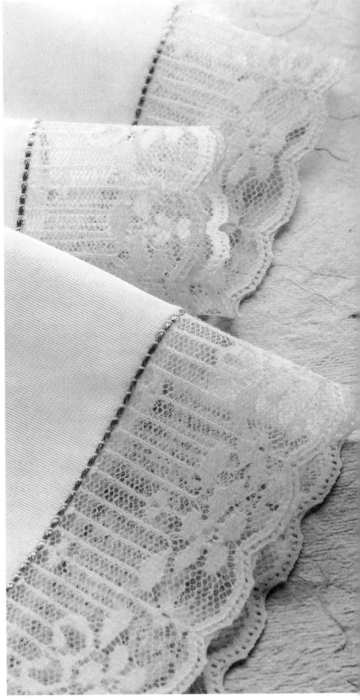

You can simulate the finish you often see on ready-to-wear lingerie and evening wear by adopting the techniques serger expert Agnes Mercik used for this tricot slip. She wove four strands of silk embroidery floss under and over the ladder (needle), stitching on the right side of the fabric. You can substitute rayon embroidery floss for the weaving—the result is just as nice looking. To attach lace to a slip in this manner, follow the "Fagoting" instructions on pages 123–124. Use the floss in Step 3.

Gathering

There are so many ways to draw in your fabric in order to create both ruffles and gathers. You can adjust the needle tension, switch to a special presser foot, and even serge on elastic. This chapter shows you several methods so that you can select the end that's most suitable for your fabric and garment.

GATHERING FOR THE REAL WORLD

Differential feed is a wonderful time-saver. But many of us don't use it to its fullest. Just as we learned to leave traditional sewing machine methods behind when we started serging, we must continue to embrace new ideas while tapping into the advanced, creative joys of sewing by serger. So, why not use the differential feed and the gathering foot at the same time?

For example, using the gathering feature on your serger simply means that you have to adjust the way that you think about how gathers are created and attached to fabric. Serger expert Mary Griffin remembers reading directions for using a sewing machine ruffler and faithfully attempting to adjust it until she had a perfect 2:1 ratio. So, too, with the serger, until she realized that life was too short for this!

Try this serger technique, and leave behind all that time-consuming measuring. Soon you won't hesitate to add yards of ruffles to skirts, attach gathered skirts to yokes, put in pretty peplums, and even ease in sleeve caps with your differential feed.

A bow and "belt" hide the gathered waistline seam. The finished bow is 5 × 2½ inches (12.5 × 6 cm). Start with an 11 × 6-inch (28 × 15-cm) piece of fabric. Using ½-inch (1-cm) seam allowances, make a tube by joining the lengthwise edges with right sides together. After turning it right side out, make a circle by overlapping the short ends. Wrap a smaller tube/circle made from a 3½ × 2-inch (9 × 5-cm) fabric piece around the center. A second, serger-made version of a bow with decorative edges is featured on pages 100–101.

SETTINGS & MATERIALS

Stitch: Almost any stitch used to create seams, even a rolled hem, as long as it's appropriate for the fabric
Presser foot: Gathering, then standard
Thread: All-purpose
Upper knife: Engaged
Differential feed: Gather

1 In this case we added a gathered panel to the back of a jacket. Measure the length of the area onto which the ruffle will be serged. Double this measurement, and add 5 inches (12.5 cm). Cut the ruffle fabric that length. The extra inches of fabric will serve as insurance.

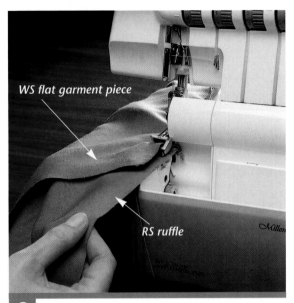

WS flat garment piece

RS ruffle

2 Place the fabric you want ruffled right side up under the foot with the wrong side against the feed dogs. Place the right side of the garment face down, through the groove of the foot. Serge the fabric pieces, gathering the ruffle onto the jacket's Upper Back panel at the waist.

3 When you're finished serging, you're left with extra ruffle hanging off the edge of the jacket Back. Place the jacket Back and Side Back right sides together. Cut off the excess ruffle with your scissors, or let your serger trim it away as you serge together the Back and the Side Back when you join the garment pieces with a safety or overlock seam.

Fast Fix

CUT IT SHORT?

My students always want to know how long to cut the ruffle. This is a tough decision if you're looking for hard-and-fast rules. The differential feed on most sergers gathers at a 2:1 ratio. In other words, a 10-inch (25.4-cm) piece of fabric will ruffle to half the original length: 5 inches (12.7 cm). Heavier fabrics gather less, and lighter fabrics gather more. Use a longer stitch length, and tighten the needle tensions to increase the gathers even more. (See "No Frills Easing" on page 130.) Since more ruffles are usually better than fewer, I set the differential feed to maximum.

Mary Griffin

GATHERING WITH ELASTIC

In "Casings" (see pages 104–108) you'll find two different ways to insert elastic at the same time you're actually stitching the fabric in place. These procedures save a lot of time when you're making an elasticized waistband, sleeves, or pant hems.

The technique on this and the opposite page is a similar procedure for gathering fabric. But you aren't wrapping the fabric around the elastic. Instead, you're simply gathering an edge.

There are times when you need to gather one edge of a piece of fabric, most often to join it to another, straight, edge. This is when a gathering presser foot comes in handy because you can make the seam at the same time you're gathering one of the fabric edges. (See "Gathering for the Real World" on pages 126–127 for complete instructions for using this presser foot.)

However, if you need to join two gathered edges, or you don't make ruffles often enough to warrant purchasing a gathering presser foot, then this technique is a great alternative.

Clear elastic is the best choice because it has such tremendous stretch and recovery. In addition, unlike many other types of elastic, you can nick the clear variety with the serger knife and it won't unravel. This makes it possible to trim the fabric edge as you serge. Before serging clear elastic to the fabric, it's a good idea to stretch it several times. This ensures that the elastic won't become longer when stitched.

Clear elastic can be used to create lush ruffles or gathers. Just catch the elastic under the stitching as you serge the fabric edge.

SETTINGS & MATERIALS

Stitch: 3- or 4-thread overlock
Stitch length: Long
Stitch width: Wide
Presser foot: Standard
Thread: All-purpose
Upper knife: Engaged
Notions: Clear elastic, fine-point permanent marking pen

Fast Fix

SIZE MATTERS

When a stitch is made, the serger needle goes down through a loop in a looper thread and then into the fabric. To avoid hitting the looper thread, keep your serger needle within a certain size range: 70/10, 75/11, 80/12, and 90/14. Your needle should be large enough to penetrate the fabric without deflecting.

Agnes Mercik

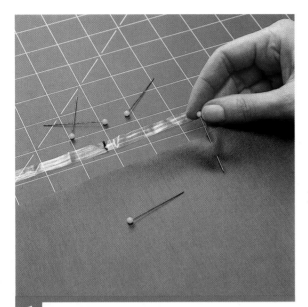

1 Cut the elastic to match the length where the ruffle will be attached plus 4 inches (10 cm). Pen-mark 2 inches (5 cm) in from each end. Pen-mark the elastic into fourths for short ruffle strips or eighths for very long strips. Quarter-mark the ruffle to match the marks on the elastic.

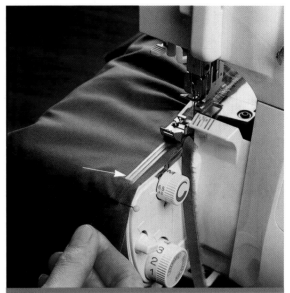

2 Place the right side of the ruffle against the feed dogs, and position the elastic ¼ inch (6 mm) from the long raw edge with the first set of marks matching. Take a few stitches to get started, then serge, stretching the elastic until the next marks match.

3 Continue serging until you have attached the elastic to the ruffle. Don't pull too hard on the elastic, as this will damage the serger's timing. The elastic is a few inches longer than the desired finished length of the gathered ruffle. So align the end of your fabric with the last mark, which is 2 inches (5 cm) from the end of the elastic.

Fast Fix

FEED THE DOGS

Clear elastic stretches like crazy. Yet there may be times when this still isn't enough to obtain as much gathering as you want. The first step, of course, is to test your settings by serging a strip of elastic to your fabric edge. Stitch a bit, and then turn your differential feed to a gather setting, and stitch a bit farther, while continuing to stretch the elastic. Continue adjusting the differential feed in small increments until you obtain the desired fullness in the finished stitching. While you add gathers by stretching the elastic, the feed dogs will be pulling the fabric in.

Barbara Weiland

NO-FRILLS EASING

Often you need a few gathers along the edge of a garment piece so that you can ease it to fit another. The hem on an A-line skirt, a sleeve cap, a released dart on a bodice, or the elbow area of a fitted sleeve are all good examples of places where a bit of easing or a few subtle gathers will enhance the appearance of your garment.

You can accomplish this little bit of easing on your serger without digging out your gathering foot. All you need is a simple adjustment to the needle tension on your serger, as explained and shown in the photos and captions at right. (This technique is also great to know if your serger doesn't have differential feed.)

If necessary, you can also enhance and adjust the easing by pulling the needle thread on your finished stitching—just as you would for traditional machine gathers.

Another way to gather is with a fabric separator or gathering attachment, used with differential feed set on gather. This will draw up one layer of fabric while stitching it to another, flatter, piece—all in one easy step.

The slot in the front of the foot separates the two fabric layers, keeping the top layer flat, while the second one is gathered in the stitching.

Step-by-step instructions and photographs that explain how to use the gathering foot are featured in "Gathering for the Real World" on pages 126–127 and "Skirting the Issue" on pages 131–132.

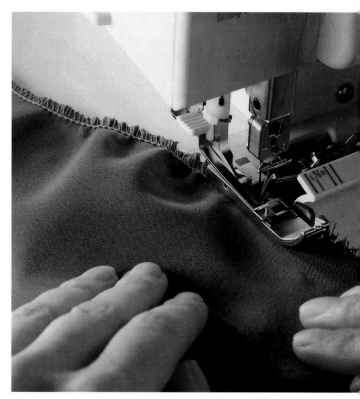

Increase the needle tension to create the desired amount of easing for a lightly gathered edge, and then serge along the edge.

To gather only a section—the curve of a shirttail hem, for example—press on the needle thread above the tension dial while you serge.

SETTINGS & MATERIALS

Stitch: 3-thread overlock

Stitch length: Medium or as desired for the fabric

Stitch width: Medium or as desired for the fabric

Presser foot: Standard

Thread: All-purpose

Recommended fabric: Light- to medium-weight knits and wovens

SKIRTING THE ISSUE

Actually, we're doing quite the opposite—and so should you. Don't avoid gathered skirts and ruffles just because you think the gathering process is long and tedious, because it's not. The secret is to do the work on your serger, using the gathering presser foot in combination with the differential feed on your machine. If you don't have differential feed, don't stop reading. You'll like the way serger expert Mary Griffin cuts her ruffles with a bit of "insurance," a method she also uses in "Gathering for the Real World" on pages 126–127.

Full dresses gathered onto yokes are a breeze to make in lightweight fabrics when you let your differential feed do all of the work.

Differential feed will rescue you. The gathers are automatically adjusted for perfect fullness, and the seam allowance is efficiently finished and controlled in one step. Note that because this is a sheer fabric, the bodice dart is converted to a short gather for a neater look. Cut out the Front Yoke fabric piece. Don't transfer the dart markings. Hand-gather the fabric at the Front Yoke seamline between the dart legs, then serge.

Mary likes the gathering foot because it gives the fullest ruffle and attaches the ruffle to flat fabric in one easy step. If you're planning to gather a ruffle but not attach it to another piece of fabric immediately, simply place the ruffle piece underneath your gathering foot, and serge to push the single piece of fabric into beautiful fullness.

SETTINGS & MATERIALS

Stitch: 4- or 5-thread safety
Stitch length: 3 mm
Stitch width: 3.5 to 4.5 mm
Presser foot: Gathering
Thread: All-purpose
Differential feed: Gather
Recommended fabric: Ideal for sheers and fabrics that ravel easily, but you can use it on any woven

Serger expert Mary Griffin made this little dress from a delicate georgette that ravels like crazy. As a sewing machine educator, she travels a lot, so finding the time to hand baste and gather the skirt was a problem. Who wants to spend hours on such a chore? Besides, while gathering the fabric by pulling the hand basting stitches, the seam allowance could fray away to nothing before the work of adjusting all those gathers was even finished. The obvious solution was to gather and seam the garment pieces in a single step, using the technique described here and on the next page.

1 Cut out the yokes. Cut the Skirt Front and Back both about 5 inches (12.5 cm) wider at one side seam. Serge the skirt pieces to the yoke pieces, gathering as you stitch. (See Steps 2 and 3 of "Gathering for the Real World" on pages 126–127.) Do not trim off the extra skirt fabric.

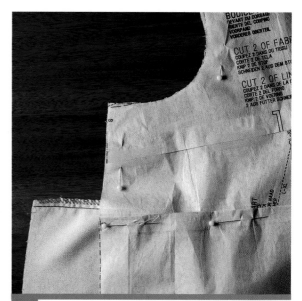

2 Pin the yoke pattern to the Skirt pattern for a few inches in from the armscye. Line up the side seams. Don't pin in the gathers in the skirt pattern. Pin the patterns on top of the joined fabric yoke and skirt pieces, aligning the centers, shoulders, and armscye areas.

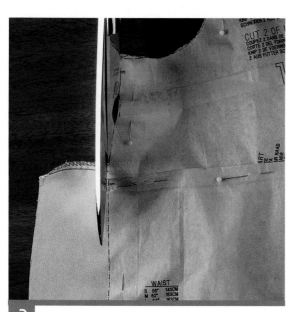

3 The Skirt fabric piece extends beyond the side seam of the pattern. Cut off the excess fabric. Serge the side seams. Repeat Steps 2 and 3 for the remaining Yoke and Skirt. If desired, rather than cutting off the excess fabric with scissors, you can let the serger knife trim off the excess side seam fabric when you join the front to the back.

Fast Fix

HOLD STILL

If you're disappointed with the amount of gathers you're getting using the gathering presser foot, try adjusting the position of your hands.

Place the ruffle under the foot and the flat fabric into the groove. Hold the pieces together so they don't slip when you begin serging. Once the needles are in the fabric, stop and grasp the top piece with your left hand. Support the ruffle with your right hand. The goal is to guide the ruffle straight while letting it flow freely. If you hold back even slightly, you'll be disappointed by the amount of gathering you achieve.

Mary Griffin

Heirloom Serging

Imagine creating delicate heirloom work on a serger. Yes—it's possible, and it's gorgeous. Combine beautiful laces and fine fabrics without any of the painstaking hand sewing that's part of traditional heirloom sewing.

UNDERSTANDING HEIRLOOM SERGING

With the precise settings and adjustments available on today's sergers, you can create a very delicate heirloom garment.

Joining entredeux, stitching fine pin-tucks—even creating a French seam—are possible practically without firing up your sewing machine.

The real artistry of heirloom serging is in the creation of the fabric from which the garment pieces are cut. A "new" fabric is

Serger expert Linda Lee Vivian introduces her students to heirloom serging by showing them several finished garments. Each one is assembled from a "fabric" created by joining strips of delicate fabric, embroideries, and laces. In this section, Linda Lee shares her years of experience with you.

lovingly assembled from strips of lace, fine fabric, and entredeux.

Even fabric strips, detailed with embroidery and pintucks if desired, can be added. These pieces are first serged together along the lengthwise edges.

The first section of this chapter (pages 135–139) offers an overview—and complete instructions—for creating your "new" fabric. Also included is guidance on selecting and cutting out a suitable garment pattern.

The specific instructions for joining together the lace, fabric, and entredeux are separate; see "Entredeux to Fabric" (page 140), "Entredeux to Lace" (page 142), "Lace to Fabric" (page 146), and "Lace to Lace" (page 148).

There are two additional heirloom serger techniques that you should consider adding to your garment: "Puffing" (page 152) and "Pintucks" (page 150).

It would be a pity to lovingly assemble a beautiful heirloom fabric, and then assemble your garment with less refined methods. For this reason, a few additional techniques are included throughout the sections of the book.

When made from sheer or fine fabric, the most suitable way to join your garment pieces is with French seams (page 144).

If the pattern calls for a neck placket or a sleeve placket, there's a delicate version on pages 180–182, also written by Linda Lee Vivian.

Two pieces of fine silk ribbon weave their way in and out of the entredeux beading that edges the neckline of this garment, called Transition in Silk by its creator, the heirloom serging expert Linda Lee Vivian.

There are several techniques on the garment, a few of which are visible here. The entredeux beading is joined to lace insertion. These two strips are joined at an angle to another piece of heirloom fabric that consists of fabric (not visible), lace insertion, and Swiss embroidery beading. (Various types of lace and entredeux are identified on page 136.)

Heirloom serging used to be done by using a rolled hem stitch and then trimming off the excess fabric while serging the embroidery to a lace. This trim-as-you-go method makes accuracy difficult to achieve. The new, 2-thread flatlock method is a better option. It's delicate, and less fabric is used in the seam. Heirloom serging expert Linda Lee Vivian likes it because the needle thread shows on the right side, contributing a touch of color or sheen to the heirloom fabric that's being created. You'll like the speed at which you can join the strips once the proper settings are in place on your machine.

CREATING "NEW" FABRIC

Before you make a single cut, you need to gather the best materials so that you can create beautiful garments that are worthy of being passed through many generations of your family.

Choose natural fabrics, embroideries, threads, and laces. Not only do they keep well for years, but they're also easier to work with than synthetics. Do, however, keep in mind that silk won't remain white. It gains a yellow patina as it ages.

When you've collected the materials, you "design" the new fabric by deciding the position of the various elements, then cut the strips, and serge them together. This section of the book, "Creating 'New' Fabric," on pages 135–139, explains the process.

The remainder of the chapter on Heirloom Serging shows you the step-by-step techniques for seaming the fabrics, laces, entredeux, and embroideries.

A tone-on-tone color scheme, with the subtle addition of another color, offers graceful style. Serger expert Linda Lee Vivian used beautiful laces, silk threads, and fine silk fabrics to create the "new" fabric from which the vest garment pieces were cut. The patchwork effect is the result of combining four different sections that each feature several heirloom techniques. The sections were then joined together with a 2-thread ladder stitch and enhanced with silk ribbon weaving. Linda Lee says it was a real treat to use all silk fabrics, beautiful laces and embroideries, as well as silk thread, to construct this beautiful vest.

SETTINGS & MATERIALS

Stitch: Flatlock, overlock, or rolled

Presser foot: Blind hem or lace

Thread: A variety of fine machine embroidery and heirloom threads*

Notions: Air-erasable marking pen; Flat Milward Bodkin for weaving ribbons; liquid seam sealant such as Fray Stop; quilt ruler, rotary cutter, and cutting mat; sharp scissors for trimming embroideries; spray water bottle with a fine spray tip, filled with distilled water; Sullivan's Spray Stabilizer; variety of silk ribbons for lacing through the beadings on laces and embroideries

Recommended fabric: A variety of heirloom laces and embroideries; heirloom fabric for the garment (see Steps 1 and 2 on page 137)

*Silk Stitch or a 50-weight silk thread from YLI, or Sulky rayon thread in a 30- or 40-weight. Fine cotton embroidery threads can also be used.

GETTING ACQUAINTED

Select your laces, entredeux, and embroideries. There are many types that you can combine to create your heirloom fabric. A selection is shown here so that you can identify the differences. (Fine cotton laces and embroideries can be hard to find. Capitol Imports carries a wonderful selection. See page 234.)

Join entredeux to other heirloom materials by placing one stitch in each hole. Some embroideries already have an entredeux edging stitched onto them.

Entredeux beading offers a space for weaving a ribbon into the beading for added color.

Lace beading has gaps so that you can weave ribbons through it.

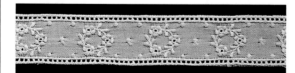

Lace edging is applied to the edge of a garment.

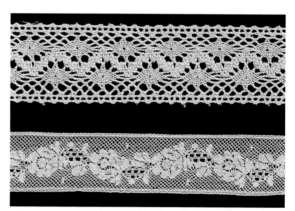

Lace insertion is placed between other laces, embroideries, or fabrics.

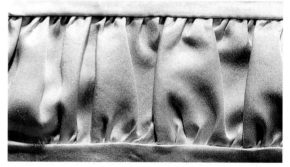

Puffing strips add a feminine touch to any heirloom garment. Make puffing by gathering both edges of a fabric strip and inserting it between other fabric or lace strips.

Swiss embroidery beading is a fine cotton fabric that's embroidered. Ribbons can be woven into the beading.

Place Swiss embroidery with entredeux between other laces, embroideries, or fine heirloom fabrics.

1 Cotton and silk are the best fabrics for heirloom serging. Choose satin, organdy, or tussah. Don't rule out cotton: Swiss cotton batiste, cotton satin, Swiss cotton lawn, cotton organdy, and piqué. Silk takes dye very well. Make any color by using a Jacquard Acid Dye, which offers great results.

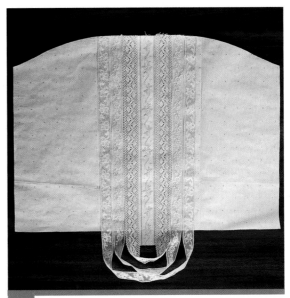

2 Determine the size of the "new" heirloom fabric. Allow a bit of extra fabric for "insurance." Arrange the embroideries and laces on top of the pattern piece. Make notes and lines for positions so you can remove items, two at a time, for serging, without losing track of your master plan.

3 Cut the laces and embroideries to the same length. They'll shrink as they're serged together so allow a few extra inches. It's always better to have more length than to be short after putting in all the work. You will spend so much creative energy when stitching into this fabric, it would be a pity if you had to start over.

Fast Fix

AVOID HANGING

Your laces and embroideries can distort during the preshrinking process, especially if you hang them to dry. Let them dry flat. You can repair the existing distortion problems with this Fast Fix.

I spray the laces and embroideries with a fine mist of distilled water. Then I press them with an iron on a steam setting. This completely dries the laces or embroideries.

The process restores the laces and embroideries to their original shape, and they're ready for you to join them to other lace or embroidery strips, to make the heirloom fabric.

Linda Lee Vivian

4 If a lace or embroidery is too limp (like a sheer fabric), apply a light coating of spray stabilizer directly onto the lace or embroidery. Iron it dry, then see if it has enough body. If it needs more body, just spray on another coat of the stabilizer, iron it, and let it dry again.

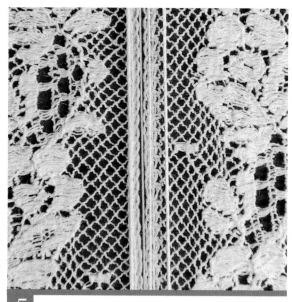

5 To choose the stitching color, lay several strands of threads between the laces and embroideries. YLI Corporation carries a wonderful color selection of 30-weight Silk Stitch and 50-weight silk thread. The company also carries a complete selection of silk ribbon for weaving into beadings.

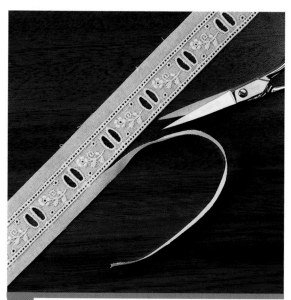

6 Embroideries are sold with fabric "extensions" on both lengthwise edges. To prepare for serging, trim this excess fabric right up to the edge of the entredeux. When you test your settings in the next step, you'll find it much easier to place one stitch in each hole of the entredeux. In the past, serger experts let the knives trim off the excess.

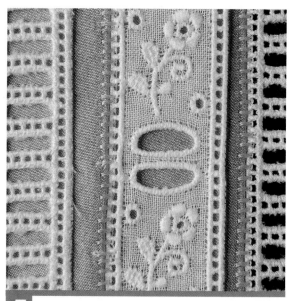

7 Test the stitch length and depth for each stitch and each lace, entredeux, fabric, or embroidery strip. The distance between the holes in entredeux embroideries varies greatly. One stitch goes in each hole. When you miss a hole, you get a skipped stitch or two stitches in the same hole. Testing the stitch flow will prevent frustration later.

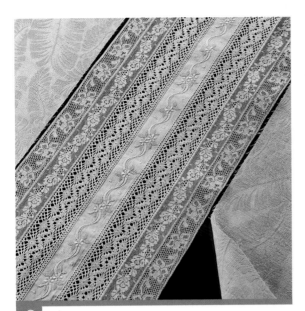

8 Seam your strips following the instructions on pages 140–153. If necessary, add fabric to the outer edges to create a large enough piece of "new" fabric from which to cut the garment piece. Cut a strip of fabric for each side, and serge it to the outer edge of the lace and embroidery.

9 The "new" piece of fabric may now be treated as normal yardage. You can cut your garment piece from it. The center of the middle lace or embroidery is now the center front line. Keep this middle piece as straight as you would keep the grainline on a normal piece of fabric.

10 Lay your garment pattern piece on the new fabric, pin it in place, and cut it out. Seal the ends of every one of the seams with a liquid seam sealant to secure the stitching. Treat this new pattern piece just as you normally would, by assembling it following the pattern instructions, to complete your heirloom garment.

11 There are several ways to finish the edges of your garment. Serger expert Linda Lee Vivian likes to bind neckline edges with bias binding. Another option is to attach a strip of lace beading, then weave silk ribbon through the holes. A lace rosette (see page 164) is this camisole's pièce de résistance. See the complete garment on page 133.

ENTREDEUX TO FABRIC

Used to join fabric, lace, and embroidery, entredeux is an integral part of almost every heirloom garment. It adds a feminine touch to the fabric you create, as well as subtle color, if desired.

Entredeux is an embroidered edge on a fine cotton fabric base. It may be a narrow trim with only entredeux holes, or the entredeux holes may be stitched along the edge of another embroidery. The holes of the entredeux offer a place for the needle to stitch into when items are joined together.

Attaching entredeux isn't that difficult. The important thing to remember is that the needle must stitch into each hole of the entredeux that you're working on.

Consider serging a number of strips of fabric to several entredeux-edged embroideries. You can then make your own design by combining these joined entredeux/fabric strips into a pleasant design for a "new" heirloom fabric.

With the aid of the stitching that you produce on your serger, you can introduce a needle thread color that separates the entredeux and the adjacent fabric strip. Or for a subtler look, use matching thread that blends into the seam. Even a close inspection won't reveal the serger stitching.

SETTINGS & MATERIALS

Stitch: 2-thread flatlock
Stitch length: 1½ to 2½ mm
Stitch width: 3 to 4 mm
Needle position: Right (if possible)
Presser foot: Lace or blind hem
Upper looper converter: Engaged or attached
Needle thread: 30-weight Silk Stitch
Lower looper thread: All-purpose
Upper knife: Engaged
Notions: Entredeux or entredeux-edged embroidery, liquid seam sealant
Recommended fabric: Fine cottons or silk fabrics such as a batiste, silk satin, silk tussah, or silk jacquard

Choose simple patterns for heirloom clothing. Avoid darts and extra design seams to ensure that the focus of the garment remains on the elegant heirloom techniques.

Serger expert Linda Lee Vivian made this blouse with a pattern from Londa's Elegant Creations. The collar on the pattern didn't suit the intended mood of the blouse, so Linda Lee simply replaced it with a bias binding.

The "new" heirloom fabric consists of a variety of fine cotton entredeux-edged embroideries and laces. The final touch is a soft pink ribbon woven through the lace beading. (See the photo on page 142.)

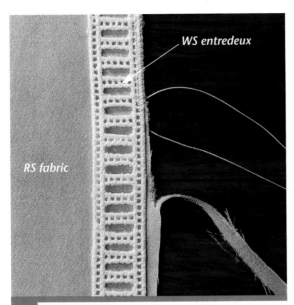

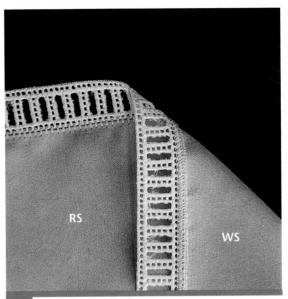

1 Lay a scrap of fabric against the feed dogs, just in front of the blade. Place the entredeux under the foot, against the guide. Lower the needle into the first hole of the entredeux. Lower the presser foot, and serge a test seam. Adjust the guide and stitch length as necessary.

2 Serge together the first piece of entredeux and a fabric strip that's cut from the same fabric yardage you're using to make your garment. Pull the seam open, and press it flat. The entredeux and fabric should be adjacent and very flat. Only the needle thread will show.

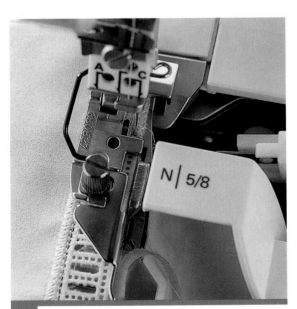

3 To add a piece of fabric to the remaining edge of the entredeux, the entredeux must always be on top so you can see the holes when serging. It's a very good idea to serge all of the entredeux-to-fabric seams for the entire garment "fabric" at the same time, thus keeping the continuity in the direction of the stitching.

Fast Fix

BUILD STRENGTH

It can be difficult to guide fabric and entredeux through the presser foot while getting enough fabric into the seam. I adjust the guide on the foot to the proper depth for the needle to align with the holes of the entredeux, then I place the fabric just in front of the knife so that I trim only a sliver off as I serge. This places a little more fabric into the seam, which makes it stronger. There's one more safeguard that ensures there's enough fabric in the seam: I adjust the stitch length so that only one stitch goes into each hole. Even small adjustments make a difference.

Linda Lee Vivian

ENTREDEUX TO LACE

This is a fast yet efficient technique for adding an entredeux-edged embroidery to a beautiful lace. It's also very attractive because the combinations of textures and stitching complements one another.

There are so many wonderful threads you can use to add a color accent to your fabric while stitching. Heirloom serging expert Linda Lee Vivian suggests selecting a needle thread color that contrasts with the entredeux and lace. The needle thread colors are usually soft accents. However, for a subtler effect, choose a thread color that blends with the entredeux or lace.

To create a larger fabric, join additional strips of entredeux and lace until the "new" fabric is large enough to accommodate the pattern for the garment piece that you'd like to cut from it. Or serge only a few pieces together to make enough for the bodice of a garment.

This technique needs to be executed with precision. As you serge the entredeux and lace together, keep in mind that it's essential that the serger be adjusted so that one—and only one—stitch is placed in each hole along the edges of the entredeux.

SETTINGS & MATERIALS

Stitch: 2-thread flatlock
Stitch length: 1½ to 2½ mm
Stitch width: 3 to 4 mm
Needle position: Right (if possible)
Presser foot: Lace or blind hem
Upper looper converter: Engaged or attached
Needle thread: 30-weight Silk Stitch
Lower looper thread: All-purpose
Upper knife: Disengaged
Notions: Entredeux or entredeux-edged embroidery, fine cotton laces, liquid seam sealant

As beautiful up close as it is from a distance, this Transition in Silk blouse includes fine workmanship. At the neckline, Linda Lee Vivian joined entredeux to the lace and then threaded ribbon through the entredeux "ladders."

The fabric for the top was created entirely on the serger using a 2-thread flatlock stitch. It's essential that you use quality fabrics, laces, embroideries, and threads so that your heirloom garment is worthy of passing on to future generations.

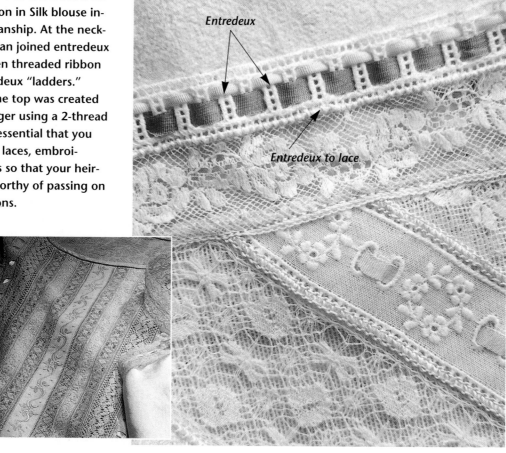

Entredeux

Entredeux to lace

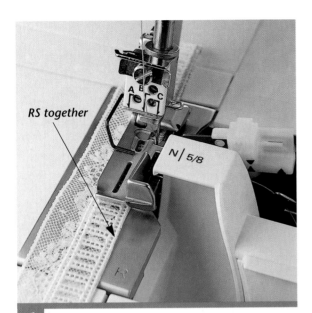

RS together

1 Lay a test piece of entredeux-edged embroidery on top of a piece of lace with the right sides together. Place them against the guide on the presser foot. Lower the needle into the first hole. Lower the presser foot, and serge. Adjust the guide and stitch length as necessary.

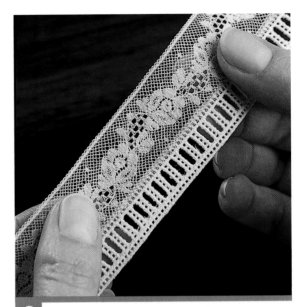

2 Serge together the first piece of entredeux and lace for your garment "fabric" as you did in your test in Step 1. Pull open the lace and entredeux seam, and press it flat. The entredeux and lace should lie adjacent to each other and be very flat. Only the needle thread should show.

3 You may add a piece of lace or fabric to the other long, lengthwise edge of the entredeux. If you do this, the entredeux must always be on top so you can see the holes when serging. Serge all of the entredeux-to-lace seams for the entire garment "fabric" at the same time to keep continuity in the stitching.

Fast Fix

SEEK "GUIDE"-ANCE

As mentioned in the introduction on page 140, it's important that you take only one stitch into each hole of the entredeux. This can be tough to do if you're new to heirloom serging.

So practice before stitching the "real thing." If, while stitching, the needle doesn't go into the center of each hole of the entredeux, I suggest you adjust the guide on the lace or blind hem presser foot. When properly positioned, the guide helps the needle to align with the entredeux's holes. Also, adjust the stitch length, doing so in small increments until you're satisfied with the results.

Linda Lee Vivian

FRENCH SERGED SEAM

At the serger it's easy to make a fine French seam. The result is a very dainty look that's a great seam finish for sheer and very delicate fabrics such as chiffon, batiste, lace, and silk. Ugly raw fabric edges don't show through on the right side of the completed garment.

While you can make this solely on your sewing machine, a French serged seam is much neater because it eliminates all the raw edges and threads that are part of a traditional French seam.

It's also possible to create a tinier French seam because the narrow 3-thread overlock used in the first step to join the fabrics is strong enough to prevent the seam from pulling out.

In addition, this stitch eliminates any stray threads. It's also very strong because you've stitched each seam twice by the end of the process.

So if you're going to put a great deal of time into your heirloom garment, make the inside as finished as the outside by using this fine seam. Even if your fabric isn't sheer, seam allowances will be visible through the material.

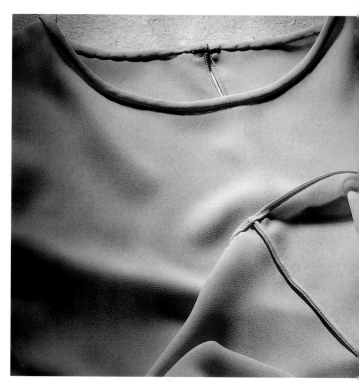

Slippery fabric like this chiffon blouse needs the differential feed at a stretch setting. This extra control also eliminates puckers.

SETTINGS & MATERIALS

Stitch: 3-thread narrow overlock
Stitch length: 2½ to 3 mm
Stitch width: 3 to 4 mm
Differential feed: Stretch
Needle position: Right*
Presser foot: Standard or rolled hem
Throat plate or stitch finger: Rolled
   (if necessary)
Upper knife: Engaged
Thread: All-purpose
Notions: Air-erasable marking pen, liquid
   seam sealant

*If you have the option of using the small stitch finger (the one you use for a rolled hem) either on the plate or foot, do so to create a narrower overlock.

Fast Fix

USE MORE

The first few times I made a French serged seam I ended up with rather wide seam allowances. I forgot that this seam finish uses twice as much fabric because it's stitched twice. (In other words, the first seam is half the width of the total seam allowance.) Now when I plan to use a French serged seam, I test the seam finish on some fashion fabric to determine how much width the seam requires. Then I make sure the pattern has the correct seam allowance widths, cut them out, and sew the garment pieces together. On average, I've found that a ⅝-inch (1.5-cm) seam allowance works nicely.

Linda Lee Vivian

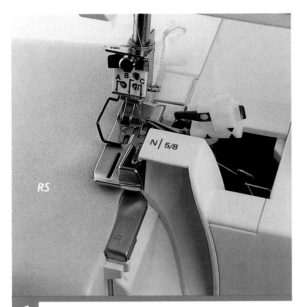

1 Place the wrong sides of the garment pieces together with the raw edges even. Serge, using the knife as a guide, trimming only a bit of fabric. For more accurate seam allowances with slippery fabrics, trim a sliver rather than keeping the cut edge against the knife.

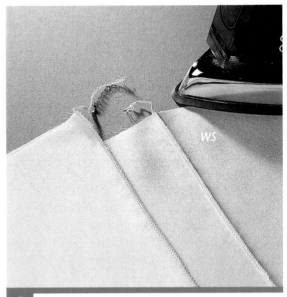

2 Press the seam allowances flat. Now press the seam allowances to one side. This two-step pressing method makes a neater seam finish. Moreover, it also keeps the fabric from accidentally shifting deeper into the seam as you stitch the final row of straight stitching.

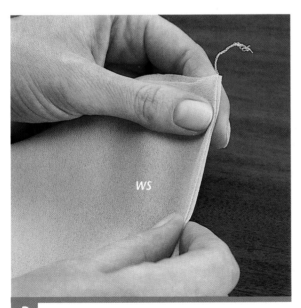

3 Fold the right sides together along the seamline to encase the seam allowances inside the fabric. Press. It's often difficult to keep the fine fabrics from shifting as you sew the second seamline in Step 4. The best way to ensure that the seamline remains the folded edge is to pin the seam in position in several places.

4 At the sewing machine, stitch a second seam just beyond the edge of the serged seam allowances. Make sure the seam allowances inside the folded fabric aren't caught in the stitching. This second seam encases the serged seam and finishes the fabric very neatly. After stitching, press the seam allowance flat, then to one side.

LACE TO FABRIC

Traditionally, lace-to-fabric stitching is created at the sewing machine with a roll-and-whip technique. Now, thanks to the serger, you can stitch a delicate seam that has less bulk than its sewing machine counterpart. In addition, you can add an accent color with needle threads and a 2-thread flatlock stitch.

At the serger, the raw fabric edge is finished as you stitch, encased inside the fabric by the looper thread. There's no need to pink, overlock, or zigzag a raw fabric edge because it's neatly rolled into the stitching.

When done properly, your serger needle "bites" into the lace just enough to make a secure seam. If the bite isn't deep enough, there may be gaps where the lace and fabric aren't properly joined. Adjusting the depth of the lace foot or the blind-hem foot helps.

The next step, opening the seam, reveals the color of the needle thread. If you want a subtler seam, choose a thread color that matches the fabric or the lace.

The stitch length and width in "Settings and Materials," below, are guidelines. Serge together a small strip of fabric and lace to determine a suitable stitch width and depth.

SETTINGS & MATERIALS

Stitch: 2-thread flatlock
Stitch length: 1½ to 2 mm
Stitch width: 3 to 4 mm
Needle position: Right (if possible)
Presser foot: Lace or blind hem
Upper looper converter: Engaged or attached
Needle thread: 30-weight Silk Stitch
Lower looper thread: All-purpose
Upper knife: Engaged
Notions: Liquid seam sealant

An elegant satin camisole showcases many heirloom techniques, several visible in this small section. At left is a lace insertion. The right edge of the lace insertion is attached to a fabric strip using the method presented on this page and the following page. At far right is one edge of a puffing strip, which was gathered and joined to the fabric strip in a single step. The horizontal lace beading is the straight neckline on the garment. Serger expert Linda Lee Vivian wove silk ribbon through the beading and then straight stitched the ribbon to hold it in place.

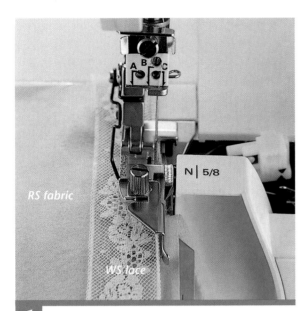

1 Place a fabric strip right side up just in front of the knife so you trim off only a sliver as you stitch. Serge until the needle makes one stitch into the fabric. Leave the needle down. Place the lace, wrong side up, against the guide on the foot. Lower the presser foot. Serge to the end.

2 Pull the seam open and press it flat. The lace and the fabric lie adjacent to each other and are very flat. When stitched correctly, only the needle thread shows on the right side. Adjust the stitch length to show more or less needle thread. If done correctly, it looks like hand stitching.

3 Add another fabric strip to the remaining edge of the lace. Always position the lace on top of the fabric so you can place it into the guide on the foot. Serge all of the lace-to-fabric seams for the entire garment "fabric" at the same time to keep continuity in the direction of the stitching on each lace-to-fabric joined strip.

Fast Fix

LOOK FOR A RAISE

When I choose a piece of lace, I sometimes have trouble figuring out which side of it is the right side. If you find yourself in the same situation, then try my trick. To help me determine the right side, I carefully examine the lace, comparing each side. I try to find the side that has a heavier, more raised effect. This is usually the right side. If you find it impossible to tell which side of the lace should face out when it's sewn into your garment, then don't worry, and just sew it in. If the difference is so subtle, then no one else will be able to tell the difference either, especially when you're wearing it.

Linda Lee Vivian

LACE TO LACE

Imagine creating a showcase for your collection of beautiful lace insertions. You can do just that by stitching many of them together and then making the resulting "fabric" into a new garment.

The first step is to lay the laces in front of you as you want them to look on your garment. Before committing to a certain arrangement, try switching the laces around to help you decide which laces look best next to each other.

Now envision how they'll look after they're serged together. Give some thought to the thread color that you want to use in the needle, as the thread separates the laces with just a hint of color. Lay strands of different color threads between the laces to help you decide.

For more interest, you may want to alternate the needle thread color, such as a light and a medium pink, as you join together subsequent lace strips.

Remember to pretreat all the laces before assembling the garment so any shrinkage happens before assembly. Always test for strength when using antique laces.

This may be the perfect place to add some lace treasures from a wedding dress or a special piece of lace from your grandmother's trunk. What a great excuse for spending a few hours sorting and admiring your delicate collection!

SETTINGS & MATERIALS

Stitch: 2-thread flatlock
Stitch length: 1½ to 2 mm
Stitch width: 3 to 4 mm
Needle position: Right (if possible)
Presser foot: Lace or blind hem
Upper looper converter: Engaged or attached
Needle thread: 30-weight Silk Stitch
Lower looper thread: All-purpose
Upper knife: Disengaged
Notions: Liquid seam sealant

This is a very close photograph of the pink blouse that's shown on page 140. The garment is made from a fine mulberry silk tussah. Serger expert Linda Lee Vivian dyed the fabric with Jacquard Acid Dye. She chose several laces, embroideries, and a ribbon to create the fabric. Use this method to make a patchwork vest or add a feminine touch to a simple dress. This same technique also works on a wedding dress. Add a piece of antique lace that has some sentimental value. Try using something old, something new, something borrowed, and something blue...a treasure worth keeping for many generations.

1 Place two pieces of lace, right sides together, against the guide on the presser foot. Adjust the guide as necessary until you achieve the proper depth for the type and weight of your lace. The depth of the seam is narrower on lightweight laces and wider on heavier laces.

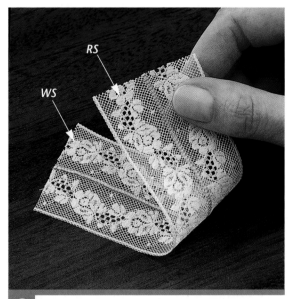

2 Serge along the entire length of the two pieces of lace that you're joining together. Now remove the lace from the serger. Pull the seam open as you would for any flatlocking procedure. For this type of work, the needle side is the right side. Now press it flat.

3 Join additional pieces of lace in the same manner. For consistency, stitch in the same direction for all seams. Once you adjust your serger to the proper settings, it's best to serge together all the laces that you plan to use in your garment. This maintains the continuity of the stitching everywhere on the finished garment.

Fast Fix

DON'T OVERBITE

It's always nice to start a technique knowing the exact settings. Unfortunately, I can only offer you ranges. So much depends on the type and weight of the fabric. The best guidance I can offer is to always test your seam width and stitch length on lace scraps.

When a serged lace seam looks too bulky, move the presser foot guide closer to the needle. This adjusts the depth of the seam. Large adjustments probably won't be necessary. When the guide is too close to the needle, the seam isn't wide enough to "bite" into the lace, thus creating holes in the seam.

Linda Lee Vivian

PINTUCKS

In contrast to the harder edge of its sewing machine counterpart, the rolled hem pintuck has a soft roll. The serger version isn't quite as delicate, but you can use a wider variety of threads.

Silk thread is a good choice. For a delicate look, use 50-weight, and for a heavier effect, choose 30-weight silk thread. Rayons also work well, as do the fine heirloom cottons like Tanne.

When selecting your thread, why not consider adding a touch of color by using a color that contrasts with your selected garment fabric?

Before stitching on your garment piece, serge a test row to check the depth of the pintuck. Then adjust the presser foot guide as necessary until you achieve the proper depth for the type and weight of fabric that you're using. As a general rule, on lightweight fabrics the depth is narrower than on heavier fabrics.

SETTINGS & MATERIALS

Stitch: 3-thread rolled*
Stitch length: 1½ to 2 mm
Stitch width: 3 to 4 mm
Needle position: Right (if possible)
Presser foot: Lace or blind hem†
Throat plate or stitch finger: Rolled (if necessary)
Needle thread: All-purpose
Upper looper thread: 30-weight Silk Stitch
Lower looper thread: All-purpose
Upper knife: Disengaged
Notions: Air-erasable marking pen, liquid seam sealant

*Leave more than 1-inch (2.5-cm) spaces between your pintucks if you want to insert decorative sewing machine stitches between the pintucks.
†If you're using a lace or blind-hem foot, test a pintuck, and adjust the guide to the proper depth.

The upper shoulder of serger expert Linda Lee Vivian's vest features a section of serger pintucking. Really a technique "sampler," this vest was created for the Pfaff Dealers convention in 1997. Linda Lee designed the vest so that she could quickly teach a number of serger heirloom techniques to the students in her classes. All of the beautiful silk fabrics, from Mulberry silk tussah to silk jacquard, are from Rupert, Gibbon, and Spider. (See the "Shopping Guide" on page 234.) The lining is a silk satin, and the fine cotton laces, from Capitol Imports, add a feminine touch. You can see more of the vest on page 135.

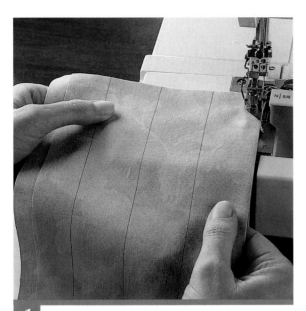

1 Draw parallel lines an inch or more apart on the right side of the fabric. If the pintucks are too close together, slight imperfections in width are more noticeable. Fold the fabric, wrong sides together, along the first parallel line, and place the fold against the presser foot's guide.

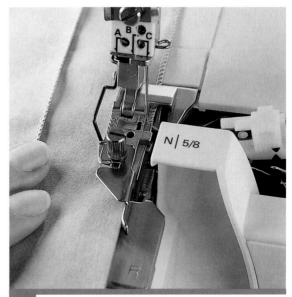

2 Serge along each fold, using the guide on the foot to maintain the proper depth. For best results, stitch pintucks from top to bottom on the left side of the garment and from the bottom up on the right side of the garment. This keeps the pintucks lying in a directional pattern.

3 Place a small drop of seam sealant onto the ends of each pintuck, and let dry. Press the pintucks away from the center. Now cut the garment piece from the pintucked fabric. Apply seam sealant to each pintuck that you cut through, in order to seal the thread ends. Take care with fine fabric because the seam sealant could seep through the fabric.

Fast Fix

HANG LOOSE

It's possible to make a pintuck using the 2-thread rolled hem stitch—a great solution if you don't have a lot of thread. If the 2-thread pintuck looks as if it's pulled in, and the fold/stitching line is very irregular, try adjusting the lower looper thread. Loosening the tension will help it lie flatter. If the stitched loops hang off the edge of the pintuck (the fabric fold), then you need to tighten the lower looper. The ultimate solution is switching your stitch. You can pintuck with a 2-thread rolled hem, but I prefer the 3-thread stitch. This version gives me more control over the tension adjustments.

Linda Lee Vivian

PUFFING

Puffing has been used for years on ladies' blouses, children's clothing, babies' christening gowns, and a large variety of garments that are intended to last for generations and are usually made of the most exquisite fabrics.

Never before has it been easier to add puffing strips to any garment; you need only exploit the differential feed on your serger.

In the past, you had to pregather the edges of the puffing and then carefully adjust the gathers to fit the edge of the fabric strip you were adding it to. At your sewing machine you then stitched the seam to hold the gathers in place.

What was normally a two-step process can now be done in one easy step with the aid of a gathering foot and differential feed. Check the owners' manual. It's possible that your machine needs a fabric separator attachment. A puffing strip is usually serged between two fabric strips, but it can also be serged to a lace or embroidery strip. After the puffing sections are created, they are added to the heirloom fabric with another serger heirloom seam.

For additional information on heirloom techniques and guidance on assembling lace, fabric, and puffing strips into "new" fabric, refer to "Understanding Heirloom Serging" and "Creating 'New' Fabric" on pages 133–135.

Two puffing strips frame central laces, embroideries, and fabric on this camisole. The silk satin tussah was "antiqued" with ecru dye.

SETTINGS & MATERIALS

Stitch: 4-thread overlock
Stitch length: 4 to 5 mm
Stitch width: 3 to 4 mm
Presser foot: Gathering or shirring*
Thread: All-purpose polyester
Upper knife: Engaged
Differential feed: Gather
Notions: Air-erasable marking pen, liquid seam sealant

*On some sergers, you need a fabric separator attachment.

Fast Fix

PUFF TENSELY

If my puffing doesn't gather enough, I adjust the stitch length and the differential setting. Even the needle tension can affect the way the fabric gathers. Increasing this tension makes the fabric gather more. In addition, the heavier the fabric, the more necessary it is to have a longer stitch length.

Linda Lee Vivian

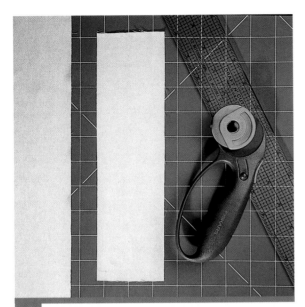

1 Cut a strip of fabric (the puffing strip) at least twice as long as the fabric to which it will be attached (the fabric strip). It's better to have a puffing strip that's too long rather than too short. You can cut the width of each of your puffing strips as wide as 3 inches (7.5 cm).

2 Place the puffing strip right side up under the presser foot so ⅛ inch (3 mm) will be trimmed. Serge. When the needles enter the fabric, stop. Lift the presser foot. Insert the fabric strip into the foot's slit, with the fabric edge against the knife. Lower the presser foot.

3 Serge the layers together, holding lightly onto the lower one and keeping the upper layer taut. Continue to serge so that ⅛ inch (3 mm) is trimmed. Don't trim fabric off the fabric strip. The differential feed automatically gathers the under layer to the upper layer. At the end of the fabric strip, serge off, then trim off the excess puffing strip.

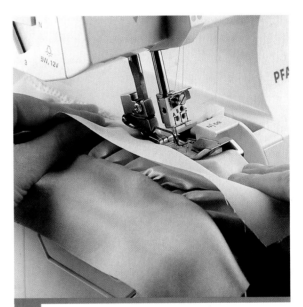

4 Serge another fabric strip to the remaining, unattached, side of the puffing strip, repeating the previous steps on this page. Serge slowly, again adjusting the layers for a couple of inches at a time. Always stop with the needles in the fabric, and reposition them before starting to stitch again.

Hems

There are an infinite variety of ways you can hem your garment. Bias-bound, blind-stitched, and cover-stitched versions are explained here. For additional ideas, see "Edgings" on pages 113–122.

BOUND TO BE ROLLED

Can you make a bias binding? Then you're set to tackle this interesting hem. Featured on upscale ready-to-wear, it combines the ease of a rolled edge finish with a splash of contrasting color.

One edge of a band of bias-cut fabric is finished with a rolled hem and stitched to the garment. You don't fold under a single seam allowance!

To make your own version, experiment with various fabric combinations, such as solids with bias-cut strips of checks, stripes, or dots. For a festive look, bind the edge of a plain garment with a holiday print.

If you're using cottons, remember to preshrink both the garment and the band fabric before assembly. Try using plaids or stripes for an interesting visual effect on the band. Or combine fabrics with different textures. A patch pocket on a bouclé jacket looks sophisticated when trimmed with velveteen. Experiment with the remnants in your fabric stash for interesting effects.

A tone-on-tone version has a subtler effect. Make the bias band from the same fabric, and finish the edge using a matching rayon thread.

Before adding your bands, practice the rolled hem on a scrap of the band fabric to ensure that you're getting the look you anticipated. If the fabric is too heavy to "roll," use a narrow overlock stitch (use the rolled hem setup, but adjust tensions for a balanced 3-thread overlock stitch). If fibers poke through the stitching, cover the edge with water-soluble stabilizer or tricot edging before stitching.

A bias band is an attractive detail on the hem of walking shorts, a sleeve, pocket, or any edge where you want a fabric accent. When applying a band, be sure to use fabrics that are similar in weight and require the same care.

SETTINGS & MATERIALS

Stitch: Rolled
Stitch length: 1.5 mm
Stitch width: 1.5 mm
Needle position: Right (if possible)
Presser foot: Standard or rolled
Throat plate or stitch finger: Rolled (if necessary)
Needle thread: All-purpose
Upper looper thread: Woolly Nylon
Lower looper thread: All-purpose
Upper knife: Engaged
Recommended fabric: Woven, any weight

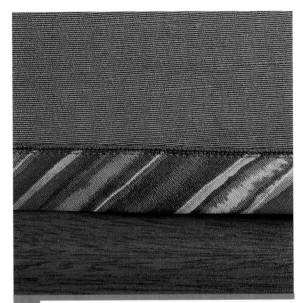

1 To make the binding for this technique, first measure the distance around the hem area you're covering. Cut a bias strip of fabric to the measurement of this hem area plus two seam allowances. The width of the strip is twice the desired finished width of the band plus ½ inch (1 cm).

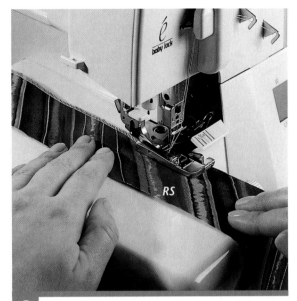

2 Finish one long edge of this bias strip with a rolled hem. Make sure you serge the bias strip with the fabric right side up so that the upper looper thread is on the correct (right) side. For added interest, use a contrasting color thread for the rolled hem stitching.

3 Join the remaining raw edge of the band to the raw edge of the garment's hem by placing the right side of the band against the wrong side of the garment. At your sewing machine, straight stitch the band to the edge of the garment with a ½-inch (1-cm) seam allowance when you join the two pieces together.

Fast Fix

WRAP 'N ROLL

Fabric ends can poke through your rolled hem stitching. Using Woolly Nylon in the upper looper can solve some of this problem because the fluffy thread fills out any holes in the stitching. But if the fabric thread ends are still "out there," place Seams Great on top of your fabric, and stitch through both layers. The right edge of the Seams Great, a tricot that tends to curl, will wrap around the edge of your fabric. Let the right edge of the tricot extend just a bit beyond the raw fabric edge so that the tricot encases those loose ends. Trim away the excess tricot after serging the rolled edge.

Pam Hastings

WS

4 After stitching has been completed, trim and grade the seam allowances to ¼ inch (6 mm). Press the seam allowances down, toward the band. Since both of the seam allowances are eventually enclosed in the finished band, you do not have to finish the raw edges on the serger.

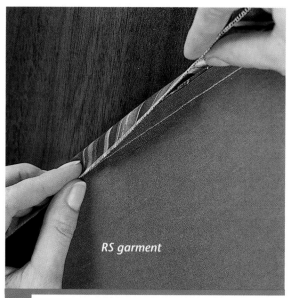

RS garment

5 Fold the band to the right side of the garment. The serger-finished edge, which is a rolled hem, is now on the outside of the garment. Fold the band enough to encase the seam allowances. The rolled edge sits just above the straight stitching. Press the band, and pin it in place.

RS garment

6 Move over to your sewing machine. Set it for straight stitching, and then sew through everything to secure the band. To do this, topstitch the band by sewing through all layers, on the band side. Sew as close as you can to the rolled hem stitching by using a zipper foot and shifting your needle position, if possible.

Fast Fix

RUNNING ON EMPTY

Occasionally, I spend a few intense hours trying to perfect the rolled edge stitch I want to apply to a garment. I fiddle with the tensions, try 2- and 3-thread versions, use different threads, and even try my other serger. I often feel as if I'm using up a mile of thread!

Inevitably, when I finally have perfect tension, I run out of thread before completing the line of stitching.

Now, before stitching on the garment piece, I look at the spools. If one spool has less thread, I move it to the needle position. The upper looper thread for a 3-thread stitch should be about eight to ten times as long as the fabric piece.

Susan Huxley

BLIND HEM

Enjoy the speed of the serger as it completes blind hems in half the time you'd spend doing a similar procedure at your sewing machine.

As with blind hemming at your sewing machine, the secret to success is the position of your fabric fold. The effect of a serger blind hem is quite professional looking if you catch just the fold of the fabric with the needle. If you do a test on a fabric swatch and discover that too much thread shows on the right side of your garment, just lengthen your stitch as much as possible on your machine.

A test also helps you determine if a serger blind hem is suitable for your garment. Some fabrics hem invisibly, while others will not. Serger blind hemming works beautifully on knits because it builds in stretch. And you can use the stitch on wovens, too.

While you can create a blind-hem with little more than your standard serger presser foot, you may want to use a blind-hem foot if you have one. There's a groove on it that protects the fabric from the knife. Usually, the foot can be adjusted with a screw, somewhat like your sewing machine blind-hem foot. This allows you to move the groove so that more or less of the fold of the fabric is caught in the stitching.

SETTINGS & MATERIALS

Stitch: 3-thread overlock
Stitch length: As long as possible
Stitch width: Test to adjust*
Needle position: Right (if possible)
Presser foot: Blind hem or standard
Thread: All-purpose
Upper knife: Engaged
Notions: Air-erasable marking pen or chalk

*The stitch width depends on the position of the fold you make in Step 2. It's usually ¼ inch (6 mm) left of the hem allowance edge. This varies if you adjust the width of the overcast on the raw edge (See Step 4).

Serging a blind hem allows you to perform two procedures in a single step: securing the hem allowance and overcasting the raw edge.

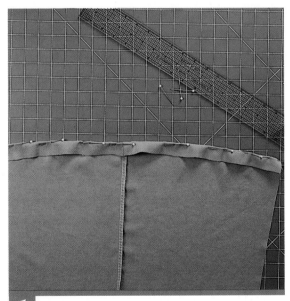

1 Join the left side seam, and press it toward the back of the garment. (This is a ready-to-wear procedure that leaves one side seam open so the hem can be serged flat.) Mark the hem. From the wrong side, fold up the hem allowance, and pin it close to the fold.

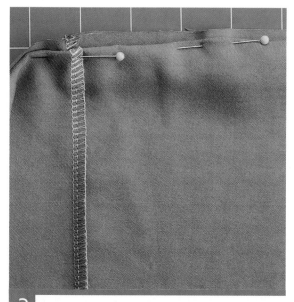

2 With the garment wrong side up, fold the hem back, underneath the rest of the fabric. Adjust the fold that forms in the garment so it's about ¼ inch (6 mm) to the left of the raw edge of the hem allowance. For a wider overcast, increase the visible raw edge, and increase the stitch width to cover it.

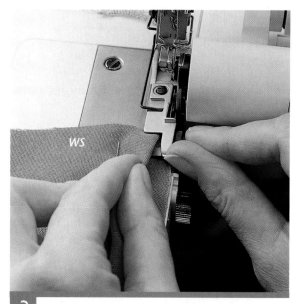

3 Pin the layers, keeping the pins away from the raw edge. Remove the first pins you placed in the hem so they won't get caught in the machine as you serge. Beginning at the open end of the hem, place the fold of the fabric into the groove of the presser foot.

4 Arrange the raw edge of the fabric underneath the foot. Serge. The needle stitches will just catch the fabric's fold, and the knife will trim the raw edge. At the same time, the loopers will overcast the raw edge. Because the left side seam faces the back, the foot will serge across it without getting caught in the seam.

5 Serge slowly over the bump formed by the seam. Complete the hem, press it, and then serge the final side seam. To secure the starting thread tail, begin serging at the top of the seam, and stop when the needle just enters the fabric. Lift the foot, and pull the thread tail forward and under the foot.

COVER-STITCHED HEM

If you have a newer serger with the cover-stitch option, you'll love using it to hem your knits. It's a one-step procedure that gives you the same look you find on ready-to-wear garments.

On the right side of your garment, the cover-stitch hem appears as two rows of straight stitching. In fact, many garment makers imitate the look of cover stitching by first finishing the raw edge of the hem allowance with 3-thread overlocking and then topstitching the garment with a wide-spaced twin needle.

The interior of a cover-stitched hem tells a different story. On this side, looper threads hold the upper edge of the hem allowance in position as well as prevent the raw edge from fraying. All this is done in a single step!

The flexibility of this stitch makes it the perfect choice for hemming knits.

When sewing on knits, hems may easily be steamed back into shape if they stretch during sewing.

Setting the differential feed to slightly gather should also help prevent stretching on knits.

Some sergers offer two needle positions for the cover stitch. The wider setting is a distance of 5 to 6 mm between the needles, while the narrow needle position has a 2.5 to 3 mm space. For hemming, a wide needle position is most appropriate.

Serge with decorative looper thread and the fabric wrong side up for a pretty effect. When you cover stitch a hem, however, serge with the fabric right side up. This will ensure that the looper thread covers the raw edge of the hem allowance so it won't fray.

Serge with the left needle the same distance from the fold as the hem allowance depth. If the hem is 2 inches (5 cm), the left needle is 2 inches (5 cm) from the fold.

SETTINGS & MATERIALS

Stitch: Cover
Stitch length: 3 mm
Needle position: Wide
Presser foot: Standard
Throat plate or stitch finger: Cover (if necessary)
Needle thread: All-purpose or decorative
Looper thread: All-purpose
Upper knife: Disengaged
Recommended fabric: Medium- to heavy-weight knits and wovens

Lace

For years sewers have used lace to soften a silhouette or add a feminine touch. With your serger you can easily attach—and even make—lace. To stitch in a traditional manner, refer to "Heirloom Serging" on pages 133–153.

COVER-STITCHED LACE

This is one of the nicest ways to attach cluny and crocheted laces that are hard to stitch with an heirloom technique.

The garment and facing are overlocked together to neaten the edges, and then the lace is cover stitched. It isn't inserted in a seam, thus avoiding a bulky seam allowance.

If your machine has two cover-stitch widths, you can easily attach any width or type of lace. A basic guideline for choosing lace for your project is to plan the lace and fabric combination according to weight. The finer the lace, the more lightweight the fabric. A heavier lace is more appropriate for medium- to heavyweight fabrics.

> ### SETTINGS & MATERIALS
> **Stitch:** 3 or 4-thread overlock, then cover
> **Stitch length:** 2.5 to 3 mm
> **Presser foot:** Standard, then cover
> **Throat plate or stitch finger:** Standard, then cover (if necessary)
> **Thread:** All-purpose
> **Upper knife:** Engaged, then disengaged
> **Notions:** Glue stick, ⅛-inch (3-mm)-wide ribbon, tapestry needle
> **Recommended fabric:** Light- to medium-weight knits or wovens, not suitable for loosely woven material
> **Recommended lace:** Edging lace (it has one straight edge) more than 1 inch (2.5 cm) wide*
>
> *You can use ruffled lace, but baste it to the fabric before serging.

When stretch lace is used on knit fabrics such as in lingerie, the cover stitch creates a built-in stretch factor. If you're still getting used to using the cover stitch on your serger, then start with a lined vest that you can make in an evening. After you're familiar with the process, you can apply the same technique to a huge variety of projects—everything from hems, sleeves, necklines, and zippers to quilting and home decorating. The stitching actually disappears into the lace design; thus it's invisible but absolutely secure, thanks to the double needle stitching.

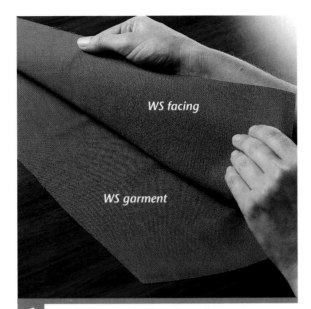

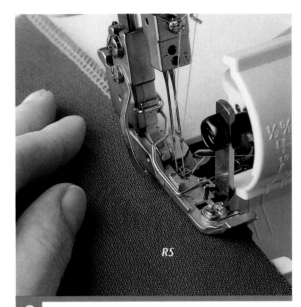

1 Cut out your garment and lining (optional) and facing pieces. You can apply the lace after assembly, but in this case we're applying it before. Select the piece to which the lace will be stitched. Place the optional facing or lining and garment pieces wrong sides together.

2 Make sure that the raw edges of your garment and lining are aligned. Set your serger for overlock, and serge the garment and facing together. Let the knife trim off all the seam allowances as you simultaneously join and neaten the fabrics during the stitching.

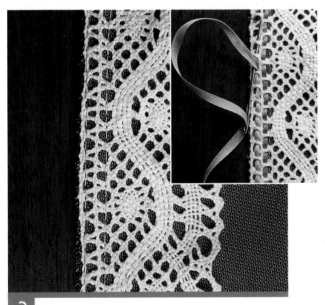

3 Pin or glue the lace, right side up, on the right side of the garment. Cover stitch the lace to the garment. Here, the needle threads are a contrasting color for better visibility. For your fashion garment, it's best to match your thread color to the lace. Thread ribbon in and out of the lace, between the cover stitches.

Fast Fix

STOP STRETCHING

It's more than likely that some parts of your garment are cut on the bias, so there's a good chance these areas will stretch when you attach the lace. (On the vest shown on these two pages, for example, the neckline areas on all pieces are prone to distortion.) If the fabric is a stretchy knit, the lining will usually take care of the problem. For other materials, simply adjusting your differential feed will bring the fabric under control, and you won't need to staystitch the bias areas. But only set the differential feed in the appropriate areas, reverting back to normal to complete the rest of the garment.

Agnes Mercik

OVERLOCKED LACE EDGING

It's possible to make a delicate, lacy edge for your garment using nothing more than a balanced 3-thread overlock stitch and some pretty, decorative threads.

Starting on a finished garment edge, you serge overlapping rows of stitching until the lace is the desired width.

This technique calls for stitching directly on the garment. Straight edges are best, but with practice you should be able to master curves and corners. If this sounds too involved, just stitch on bias-cut fabric strips, and insert this lace piping into the seam.

Have fun experimenting with decorative threads for a customized touch. Try rayon embroidery, metallic, and even some of the variegated threads.

If using three different threads, experiment on fabric scraps first, and look at the wrong side. You may like it better. For example, if you use a metallic thread on the upper looper and a rayon in the lower looper, the metallic thread shows more on the right side. On the back of the lace you get just a subtle glimmer between the layers of rayon thread.

Building on the feminine theme established by the print on this blouse, narrow serger lace accents the center front closure and collar. The gentle loops imply expensive detailing but can be replicated on even the most basic serger. Seamstress Sue Nester mastered the more challenging aspect of the overlocked lace technique—stitching around corners—but you can substitute lace piping that's made in the very same manner.

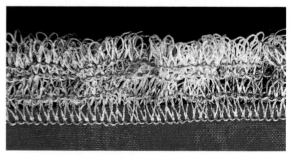

For ruffled lace, adjust the differential feed setting, or try using Woolly Nylon in the loopers. After stitching with Woolly Nylon, gently stretch the last row of stitching.

SETTINGS & MATERIALS

Stitch: 3-thread overlock

Stitch length: Short to medium (1.5 to 3 mm)

Stitch width: Wide (5 to 9 mm)

Needle position: Right (if possible)

Presser foot: Standard

Needle thread: All-purpose or lightweight decorative*

Looper threads: Decorative

Upper knife: Disengaged

Differential feed: Normal for the first row, then adjust to gather

*When using a heavier thread in the loopers, place matching all-purpose thread in the needle.

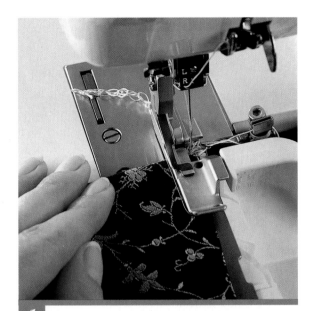

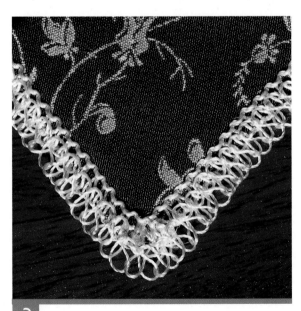

1 Assemble your garment, and finish the edge or hem to which you plan to stitch lace. Choose an unobtrusive location on the edge to start stitching. Position it under the presser foot so that the needle just catches the garment edge and half of every stitch hangs off the edge.

2 Serge along the garment edge for the first row of stitching, with the differential feed setting on normal. In subsequent rows you can adjust the differential feed as desired. At a gather setting, the lace is flat. Adjust the differential feed to stretch the lace ruffles.

3 Adjust the differential feed, if desired, for flat or ruffled lace. See the detail photo of ruffled lace, at bottom right on the opposite page. Serge a second row over the right-hand edge of the previous row. Stitch slowly to be sure that the needle catches the lace with every stitch. Continue adding as many extra rows of stitching as desired.

Fast Fix

BE "CORNER"-WISE

Turning a corner takes a lot of practice and wastes a lot of precious decorative thread. When the garment that I want to edge has square corners, I switch to lace piping. This is a bit of a shortcut, and it's very easy because you stitch on a fabric strip and then insert this piping into the seam when assembling the garment. The process is simple. Cut a 1¼-inch (3-cm)-wide bias fabric strip. Fold it in half lengthwise, and press lightly. Then follow the directions in Steps 2 and 3 on page 163 to serge along the folded and pressed edge. You'll end up with a ⅝-inch (1.5-cm)-wide seam allowance to catch in the seam.

Barbara Weiland

ROSETTE

If you want to add a ribbon or bow to gathered lace or eyelet, it usually takes several steps to get to that point.

But on a serger, in one simple step, you can stitch a ribbon onto the lace at the same time you're creating the casing.

When it's complete, you have the option of creating a rosette. All that's left is gathering the lace by pulling the ribbon and then tying it into a neat bow.

The application is quick and easy and can be used in a variety of ways on a garment. Used as an accessory or sewn directly onto the garment, a rosette creates a lovely Victorian style of embellishment. Substitute rosettes for buttons. (Sew snaps for the closures, and then stitch the rosettes in the button positions.)

Serger expert Agnes Mercik embellishes vests with small rosettes, scattering them across the fabric in a pleasing arrangement.

Don't stop at lace! Create your own flower embellishments from any lightweight pretty fashion fabric in order to coordinate with specific fabrics. Just stitch a rolled hem to the edges of narrow strips of fabric, and gather.

SETTINGS & MATERIALS

Stitch: 3-thread overlock
Stitch length: 4 mm
Stitch width: 2 to 3 mm
Needle position: Left
Presser foot: Lace
Thread: All-purpose
Upper knife: Disengaged or engaged
Notions: 1/8-inch (3-mm)-wide ribbon, liquid seam sealant
Recommended fabric: 2- to 4-inch (5- to 10-cm)-wide heavy- or lightweight edging lace, 18 inches (46 cm) of ribbon, liquid seam sealant*

*Layer a variety of lace widths to achieve a fuller look. Pregathered lace can also be used for a much fuller rosette.

Needle position is very important when serger-stitching a ribbon casing. You must use the left needle. Stitching with the right needle makes the looper thread casing too narrow for the ribbon—you'll end up stitching into the ribbon.

As serger expert Agnes Mercik says when she teaches, "You have to realize that not all machines do all things. Consider this when you purchase a serger, and ask the right questions."

If you own a 3-thread serger, you can make rosettes, as described in the following steps, but you'll have trouble with the ribbon. So switch to decorative cord.

1 Lower the needle. Insert one end of the ribbon through the presser foot and to the right of the needle. Place the start of 12 to 15 inches (30.5 to 38 cm) of lace under the presser foot with nothing extending past the right edge of the foot.

2 Without stitching through the ribbon, serge to the end (even if you've gone off the lace). Remove the joined lace and ribbon from the serger. Cut the excess stitches off the ribbon. Seal both of the ends with liquid seam sealant.

3 If desired, you can make the lace into a circle by serging together the short ends. Pull on the lace to draw up the ribbon until you have a tight center. Secure the tight circle by tying a nice bow with the ribbon. Hand stitch the center of the rosette to your fabric. This will prevent the rosette from coming undone.

Fast Fix

SLIP SLIDE AWAY

Your lace won't slide along the ribbon. What's wrong? When making a rosette, it's especially important to test your fabric and stitch before working on "the real thing" because you don't want to stitch through the ribbon. Rather, the upper and lower looper threads should wrap around it. The looper stitches actually create the casing for the ribbon to slide through. After you've inserted the ribbon into the foot, and before you add the lace, begin the stitching process by turning the handwheel a few times to ensure that the needle won't stitch through the ribbon.

Agnes Mercik

Neck Bands

Bands not only stabilize the neckline of a garment but also give you the opportunity to add interesting detailing. This chapter explains ways to both attach and detail neck bands using your serger.

COVER-STITCHED BAND

The cover stitch is the perfect finish for a banded neckline.

In one easy step the outside of the garment is finished with two perfectly parallel rows of topstitching, while the bottom (looper side) of the cover stitch encases the neckline seam—resulting in a smooth finish for the raw fabric edges.

The step-by-step instructions on this and the following page show the procedure on a woven fabric, but don't limit yourself. Bands can be constructed of woven fabrics or even ribbing yardage.

Self fabric or matching rib knit are used for a classic look, but for variety and interest, consider a contrasting color.

When using a woven fabric, the band must be cut on the bias, whereas ribbing should be cut in the direction that has the most stretch.

A cover-stitched band can be incorporated into any area of a garment. In this case, the stitching is on the round neckline of a blouse, positioned below the seamline. The stitching can just as easily straddle the seamline, or appear completely on the garment side.

Perfectly parallel topstitching is only one of the advantages of using a cover stitch to detail the neckline of a blouse. It's easy to apply, and you end up with a nice, flat edge.

Try using the same procedure to accent the edge of a pocket, sleeve, or hem that's finished with a band of contrasting or self fabric.

1 For the band, cut a piece of fabric 1¼ inches (3 cm) wide and the length of the area to be covered plus two seam allowances. If you're making a neckline band, cut the fabric on the bias. Fold and press the band in half lengthwise with the wrong sides together.

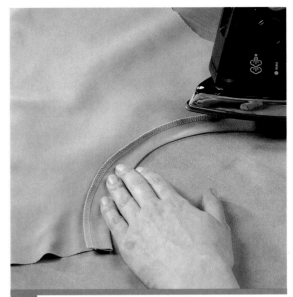

2 Overlock the folded band to the right side of the garment piece, with the raw edges even. Press the seam allowances toward the garment. If you want your cover-stitch topstitching to straddle the seamline (see Step 3), don't overlock the band to the garment; straight stitch instead.

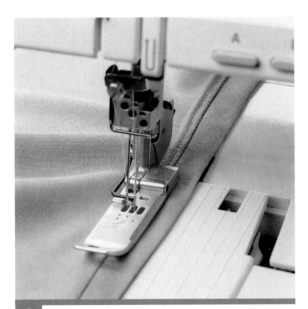

3 Change the serger settings, throat plate, presser foot, and needle plate (if necessary) for the cover-stitch option. With the garment right side up, sew a row of stitches on the right side of the garment. At your serger, position your garment under the presser foot. Place the right needle just to the left of the seamline if desired (see Step 4).

4 There are two ways you can position the stitching. For the first method (Step 3), you're sewing on the garment, not on the band. For a slightly different effect, you need to straight stitch the band to the garment in Step 2. At this step, press the seam allowances open, and sew so that the cover stitch straddles the seamline.

DOUBLE RIBBING

Like most people who sew their own garments, you've probably snooped through the clothing racks at your favorite stores and noticed the popularity of the double-ribbed neckline on knits.

This contemporary look combines a crew and mock turtle, thus simulating a layered look without the bulk of two garments.

If you desire only a mock turtleneck, you can still use the instructions by serger expert Agnes Mercik. Follow the steps on pages 169–170, and simply ignore all the references to the narrow ribbing in all of the instructions.

Knits are probably the easiest and quickest fabrics to serge. They're also comfortable to wear and easy to fit. Patterns for knits are designed with less complicated seaming, which makes for some really fast and fun serger projects.

In addition, you have so many choices because knit fabrics are available in a wide variety of natural and synthetic fibers, weights, and even textures.

The trendy look of multiple collars doesn't have to be uncomfortable. Rather than layering two tops, why not attach two bands to a neckline?

SETTINGS & MATERIALS

Stitch: 3- or 4-thread overlock, then cover (optional)*
Stitch length: Medium (2.5 to 3 mm)
Stitch width: Medium (2 mm)
Thread: All-purpose
Presser foot: Standard, then cover (if necessary)
Throat plate: Cover (if necessary)
Upper looper converter: Engaged or attached
Upper knife: Engaged
Notion: Ribbing†

*Thread the machine for a balanced overlock stitch. But to obtain the greatest amount of stretch, place the converter on the upper looper, and stitch the seams with two needles and lower looper.

†Self fabric such as interlock can be substituted for ribbing if the new fabric stretches and recovers sufficiently.

Fast Fix

BE ON THE BALL

Usually a universal needle is sufficient for stitching on knits. But when you stitched your test sample on a piece of knit, did you end up with snags or holes in the seam?

When this happens to me, I switch to a ballpoint needle type. In this situation it's also best to choose the smallest size needle that's suitable for the fabric.

Agnes Mercik

1 Join the shoulder seams on your garment. Set aside. Cut a piece of ribbing ⅔ to ¾ of the length of the neckline plus another ½ inch (1 cm) for the seam allowances. Cut a narrower piece of ribbing 3 inches (7.5 cm) wide. Cut another piece 5 inches (12.5 cm) wide.

2 Make each ribbing strip into a separate circle. You do this by serging the short raw fabric ends together with a balanced overlock stitch. After seaming, individually fold each ribbing circle lengthwise, with wrong sides together, so that the raw lengthwise edges are matching.

3 Layer the narrow and wide ribbing together. Align both the raw edges and the seamlines. Pin-mark the joined ribbing into quarters, ensuring that one of the pins is positioned at the aligned seams. This is center back. Cut the neckline down by ¾ to 1 inch (2 to 2.5 cm) in order to make room for the ribbing.

Fast Fix

WASH 'N WEAR

Limp ribbing could be caused by a habit that is usually reliable: pretreating fabric. Doing this could reduce or destroy the stretch and recovery characteristics of ribbing. So for more bounce to the ounce, I don't pretreat my trim. But I do pretreat all of my knit fabric before I begin assembling a garment. Let fiber content be your guide. For example, if the fabric is made partially— or totally—of a natural fiber such as cotton, it may require more than one washing and drying cycle. This multi-step approach reduces the possibility of residual shrinkage after you completely assemble your garment.

Agnes Mercik

4 Pin-mark center front and center back on your garment. Match these pins, and pin-mark the sides. Put the ribbing on the right side of the garment neckline with the ribbing seam at center back and the narrow ribbing closest to the garment. Match the quarter marks.

5 With the ribbing on top, serge, starting at center back. Since the ribbing is smaller than the neckline, stretch it to fit while serging. (Stop at each quarter mark to make adjustments.) To avoid losing stretch continuity, sink the needle(s) into the fabric every time you stop to adjust the layers.

6 Remove the garment from the machine, and press the seam allowances toward the garment side of the top that you're making. On the right side of the garment, you can topstitch along the seamline with a cover stitch. Or, if desired, you can topstitch at your sewing machine, using a double needle for the stitching.

Fast Fix

BE EDGE-WISE

There's nothing more disappointing than making a garment from a stretch fabric and then discovering that it doesn't fit right. You can alter the pattern, preshrink, cut carefully, and assemble without stretching, but if the fabric isn't suitable, all your hard work is wasted. Since the degree of stretch varies from one type of knit to another, it's important to choose a pattern that fits the fabric. I check the fabric against the stretch gauge printed on the pattern envelope by folding the crosswise edge 4 to 5 inches (10 to 12.5 cm) from the cut edge. Don't test the stretch on the cut edge.

Agnes Mercik

V-NECK PERFECTION

The thought of sewing a banded V-neck may seem daunting at first, but with a bit of practice it's as easy to construct as a curved neckline—even when assembled almost entirely on a serger.

So take out that top pattern you wanted to tackle and select the view with the V rather than the usual rounded neckline. It won't take you any longer to make a perfect V-neckline.

V-necks aren't limited to stretch fabric. They can be constructed from a rib knit or from a contrasting or matching woven fabric. As with curved necklines, you'll achieve the best results if you always construct the neckbands from the area of fabric with the greatest stretch. On a rib knit, the most stretch is across the ribs. On a woven, you should cut the neckband on the bias.

If you want to follow ready-to-wear standards, the neckband is a finished width of $3/4$ (2 cm) to 2 inches (5 cm).

You can make your neckband any width. You may want to fine-tune the measurement to suit your neck. (One of the major advantages of sewing your own clothes is being able to make a garment that looks best on you.) The cut width of the neckband should equal twice the desired finished width plus two seam allowances. In other words, a 2-inch (5-cm) finished neckband has a cut width of $5\frac{1}{4}$ inches (13 cm).

When serging a V-neck, it's a good idea to stitch it using the flat method of construction. This is an easy process in which you join one shoulder seam, apply the rib, and then sew the remaining shoulder. Then the sides seams are joined, and the sleeves are inserted. Hems are the last step.

The V-neckline may seem difficult to make, but it's truly as easy to create as a traditional neckline, even when constructed almost completely on the serger.

For added interest, topstitch the neckline seam with a single or twin needle on the sewing machine, or try adding a ribbed-knit neckline to a woven fabric garment.

Once you perfect this neckline, try it on garments other than sweatshirts and T-shirts. Add a contrasting or self-fabric woven band to a favorite chemise or shift-style dress. If your favorite pattern doesn't have a V-neck, you can easily draw one in and change the neckline.

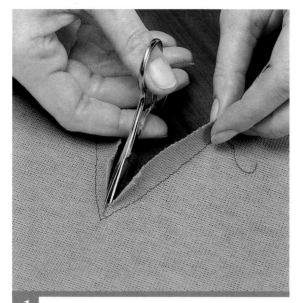

1 At your sewing machine, use a straight stitch to stay stitch the V-neckline along the seamline of the garment, beginning and ending the stitching 3 inches (7.5 cm) from the V. Clip the seam allowance to, but not through, the stay stitching. Get as close to the stitching as possible.

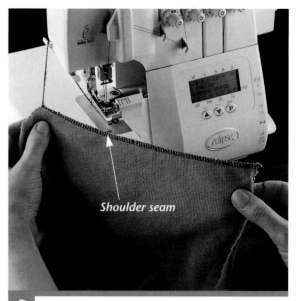

Shoulder seam

2 For best results when sewing a V-neckline, apply ribbing with the flat application method. As explained in the introduction on the previous page, the neckband is joined before the garment is assembled. With right sides together, serge only one shoulder seam together. Don't join the side seams.

3 Cut the neckband ribbing from your fabric, with the length positioned along the direction of the fabric with the most built-in stretch (this is usually across the "ribs"). See "Pinch Hit," at right. Make the neckband twice the desired width (plus two seam allowances) by the length of the neckline (plus two seam allowances).

Fast Fix

PINCH HIT

I'm lucky enough to live in an area where it's easy to find matching ribbing. And I don't mind ordering material by mail order when I'm not in a hurry. But if I'm stuck with an unusual color and can't find matching rib, I know I have options. I can add a splash of color to my garment by using a contrasting neckband. Or if my garment is a knit fabric, I make my own self ribbing. To do this, cut a band across the knit (in other words, across the "ribs") so that the fabric has as much stretch as possible. The length and width of the neckband are the same as described in Step 3 at left.

Pam Hastings

4 Fold the neckband lengthwise with the wrong sides together. Finger press the neckband along the folded edge. Place the neckband and the garment right sides together, and insert the layers into the serger with the ribbing on top and the garment on the bottom.

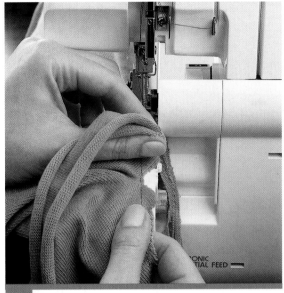

5 As you serge, stretch the neckband at the back of the neckline, and pull the edge straight at the point where you cut into the V in the garment. Don't lift the neckband off the neckline. It's removed here so you can see the V, on the bottom layer, as it's being stretched.

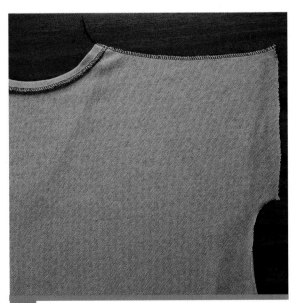

6 Your neckband is now attached to the neckline. If desired, topstitch or cover stitch along the seamline. With the right sides of the fabric together, serge the remaining shoulder seam. Thread the serger chain onto a hand sewing needle, and bury the chain under the serger stitches at the shoulder.

7 This is the finishing touch. At center front of the neckband, fold the front in half with the right side together. Take the garment to your sewing machine. At the center front fold, stitch diagonally through all layers of the neckband. Open the neckband and press the neckband "dart" flat. Join the garment's side seams and hems as desired.

Piping

Explore imaginative applications and the innovative use of stitches and materials to create your own piping without bias-cut fabric strips.

MOCK PIPING

A visit to almost any fabric store confirms that when it comes to piping, there just aren't that many options because both the color and the fabric choices are limited. You can make your own at the sewing machine by wrapping bias-cut strips of fabric around cord and securing the layers with stitching. But with the serger you have another faster, easier option.

Thread a coordinating or contrasting decorative thread in the upper looper. Now roll edge–stitch over the folded edge of one seam allowance with the fabric positioned right side up, and then topstitch it to the corresponding garment piece.

The serged, folded edge of the fabric defines the seamline, and your color choice is only limited by the decorative thread that's available to you.

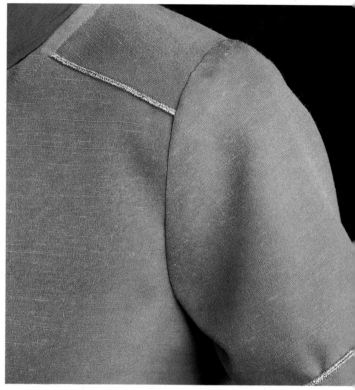

Any straight seamline is a good candidate for a mock piped edge. Consider shoulders, hems, and princess seams.

SETTINGS & MATERIALS

Stitch: Rolled
Stitch length: Short (2 mm)
Stitch width: Narrow (1.5 mm)
Presser foot: Standard or rolled
Throat plate or stitch finger: Rolled (if necessary)
Needle thread: All-purpose for the serger, monofilament for your sewing machine*
Upper looper thread: Decorative
Lower looper thread: All-purpose
Upper knife: Disengaged

*At your sewing machine, use all-purpose in the bobbin.

Fast Fix

CHOOSE QUALITY

I prefer to use a long-staple polyester thread whenever possible. The manufacturers of top-notch threads use longer fibers to make the threads. This results in a thread that is both stronger and smoother. (You can identify poor-quality thread because it's fuzzy.) Using better thread also makes it easier to maintain the desired stitch, and your tension will remain consistent. I've noticed that the inexpensive serger thread made in Mexico is of inferior quality and should be avoided.

Buy the best-quality thread you can afford. You'll discover that your serging will greatly improve.

Linda Lee Vivian

1 Turn under the seam allowance on one of the two garment pieces that will be joined. Straight stitch baste on the seamline of the other garment piece, using matching thread. (It contrasts in this photo only for better visibility.) Don't sew the garment pieces together.

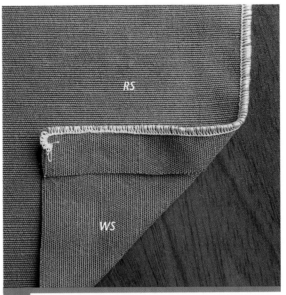

2 In this step work only with the garment piece that has the seam allowance folded to the wrong side. Insert it right side up under the presser foot with the folded edge to the right. Position the fold so that the rolled hem stitches run along the fold without curling the fold to the wrong side.

3 If desired, for better control while topstitching, fuse-baste the garment pieces together. Attach a narrow strip of fusible web to the seam allowance (the underside) of the serged piece. Remove the paper, position the serged edge along the basting, and fuse for two to three seconds. Now you can proceed to your sewing machine.

4 At your sewing machine, join the two garment pieces along the seamline. Install a standard, zipper, or cording presser foot. If desired, hold the pieces together with a temporary glue, or baste. With both garment pieces right side up, place the serged folded edge on top of the basting on the other garment piece. Topstitch through both layers.

STRETCH PIPING

Flexible piping that gives with every movement is a plus for activewear like dancewear, lingerie, and swimwear. Isn't it nice to know that you can make your own on a serger?

Overlocking along one edge of transparent elastic with stretchy nylon thread—while leaving the remainder of the elastic free of stitching—creates colorful, lightweight, flexible piping with built-in resilience.

Since you only serge along one edge of this space-age "plastic elastic," the remaining lengthwise edge of the elastic becomes the piping's seam allowance. This exposed elastic edge is stitched into the seamline, sandwiched between two garment pieces, just as you would insert standard fabric-covered piping.

Seamstress Sue Nester warns that this technique is not for the serger-timid. The stitch quality and tension will be inconsistent until you hit on the right combination of settings. Another problem is keeping the elastic evenly stretched. Once you master these hurdles, you'll be satisfied with the results. As you can see in the photos, Sue achieved a quality look.

Elasticized piping defines the seam of a two-piece sleeve on a bodysuit. Its built-in "give" ensures that the edging bounces back after every arm movement. There are no broken threads or out-of-shape piping fabric to spoil the appearance of your garment.

The effect of your piping can be subtle or dynamic, depending on your thread selection. Woolly Nylon thread comes in a wonderful array of colors so you can customize this unique trim to any knit garment fabric. This stretchy thread is the best choice, but you can also try any decorative thread.

SETTINGS & MATERIALS

Stitch: 3-thread overlock
Stitch length: Short
Stitch width: Narrow
Needle: Standard or stretch
Needle position: Right (if possible)
Presser foot: Standard or cording for thicker piping
Needle and lower looper thread: All-purpose or Woolly Nylon*
Upper looper thread: Woolly Nylon or decorative
Upper knife: Engaged
Notions: Clear elastic, 3/8-inch (9-mm)-wide or wider; elastic cord (optional)

*Try the thicker version of Woolly Nylon for superior coverage, or use two strands of regular Woolly Nylon in the upper looper.

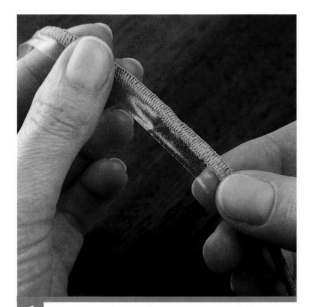

1 Insert the clear elastic under the presser foot, and prepare to serge along the entire length. Let the knife cut off just a bit of the edge of the elastic as you stitch. It's best to slightly stretch the elastic as you stitch, while holding it firmly behind and in front of the foot.

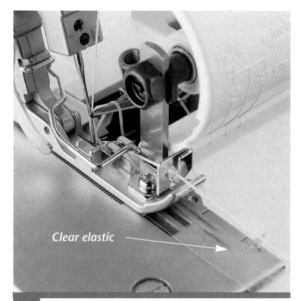

Clear elastic

2 For thicker piping, stitch with elastic cord layered on top of the clear elastic. Widen the stitch, change to a cording foot, and feed the elastic cord through the presser foot. The elastic cord is caught on top of the elastic. Instead of cord, you may want to fold the clear elastic in half.

3 At the seamline, place the stretch piping between the garment pieces. The garment pieces are right sides together, and the upper looper side of the piping faces the front garment piece. The un-stitched portion of the elastic (which is the seam allowance) is aligned with the raw fabric edges.

Fast Fix

STOP STRETCH

If you've experienced the frustration of elastic that grows after the garment is worn, you'll appreciate this Stretch Piping. How did we ever do without clear elastic? However, even clear elastic has its limitations. Like other types, you need to do some prep work. Here's my sanity-saving solution for preventing baggy, saggy elastic. Before serging on the elastic to make your own Stretch Piping (or use in any other application, for that matter), hand-stretch the elastic. By pulling on both ends a couple of times, you'll ensure that it's already its permanent length before you insert it in your garment.

Barbara Weiland

ZIPPER COIL SEAMING

As a less functional but unique and ornate detail, a zipper can substitute for piping. In this case only half (one side) of the zipper coil is used. It's inserted into the seamline so that the coil is exposed.

It's easy to insert a zipper coil if the garment pattern already has suitable seams. During the planning stage, try looking for a color-blocked garment pattern for your zipper coil seaming. You can highlight other general seams as well, such as side seams, and even gentle curved seamlines.

Select a pattern with interesting seam configurations, or use a basic pattern and apply creativity. Just divide the pattern into an interesting seam arrangement, cut it apart, and then add seam allowances to the new pieces.

Measure the distances for each seam's requirement for zipper lengths, allowing some extra length. You use only one side of the zipper coil per seam, so plan your seams to get the most economical use of the zippers.

Zipper coil seaming is also environmentally friendly. It's an excellent project for using up broken zippers. There are so many fun zippers you can use. But don't use a zipper with metal teeth. If one of the teeth accidentally slips too far to the right, the cutting knives on your serger will be damaged.

This is an excellent project if you have a collection of zippers that can't be repaired, but you just haven't the heart to toss them out.

The sky's the limit with zipper color selection and length. But to avoid damaging your serger's cutting blades, don't use any zippers that have metal teeth.

Any garment pattern that's pieced together is worth considering for this treatment. For a more creative application, purchase or collect a variety of colored nylon coil zippers, and use a crazy-patch theme to highlight the zippers. The variations are endless, and they're very easy to create on your serger.

SETTINGS & MATERIALS

Stitch: 3-thread, then 4-thread, overlock
Stitch length: 2.5 to 3 mm
Stitch width: 2 mm
Needle position: Left
Presser foot: Piping or multipurpose*
Thread: All-purpose
Upper knife: Engaged
Notion: Zipper with plastic coils, 3 to 4 inches (7.5 to 10 cm) longer than the seam

*Most sergers have an extra accessory or presser foot for applying piping, beads, and sequins. The Bernina multipurpose presser foot is designed with a long groove underneath to accommodate the extra thicknesses of zipper coils.

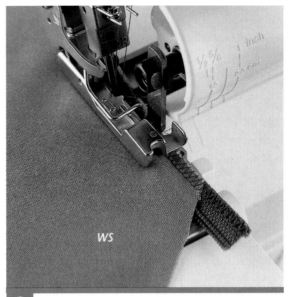

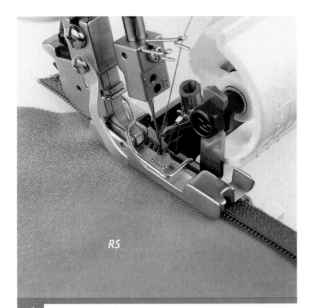

1 Separate the zipper, and place one side of the zipper tape on the fabric, with right sides together. Set your machine for a 3-thread overlock. With about 1 inch of tape extended at both ends, serge onto the zipper tape and then onto the fabric. Serge the entire seam.

2 Switch to a 4-thread stitch. Place the second fabric piece on top of the zipper with the raw edges even and right sides together. The zipper is sandwiched between the two fabric pieces. Serge the seam again, with the coil piping situated between the two fabric seams.

3 The ends of the zipper still extend beyond the fabric. These coils will be in the way in cross seaming when completing the garment. Open the fabric, and cut out all of the nylon zipper coil in the seam allowance area at both ends. Keep the zipper tape intact, though you may want to cut it off so it's even with the raw edges of the seam allowance.

Fast Fix

BUY BULK

Since this technique is primarily used for embellishment, the zipper lengths can be fudged. In basic zipper insertion, I usually suggest that you purchase a zipper 4 inches (10 cm) longer than the opening. In this case, since you're using neither the tab nor the stop, you can cut these off first and then insert the coils into the seamlines. If you plan a rather elaborate project and don't require special colors, then purchase the zippers by the yard, so that they're one continuous roll. The colors are limited, but this may be more economical for the right combination of fabrics and zipper coils.

Agnes Mercik

Placket

You don't have to bind your raw fabric edge with a strip of fabric. On finer fabric, the neckline or lower sleeve opening can be finished with a delicate edge finish.

DART-STITCHED PLACKET

For quite a few years, serger expert Linda Lee Vivian finished her beautiful heirloom garments by attaching bias strips to the placket openings at center back. Then she realized that the serger gives her the option of a faster way to finish this garment detail.

Since interior details are visible in garments made from fine fabrics, using this placket immensely improves the appearance. There's less bulk, and the placket has a tidy, daintier effect. Try it on any blouse or even a nightgown. Add a pretty button and a thread chain loop to complete your closure. To make the loop, set your serger to roll edge–stitch, and serge several inches without fabric. See "Using Rolled Edge Chain" on page 38.

This placket technique is simply a variation of an inside corner, except Linda Lee folds tiny pleats at the bottom of the placket. It's easier to maneuver the fabric as she stitches through the end of the slit, then continues along the remaining edge of the placket opening.

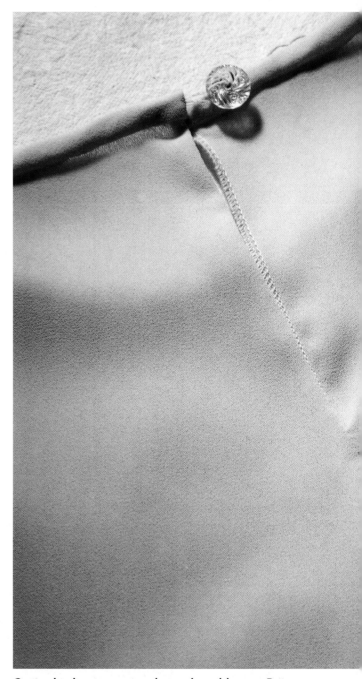

Center back seams are ugly on sheer blouses. But you need an opening to make the garment's neckline wide enough to pull a blouse over your head. A serged placket solves this problem by finishing the fabric edges without adding bulk.

The technique is also an excellent way to create a sleeve closure on fabric that's fine, sheer, or even delicate. Serge the placket according to the directions that follow, and then stitch the cuff to the edge of the sleeve. Just like a placket opening at the center back neckline, this technique speeds up your sewing time by eliminating a bias-strip placket finish at the bottom of the sleeve.

SETTINGS & MATERIALS

Stitch: 3-thread rolled
Stitch length: 1½ to 2 mm
Stitch width: 3 to 4 mm
Needle position: Right (if possible)
Presser foot: Standard or rolled
Throat plate or stitch finger: Rolled (if necessary)
Thread: All-purpose
Upper knife: Engaged
Notions: Erasable marking pen, seam sealant

1 Cut a slit in the fabric the length of the desired opening (4 to 5 inches, or 10 to 12.5 cm, is good). Place the cut fabric edge against the serger knife, and stitch until the bottom of the slit is ½ inch (1 cm) in front of the presser foot. Keep the cut fabric edge against the knife at all times.

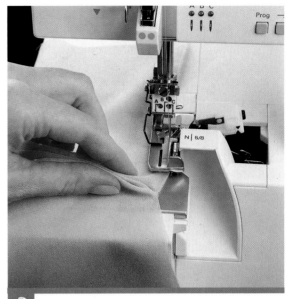

2 Fold the fabric at the bottom of the slit into a group of tiny pleats (three is usually enough). These pleats enable the cut edge to lie in a straight line against the knife. It's very important that you do this before the bottom of the placket goes under the presser foot.

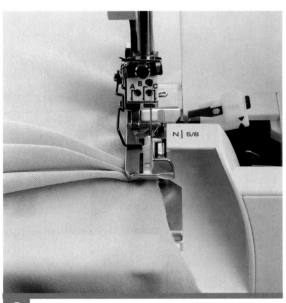

3 Continue serging, ensuring that the cut edge of the fabric placket is against the knife at all times, until the pleats are held in place just under the presser foot. Stop with the needle down in the fabric. At this point you haven't quite reached the bottom of the placket. This is important because you need to hold the fabric to complete the stitching.

Fast Fix

POINT A FINGER

Do you find it bothersome to stop stitching in order to measure something that's mounted in your serger? Experts often "sight," using marks on their machine or details (such as a certain point on the print) on the fabric. For more information, see page 3.

I don't rummage for a ruler to determine the ½-inch (1-cm) distance needed for Step 1. (The distance is a guideline only; it needn't be exact.)

Instead, I stop when there's a finger width between the front of the foot and the end of the placket. This gives me enough space to tuck without the interference of the foot.

Linda Lee Vivian

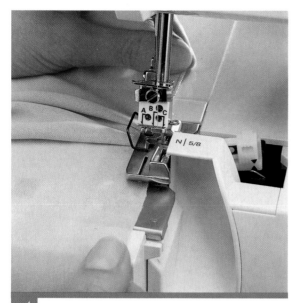

4 Hold the fabric taut behind and in front of the presser foot to prevent a pucker at the end of the placket. Serge through the end, letting the machine feed the fabric. Don't pull the fabric, or you'll risk bending or breaking a needle. Relax the fabric, and stitch the remaining side.

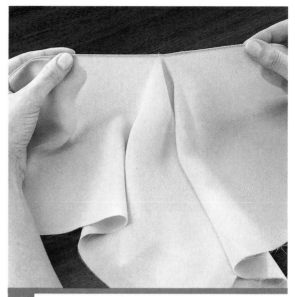

5 Remove the stitched placket from the machine. As you can see, when the placket is opened into a straight line, there is additional fabric at the end of the placket, which is the midway point on the straight line. Continue assembling the garment as desired.

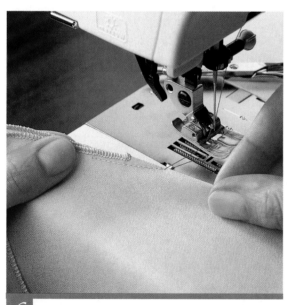

6 For a neater, hidden rolled hem, there's one last (optional) step. At the sewing machine, stitch a tiny dart at a point that's about ½ inch (1 cm) above the end of the placket. Backstitch, lock, or knot thread ends by hand at the stitches at the beginning and end of the dart. Press the dart to one side.

Fast Fix

DON'T STRAY

If I end up with a tuck at the end of the placket instead of a smooth seam, the stitching at the end of the slit is too far into the fabric because the needle took a deeper bite than needed. The solution, unfortunately, is to rip out the stitching and try again, this time making certain that the cut edge is just butted against the knife. I'm careful not to stitch any deeper into the fabric, and I don't trim off fabric as I serge.

On the other hand, if the stitching misses the fabric at the end of the slit—and I have nothing but a short serged chain—then the fabric strayed away from the knife.

Linda Lee Vivian

Quilting

You don't have to buy designer clothes to add dynamic garments to your wardrobe. The curved flatlock piecing and reversible channel quilting techniques in this chapter produce great-looking garments.

CURVED FLATLOCK PIECING

A complex appearance belies the simplicity of this technique, which uses rotary cutting, strip piecing, and serger stitching for fast and pretty results.

It's great wherever you want to introduce decorative threads and two different fabrics, and it looks particularly good on a vest or jacket front or as a patchwork garment.

Curved flatlock piecing does, however, use more fabric. You'll need to buy enough to make an entire garment in both of the fabrics so you'll have enough to layer one on top of the other to create the final pieced effect.

The fun part of this technique is joining the curved fabric strips. When placed right sides together, the inner and outer curves appear to be mismatched. To join them correctly, the serger secret is to make horizontal alignment marks across the fabric strips before flatlocking. When you open a seamed strip, the curves then fit together perfectly.

While working on these instructions, it dawned on serger expert Linda Lee Vivian that curved flatlock piecing is a suitable background for an underwater scene. Build the base fabric and then couch decorative threads so that they look like seaweed.

SETTINGS & MATERIALS

Stitch: 2-thread flatlock
Stitch length: 3 to 4 mm
Stitch width: 3 to 4 mm
Needle position: Left (if possible)
Presser foot: Standard
Upper looper converter: Engaged or attached
Needle thread: All-purpose
Lower looper thread: Decorative, such as Candlelight, Pearl Crown Rayon, Glamour, or Jeans Stitch
Upper knife: Engaged
Notions: Air- or water-soluble fabric marking pen or chalk; liquid seam sealant; rotary cutter, and self-healing cutting mat (optional)
Recommended fabric: Two contrasting or complementary pieces

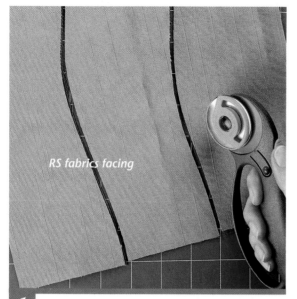

RS fabrics facing

1 Position both pieces of fabric right side up, and place them on top of each other on a self-healing cutting mat. Cut very gentle, elongated, curved strips through both layers of fabric. Don't cut the strips any narrower than 2 inches (5 cm)—they get too difficult to handle. If desired, vary the widths.

2 Remove the top layer of every other curved strip along the entire width of your layered fabrics. Set aside these extra top layers, keeping them in the same order that they were taken off the cutting mat. Back at the cutting mat, you can now see strips of alternating top and bottom fabrics.

3 Draw horizontal placement lines every 3 inches (7.5 cm) along all of the strips. These lines help match the strips when serging. Don't mark the lines before cutting the strips because the alternating fabric layers need to be properly aligned. This sample was marked with chalk for better visibility. Don't use chalk because it smudges.

Fast Fix

STOP FRAYS

The curves on your strips may not fit together if the fabric ravels so much that it loses the shape of the original edge. Tightly woven fabrics are best suited for this technique.

You can use a fabric that ravels easily if you apply a fusible knit interfacing to the wrong side before cutting the curved strips. This interfacing adds the necessary body and helps keep the stitches from pulling out of the seam. When stitching strips of knit fabric, increase the differential feed to a gather ("+" or number above 0) setting to keep fabric from stretching and rippling.

Linda Lee Vivian

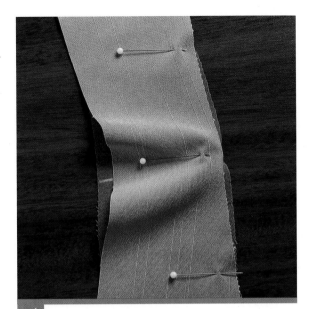

4 Working from left to right, place Strip 1 on top of Strip 2 with the wrong sides together. Match and pin at the placement lines. The curves will not match. (They do match when they're side by side and right side up.) Place the pins so they won't hit the serger knife.

5 Place the raw edges of the pinned strips beside the knife so it doesn't cut the edges but acts as a guide. Serge for a couple of inches, and stop with the needle in the fabric. Match the edges of the strips for the next few inches, and serge, always stopping with the needle down.

6 When you get to the end of the seam, serge off, leaving a 2-inch (5-cm) tail. Repeat Step 5 along the entire length of the pinned fabric strips. Remove the strips from the serger, and pull the strips apart so that the seam is flat. Press the strips flat from the wrong side. To reinforce the seam, apply a strip of fusible interfacing to the wrong side.

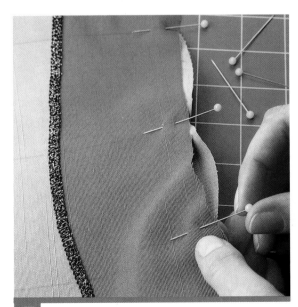

7 Back at the cutting mat, pick up fabric Strip 3. This is the same fabric as Strip 1. With wrong sides together, match the left edge of Strip 3 to the remaining raw edge of Strip 2. Match the placement lines, and flat-lock together, following Steps 4, 5, and 6. Join the remaining fabric strips. Check the order to avoid ripping out serging.

REVERSIBLE CHANNEL QUILTING

If you've ever added parallel rows of top-stitching to a garment, you've already come quite close to channel quilting; just add a thin layer of batting and a backing fabric to end up with the "real thing."

Traditionally, the channel quilting process is worked by basting the top fabric to a batting and backing and then quilting through all of the layers with parallel rows of straight stitching.

But there's an easier way. On the serger, basting is minimal, and your completed fabric has a quilted look without obvious stitching lines. The stitch is there—it's just hidden inside multilayer seams.

The result is a reversible fabric that is great for a vest without front closures. On a smaller scale, you can use the technique to make pocket flaps, a fabric tie belt, or even a stand-up collar. It's worth considering wherever both sides of the part of the garment are visible and where additional stiffness is an asset.

This process is easiest when you make the fabric and then cut out the garment pieces. In addition, if you don't use fashion fabric for the backing, you can purchase a less expensive material. Don't go this route if you want a reversible garment or garment piece. To join the garment pieces, cut off the seam allowances, then butt the raw edges together and finally zigzag along the seamlines. Then cover the seams with binding.

To pull together a jacket, channel-quilt leftover fabrics into a chic cuff. Since the fabric is reversible, the wearer never needs to worry that the wrong side will show.

Used in strategic locations on your garment, channel quilting creates visual texture and body and draws the eye to a particular spot. Suitable for fabrics with body, channel quilting can also be used for a collar, waistband, or straight hem. (Earthy wool tweeds, cotton flannels, sweatshirtings, luxurious velveteens, shiny satins, and sparkly lamés—all are wonderful fabrics for this artistic treatment.)

SETTINGS & MATERIALS

Stitch: 3- or 4-thread overlock
Stitch length: Medium (3 mm)
Stitch width: Widest possible (5 to 9 mm)
Thread: All-purpose
Presser foot: Standard
Upper knife: Engaged
Notions: Rotary cutter and mat (optional), ruler, Thermore by Hobbs (lightweight quilt batting)

1 Make your fabric before cutting out the garment piece. Decide the finished width of each row. Add 1¼ inches (3 cm) to each row, for two ⅝-inch (1.5-cm) seam allowances. (Later, the serger knives will cut off some of the seam allowance.) Cut batting and a pair of fabric strips for each row.

2 Row 1 is made differently than subsequent rows. Place a fabric strip, wrong side up, on your work table. This is the "backing." Layer a strip of batting and then another fabric strip on top. Position the strips with all of the raw edges even and the top fabric strip right side up.

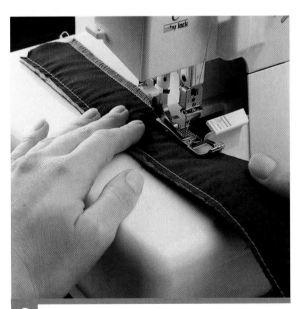

3 At your sewing machine, machine baste the layers of the fabric/batting/fabric "sandwich" together along one long edge, using a ¼-inch (6-mm) seam allowance. (To obtain the narrow seam allowance, let the knives cut off ⅜ inch (1 cm). At your serger, stitch the layers together along the length of the remaining long edge, using an overlock stitch.

4 For the next row you need a pair of fabric strips and batting. Position the Row 2 backing right side up. Put the Row 1 sandwich on top, with the right sides of the Row 1 and Row 2 backings facing. Put the Row 2 fabric top on the Row 1 top with right sides facing. Align the edges of all of the fabric and batting layers.

5 Pin all the layers together. Make sure that you place the pins to the left of the area where the serger's presser foot will ride on the fabric. (This ensures that the pins don't hit the knife when you're stitching.) Place a strip of batting on the bottom underneath all of the stacked layers.

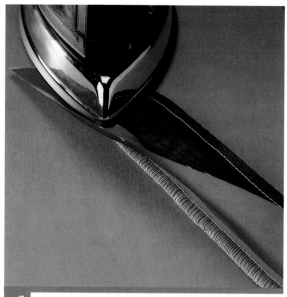

6 Serge the layers together along one long edge, the same edge that you already serged together for the Row 1 sandwich. To "finish" Row 2, press the Row 2 batting, backing, and top toward the seam allowance and away from the Row 1 layers along the newest seamline.

7 Align the unstitched, raw edges of the Row 2 strips and batting. Arrange the layers so that the raw edges of the batting are also even with the Row 2 top and backing. Serge together the raw edges of the Row 2 strips and batting. Repeat Steps 4 through 7 for the additional rows until you have joined enough strips for yardage for your pattern piece.

8 Continue joining rows until the quilted fabric is just a bit larger than the pattern piece. Cut the pattern piece from the fabric. Serge or machine baste the layers together ½ inch (1 cm) from the cut edges to create a stable edge for sewing the garment pieces together. Now assemble your garment according to the pattern instructions.

Reversible Garments

It's easy to think that sergers were designed for reversible garments because they're perfect for this type of sewing. There are several construction methods. This is the simplest.

DOUBLE-LAYER BLOUSE

Reversible garments are a wonderful way to mix and match a wardrobe. They offer flexibility and are perfect take-alongs for travel. Any simple garment, such as a blouse, jacket, skirt, slacks, or vest, can easily be made into a reversible garment.

The technique described here is double-layer construction. Two "garments" are assembled and then joined wrong sides together by edge-finishing. Your choices for this last, joining step are simple—bias binding or serging—but any sewer knows that the first option, bias binding, isn't all that great. Serging the edges, however, is very easy and beautiful.

SETTINGS & MATERIALS

Stitch: 3-thread balanced or 2-thread wrap

Stitch length: Adjust to suit the thread's thickness

Stitch width: 1.5 to 2 mm

Needle position: Right (if possible)

Needle thread: All-purpose

Upper looper thread: All-purpose (optional), then decorative*

Lower looper thread: All-purpose (optional), then decorative*

Presser foot: Standard

Upper knife: Engaged

Notions: Fusible or sew-in interfacing, liquid seam sealant

*If you assemble the garment entirely on the serger, then you need to chain or overlock stitch the garment pieces together with all-purpose thread in all positions. (See Steps 4 and 5.) The last procedure, Step 6, requires decorative thread in the loopers.

The burgundy decorative thread on this top is a subtle finish for both sides. If contrast threads had been used, they would highlight the edge and simulate a bound or piped appearance. A fun variation is variegated thread that stitches out in color "blocks." Or try using two variegated threads in the same looper to downplay the color-block effect. In this case, place an extra cone holder on the table behind the looper thread holder, and run both threads through the guides as if you were using a single thread. For two or more compatible threads, such as fine rayons and any of the smooth metallics, use a Thread Palette.

1 Select a garment with a minimum of pattern pieces, like the vest or full pants in Sandra Betzina's *No Time to Sew*. Collarless jackets and blouses can be used with some adjustments, such as eliminating facings. Choose a top without a defined front and back neckline.

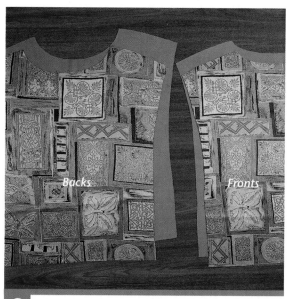

2 Cut out fabric pattern pieces for two "garments." These instructions are for a blouse, but you can apply them to other garments. Cut four garment pieces from two compatible fabrics. You need a Front and a Back from fabric #1 and a Front and a Back from fabric #2.

3 Cut out only one Front and one Back interfacing piece. Use the Back and Front Facings as the patterns, and cut the interfacing pieces 2 inches (5 cm) wide. Baste or fuse the interfacing pieces to the wrong side of the fabric #1 Front and Back fabric pattern pieces.

Fast Fix

GLUE-BASTE

At times, I find silky fabrics difficult to handle. They're so slippery that it's hard to join them. I glue-baste the raw edges together and then baste them on the sewing machine prior to serging. (Sometimes I just machine baste without gluing.) Before glue-basting, apply seam sealant to the edges of the two separate "blouses." This will prevent ravelling while handling during the serging process. You'll also be more comfortable knowing that the stitching won't come apart when you're wearing the garment. Be sure to trim or notch all curved edges so that they lie flat.

Agnes Mercik

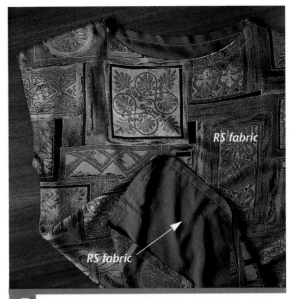

4 Pretend, for this step, that you're making two separate blouses. Sew the Fronts to the corresponding Backs at the shoulder and side seams. You can seam them using a 4-thread overlock, a chain stitch, or a sewing machine straight stitch. Press the seams flat or to one side.

5 Insert one "blouse" inside the other, with the wrong sides facing. Machine baste together the raw edges at the neckline, armhole, and hem. You may want to try basting the pieces with a serger chain stitch, because it's so easy to remove this stitching after finishing Step 6.

6 With decorative thread in the loopers and your serger stitch of choice, serge-edge-finish the edges you basted together in Step 5: neckline, sleeve, and hem. As you stitch, let the knife trim off a bit of the double-layer fabrics for the best stitch. Now give the serging a final pressing (unless this will damage the decorative thread). Your garment is ready to wear.

Fast Fix

STOP FRETTING

How on earth do you end your seams without ending up with an ugly mess of overlapped stitching? Students ask me this all the time when I'm teaching classes—even folks with lots of serging experience. My first bit of advice is to start and end your stitching in inconspicuous areas. In addition, I tell them to overlap the start and end of the serging by only one or two stitches.

For more guidance, see "Going in Circles" on page 54. Instructions in that section include the notch-out and stop-and-fold methods for ending a continuous line of stitching.

Agnes Mercik

Shirring

The romance of a ruffle is as close as your serger. This chain-stitch shirring technique is easier and the stitch stronger than the sewing machine version.

PAINLESS SHIRRING

Known as chain-stitch shirring, this technique uses elastic thread in the looper and creates perfectly parallel rows of gathered fabric. It's a great way to add gathering to garment parts as diverse as cuffs, bodices, and waistlines, and it's much prettier than adding elastic casings. Simply sew parallel rows of chain stitching until you achieve the look you want. As long as your first row is straight, you can make subsequent rows by using the edge of your presser foot as a guide while serging.

These instructions explain how to use shirring on a sleeve; when shirring is applied, it pulls in the fabric at the wrist and then releases it to create a feminine cuff. However, you can apply this technique to many areas other than sleeves. Try it when you want to gather a small portion and there isn't a seam. The back waist of a dress, for example, can be shirred with chain stitching and elastic so that your garment nips in at the waist but has sufficient give for you to pull it over your head when you get dressed.

SETTINGS & MATERIALS

Stitch: 2-thread chain
Stitch length: 2 mm
Presser foot: Standard
Needle thread: All-purpose
Chain-stitch looper thread: Elastic
Upper knife: Disengaged
Notions: Chalk, fabric marking pen, or pencil; ruler

Several rows of shirring shorten the length of the sleeve. It's a good idea to add about ½ inch (1 cm) to the sleeve length. Or else you can test your shirring on a scrap of fabric, measuring the length of the scrap before and after stitching to determine the amount of "shrinkage." Chain-stitched shirring works best on light- to medium-weight fabric.

To complete this shirring technique, your serger must be equipped with a 2-thread chain stitch. While shirring on a sleeve is shown here, the same method is also applied to other garment areas.

1 Lengthen the sleeve pattern, as explained in the photo caption on the opposite page. Don't join the underarm seam. Finish the sleeve edge with a rolled hem. Draw a line parallel to the finished edge on the wrong side of the fabric. The first row of the shirring is stitched along this line.

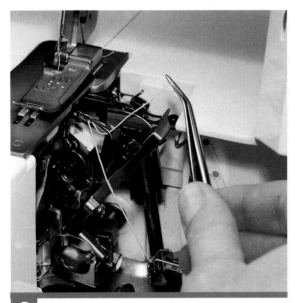

2 Thread the chain-stitch looper with elastic thread, and thread the needle with all-purpose thread in a color matching your garment. Using a scrap of fabric from the garment you're making, test the stitching, and adjust the stitch length and tensions if it's necessary.

3 Serge along the marked line with the fabric right side up. Stitch additional parallel rows one presser foot's width away from the previous row of serging. You'll need to stretch the fabric flat when stitching subsequent rows. When all the shirring is complete, sew the sleeve's underarm seam.

Fast Fix

FEED MORE

Using elastic thread in the chain-stitch looper will probably be all that you need to do to draw up light- to medium-weight fabrics. This should be enough for the shirring on your garment pattern piece.

With heavier fabric a little extra "something" is needed to encourage the fabric to draw up more, since it's harder to gather the bulk.

Whenever I need some additional shirring, I use the elastic thread and then adjust the differential feed. When it's set to gather, additional fabric is pulled into each stitch.

Pam Hastings

Tucks

There are many variations of tucks, each serving a different purpose, and some intended for particular types of fabrics. Whatever your stitch preference, you're sure to find a technique in this chapter that appeals to you.

AGGIE'S TUCKS

The special significance of this tuck design is that it uses a simple cover stitch as a base and also is very easy to execute.

First you use the cover stitch to serge all of the parallel rows of tucks, then you serge perpendicular rows. This forces the tucks to lie flat or else stand up. The rows of cover stitching are serged in alternating directions. A medium-size tuck width is very easily acquired by using the edge of the presser foot as a guide.

In her quest to research and develop unique sewing machine and serger applications, Agnes often tests the limits of her machines. At times she likes to take a basic technique and try a different approach. Since Mexican tucks are widely accepted as a popular sewing machine technique, she decided a serger stitch would add a special touch to this variation.

Since tucks add weight to a garment, visually and physically, take care to choose a light- to medium-weight fabric to avoid a bulky look. If you're planning to use this method at the edge of a sleeve or hem, stitch the hem before pleating the fabric.

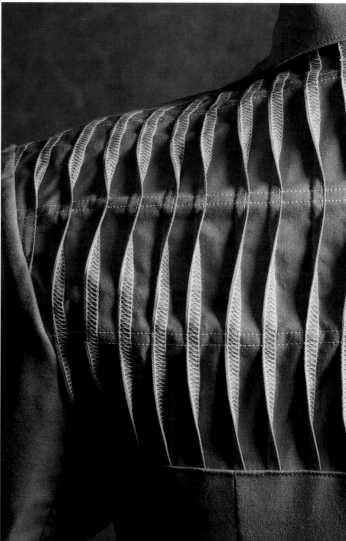

A yoke is the obvious place to use tucks; however, you can try placing them in unexpected areas. On collars, cuffs, pockets, or sections of a garment, tucks simulate a "blocked" design that stimulates an otherwise boring or basic style. For further versatility, use a woven fabric for the tucked portion of the garment, and incorporate a coordinating knit for the remainder of the garment.

Agnes Mercik's thread choices vary from very fine rayon and cotton embroidery threads (#30 and #40) to both a thicker twisted and non-twisted rayon.

SETTINGS & MATERIALS

Stitch: Cover
Stitch length: 2.5 to 3 mm
Presser foot: Cover (if necessary)
Throat plate: Cover (if necessary)
Needle thread: All-purpose or decorative
Lower looper thread: Contrasting color
Upper knife: Disengaged
Notions: Chalk or fabric marking pen, ruler

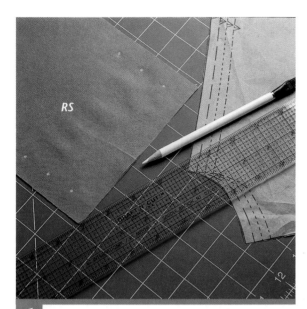

1 Cut a rectangle of fabric 2 to 4 inches (5 to 10 cm) longer than the pattern piece and three times the finished width. Draw a dot every 1¼ inches (3 cm) along the top of the rectangle, on the right side of the fabric. Mark the bottom of the rectangle in the same manner.

Fast Fix

STOP JAMMIN'

I've seen more than a few students jam the threads when they first start using the cover stitch. It's easy enough to do because sewers are accustomed to serging onto and off fabric. But cover stitching is started on the fabric and ends on the fabric. In addition, the completion of each stitch ends with the needles in the fabric. (This makes it pretty hard to take the fabric out of the machine, doesn't it?) To remove the fabric, turn the handwheel in the opposite direction of normal use (on most machines this is toward you). This last movement releases all of the threads.

Agnes Mercike

2 Make the first fold for a pleat using the dots made in Step 1 as guidelines. With the wrong sides facing, bring together the first two dots at the top and bottom of the fabric. Press along this vertical fold. Bring together the third and fourth dots to make a second pleat. Press. Repeat across the entire width of the fabric.

3 There's another way to mark pleats, but don't try it with knits. This alternate method ensures that all of your pleats are on grain and perfectly spaced. Decide the location of the fold for your first pleat. Find the lengthwise grainline, and pull a thread. Fold the fabric, with the wrong side together, on the "run."

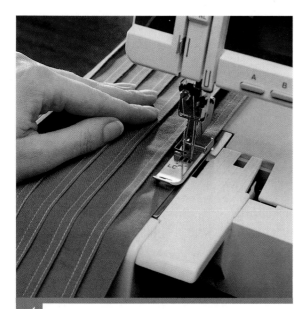

4 Place the first pressed fold under the presser foot. Align the right side of the presser foot toe with the fold. Stitch slowly to the end of the pleat. Serge along every fold in the same manner, always serging in the same direction: from the top of the fold to the bottom of the fold.

5 On the right side of the fabric, draw lines perpendicular to the tucks, across the folded, stitched tucks. The lines go across the width of the fabric, and they're spaced approximately 2 inches (5 cm) apart. Draw the lines across the entire fabric rectangle in this manner.

6 Centering the presser foot on the first marked line, serge down the fabric so that the pleats are all stitched down. Turn your fabric around (so the bottom is now the top), and serge along the second line. The presser foot toe will push the pleats in the opposite direction. Let this happen. It's this action that gives you the wave effect—with little effort.

7 Again, turn your fabric so the bottom is at the top, and the top is at the bottom. Serge across the fabric again, along the line adjacent to the last row of stitching made in Step 6, so the pleats are all stitched down. Stitch along the remaining lines in the same manner, always reversing the fabric so the tucks are alternately stitched flat and then folded back.

CHAIN-STITCH TUCKS

Beautiful thread and a stitch with depth and character are unlikely—but pleasing—accents for decorative tucks. Chain-stitched tucks serged as parallel rows in even or uneven tuck formations add exciting details to a basic tailored garment. The chain stitch is created with the combination of a needle and looper. The looper side creates the triple-thread effect. While technical needs limit your designs to parallel rows, there's room for creativity. Your tucks can be as narrow as the presser foot's width or as wide as is practical.

Placing a decorative thread in the looper enhances the triple-thread effect of the looper side of chain stitching. It's this side that's visible on the fabric that you're tucking and then using to cut out a pattern piece.

SETTINGS & MATERIALS

Stitch: Chain
Stitch length: 2.5 to 3 mm
Presser foot: Standard or chain (if possible)
Upper knife: Disengaged
Needle thread: All-purpose
Looper thread: Decorative: fine rayon, fine metallic, twisted and untwisted heavier rayon, or topstitching
Notions: Fabric marking pen or seam (stitching) guide, paper (optional)*
Recommended fabric: Light- to medium-weight (such as cotton, rayon, silk, and some blends)

* A piece of paper larger than the garment piece can help you plan your design. See "Plan Ahead" on page 198.

Tucks offer considerable design flexibility for your garment. You can create a series of tucks that progressively graduate in width, or as shown in the garment at right, you can stitch tucks on both the lengthwise and crosswise grains to form a lattice pattern. The cross-tucking approach has several variations. If, for instance, the vertical tucks are completely stitched as the first step, then the horizontal tucks will dominate the design. If, however, the stitching alternates back and forth between the vertical and horizontal tucks, then the overall design appears interwoven.

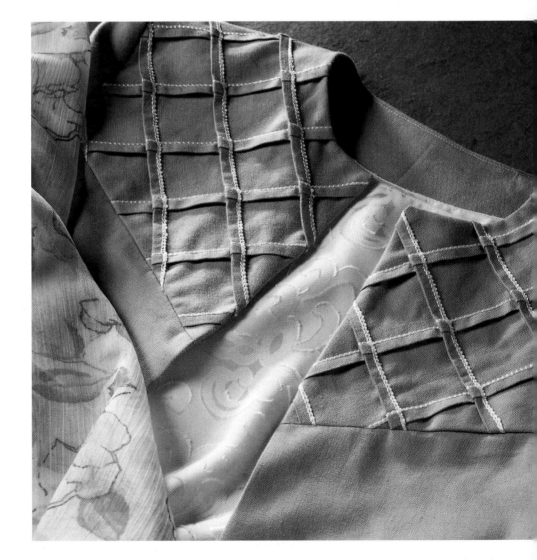

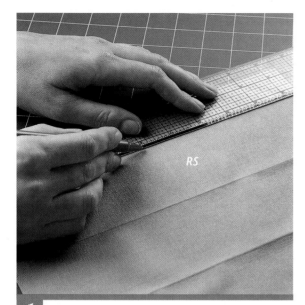

1 Plan your tuck spacing and placement. Cut a piece of fabric 2 to 3 inches (5 to 7.5 cm) larger than your pattern piece on all sides (for pattern placement and seaming). Mark the tuck fold lines on the right side. If you're using a seam guide, mark only the first line.

2 Fold and press each parallel tuck, wrong sides together, along the placement lines. Chain stitch along each fold, using the foot (or seam guide) as a guide. The looper stitch side is eventually visible, so consider the direction the tuck will lie in, and stitch all in one direction.

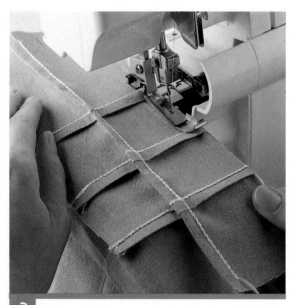

3 Set the tucks by first pressing on the needle side, then press again, but do so with the looper side of the fabric facing your ironing surface. Fold, press, and stitch all the vertical tucks. To maintain consistent stitch quality, slowly serge over the previous tucks. Cut the pattern piece from the tucked fabric.

Fast Fix

PLAN AHEAD

Are you having trouble estimating how much fabric you need? Step 1 offers basic guidelines, but more or less is necessary for extra-large—or small—garment pieces.

Before cutting out any fabric, start with a plan. You don't need to do any fancy calculating because you can mock up the tucks with paper.

I like to fold paper or pattern-making material to try out different tuck arrangements. By doing so, I can measure the paper before and after I fold it to reach a more accurate estimate of yardage required for the area that I'm going to tuck.

Agnes Mercik

SOUTACHE TUCKS

Who needs soutache braid when you have decorative thread and a flatlock stitch? The serger secret is using a heavily textured decorative thread in the upper looper. The stitching on the right side of the garment lies flat in a manner that simulates the look of expensive trim such as soutache.

There are unique design options because the tucks can be vertical or horizontal. They look great on yokes, sleeves, collars, cuffs, pockets—even a complete garment.

Serger expert Agnes Mercik likes to create a patchwork design on a jacket or vest by cutting sections of tucked fabric and then re-stitching them into an interesting abstract design.

You can also use tucks to enhance existing stripes or plaids on a fabric or to simulate the pattern that's on a matching solid fabric.

Other visual illusions are possible. For example, narrow tucks lend slimming lines to a garment, particularly when used as an accent color.

Successful tucks often depend on the manner in which they're arranged. They look best when stitched as a group or groupings. The spacing between the tucks can vary, depending on the desired effect.

Try combining pintucks with embroidery that's stitched on your sewing machine. Use a stabilizer on delicate fabric.

SETTINGS & MATERIALS

Stitch: 2-thread flatlock*
Stitch length: 2 to 3 mm
Stitch width: Narrow (1 to 2 mm)
Needle position: Right (if possible)
Presser foot: Standard
Upper knife: Disengaged
Needle: All-purpose
Lower looper thread: Decorative
Notions: Chalk or marking pen; seam (stitching) guide (optional)
Recommended fabric: Light- to medium-weight

*You can use a 3-thread flatlock. Insert decorative thread in the loopers and all-purpose thread in the needle.

Fast Fix

"SEE" WITH A FOOT

I like to use my blind-hem foot for consistent narrow tucks and flatlocking. I simply adjust the guide, then align the fabric fold with the guide. Since the blind-hem foot is made to be used with only the right needle, don't attempt to use the left needle. For a similar application, see "Plan Ahead" on the opposite page.

Agnes Mercik

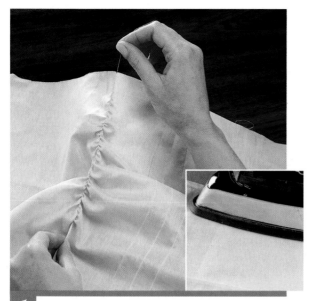

1 Plan your tuck sizes, spacing, and placement. Test your plan by stitching several tucks on fabric scraps. Cut a piece of fabric larger than your pattern. On the right side, pen-mark (or pull a thread) for the tuck fold lines. If you're using a seam guide, mark the first line. Starch and press each fold.

2 Serge a line of flatlocking along the first fold in the fabric. Try aligning the fold with the right needle guideline on the presser foot, if one is marked on the foot. This way the stitched loops partially hang off the edge of the fold, as needed for this technique.

3 As each tuck is stitched, gently pull the fabric to flatten the stitch. When the fabric is completely covered with opened tucks, place your pattern piece on the tucked fabric, and cut it out. If duplicate garment pieces need to be cut, use a "with nap" layout so both sides look the same. You use the nap layout because the stitching direction is subtly visible.

Fast Fix

FIGURE IT OUT

Since the garment pieces are cut out after you make the tucks, you need to estimate the amount of fabric that's taken up by cutting and tucking. I add 2 to 3 inches (5 to 7.5 cm) to the total length and width of the desired finished size. I also add ¼ inch (6 mm) for each tuck to either the width or length, depending on the direction that the tucks run in. Though these are flatlocked tucks, the fabric is still taken up a bit by the decorative stitching.

If you're uncomfortable working out the yardage with a calculator, adapt the paper pattern method that I explain in "Plan Ahead" on page 198.

Agnes Mercik

Waistband

For a timesaving, professional-looking waistband, finish the inside edge with your serger. This is a lot faster than hand stitching it in place.

STITCH-IN-THE-DITCH WAISTBAND

Waistbands that are finished with a serger not only save time in garment construction but also reduce bulk in the waist area and leave a nice finished edge on the inside. There isn't any tedious hand sewing.

If you've sewn a waistband recently, you'll be very comfortable with this waistband technique. It's quite similar to many versions that are made solely on the sewing machine. The finishing of the interior of the waistband is the difference here.

The waistband is stitched to the garment with a serger or conventional sewing machine, and the remaining edge, which has been overlocked, is simply straight stitched in place using the "stitch-in-the-ditch" technique (sewing in the seamline).

This technique is also applied to tailored button cuffs on blouses and shirts. As with the waistband, one edge of the cuff is finished at the serger, the cuff is applied to the assembled sleeve, and then the remaining cuff edge is secured with the stitch-in-the-ditch technique.

For less bulk in the waistband when working with wools and tweeds, use this technique—one seam allowance isn't folded into the waistband, so your waistband won't be as thick.

SETTINGS & MATERIALS

Stitch: 3-thread overlock
Stitch length: Medium (3 mm)
Stitch width: Determined by fabric type
Needle position: Left or right
Presser foot: Standard
Thread: All-purpose
Upper knife: Engaged

Fast Fix

CHECK THE LOCK

I recently learned of a woman whose serger was giving her trouble. The cutting width was erratic, and the fabric edge curled under, even though she made the stitch as wide as possible. She had previously serged with the knife disengaged. When she adjusted it at the end of the session, it wasn't fully locked in position.

Susan Huxley

1 Interface the waistband as directed in your pattern, then overlock the long un-notched edge of the waistband. At your sewing machine, straight stitch the waist-band to the garment with right sides to-gether. Press the seam allowances toward the waistband.

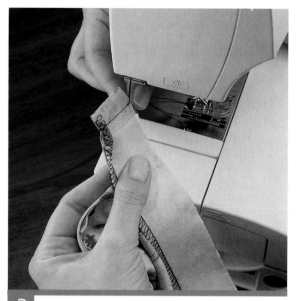

2 Fold the waistband right sides together. Again at your sewing machine, straight stitch across the short ends of the waist-bands from the fold to the raw edges of each of the short ends. Remember to ex-tend the right side of the waistband (the underlap) past center back.

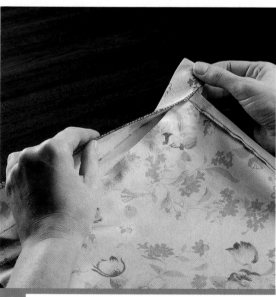

3 Turn and press the waistband right side out. Press the seam allowances up. Pin the unattached, overlocked edge to the interior of the skirt so it extends past the waistline seam. Tuck the seam allowances inside the underlap. At your sewing machine, stitch in the ditch to secure the loose, interior portion of the waistband to the rest of the skirt.

Fast Fix

GOOD HOUSEKEEPING

Thread lint and fabric fibers leave quite a mess inside a machine. While cre-ating the photographs for this book we needed pristine interiors, despite all the stitching that was done on these sergers. A shot of canned air provided a quick cleanup.

I rarely clean my own serger in this manner because the lint is blown far-ther into the mechanisms. My vacuum sucks out the mess with easily attached small nozzles and brushes I bought in a kit from a sewing notions mail-order source. Some sewing shops may also stock this item.

Susan Huxley

Weaving

From ribbons to serged fabric strips, it's possible to enhance any plain fabric surface with interesting texture and beautiful threads.

RIBBON WEAVING

The drama and beauty of ribbon weaving look as if it takes a lot of time to achieve, but that's not the case. Since it's fast, it's the perfect way to embellish a yoke, blouse front, or part of a pieced garment.

For a colorful effect, weave different colored ribbons in and out of the needle "ladder" stitches.

The secret to creating a high-quality effect is using a heavier thread in the needle. This makes the needle stitches more prominent—almost like hand stitching.

Ribbon weaving is usually done before cutting the pattern shape, but you can work on a garment piece as long as the serging is very flat. Keep in mind that the fabric will "shrink" if you take up too much fabric in each stitch.

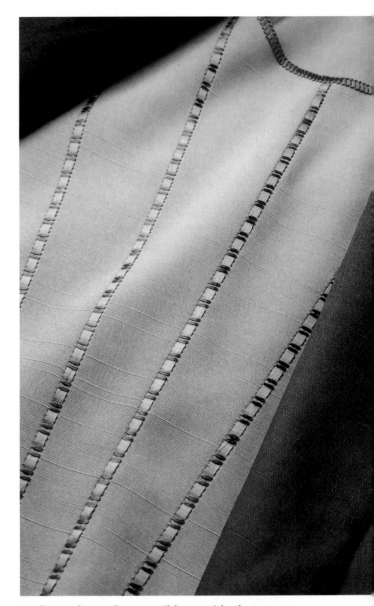

Radiating lines of woven ribbon guide the eye away from the waist area and up to the face. The flattering effect is an ideal application of ribbon weaving, since the design lines for the stitching are straight.

Each ribbon is secured under a row of stitching made with 2-thread flatlocking. Unlike couching, where the filler material is inserted during the stitching, ribbon weaving entails making the stitch and then running the contrasting ribbon in and out of the needle stitching that's visible on the right side of the fabric. (In other words, you can't accidentally stitch through the ribbon.)

SETTINGS & MATERIALS

Stitch: 2-thread flatlock
Needle: 100/16 topstitching
Needle position: Left
Presser foot: Standard
Upper looper converter: Engaged or attached
Needle thread: Designer 6, Decor 6, or 30-weight Silk Stitch*
Lower looper thread: All-purpose
Upper knife: Disengaged
Notions: Air-erasable marking pen, liquid seam sealant, 4-mm-wide silk ribbon

*It's best to use a slightly heavier thread in the needle so the needle thread will be prominent. It will be further accented by the silk ribbon weaving.

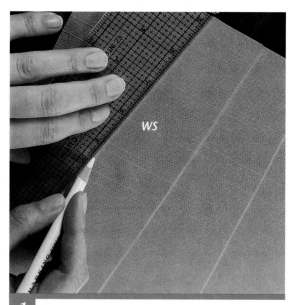

1 Draw straight lines on the fabric's wrong side, at least 1½ inches (4 cm) apart. The closer the lines, the more likely slight irregularities will show. Several rows look best, and an odd number is even better. The lines should go across the entire length or width of the piece of fabric.

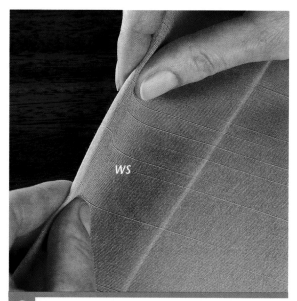

2 Ribbon weaving needs a very flat flatlock. When you open the fabric, there shouldn't be a tuck underneath the stitches. Practice the steps before stitching on your fabric. With right sides together, fold the fabric along a line. It doesn't matter which line you start with.

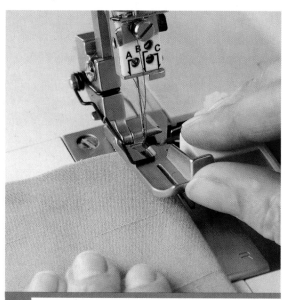

3 Lift up the front of the presser foot with your thumb. Place the fabric fold under the toe and center of the presser foot, just in front of the needle. Position the fold so half of each stitched loop will hang off the edge of the fold. (The stitch finger holds the loops, even if there is no fabric in half of the stitch.)

Fast Fix

STAY STRAIGHT

Sometimes I find it difficult to keep the fabric positioned in a straight line as I serge along the fold. This straight, even stitching is the secret to success with ribbon weaving, so it's important that I spend the time to work this out before starting to serge on my garment fabric. I find it helps when I attach a piece of drafting tape to the throat plate of the serger just in front of the presser foot. Then I align the fabric fold against the edge of the tape and use it as a guide. Sighting in this manner helps me maintain consistent stitching.

Drafting tape is wonderful because it doesn't leave a sticky residue.

Linda Lee Vivian

4 Flatlock along the fold. Keep the needle stitches a consistent distance from the fold. This is very important because you need to weave the ribbon through the ladder stitches made by the needle thread. The ladders won't be the same width without consistency.

5 Serge off the fabric, leaving a 2-inch (5-cm)-long serged tail. Pull the fabric on both sides of the seam in order to open it up. The fabric must be flat, without a tuck under the stitching. Sew the remaining lines on your fabric following Steps 1 through 5. Press if desired.

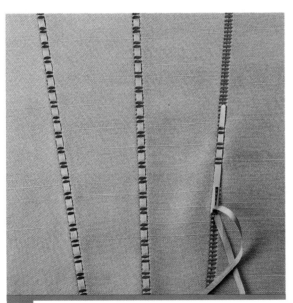

6 Weave a 4-mm silk ribbon into each line of ladder (needle) stitches, with the aid of a Flat Milward Bodkin. This bodkin is the best tool for you to use because it keeps the ribbon flat while you weave in and out of the stitching. It's also the perfect size for the 4-mm silk ribbon. Seal the ends of your seams with a seam sealant.

Fast Fix

USE A "SUB"

You may not want to buy a Flat Milward Bodkin if you don't plan to do much ribbon weaving. You can substitute, although this means working a bit harder. Sometimes I use a double-eyed bodkin or a tapestry needle to help me weave the ribbon into the ladder (needle thread) stitches. I have to be more careful, but it is possible to do the work this way. I weave only a few stitches at a time, and I pull the ribbon through until it lies completely flat. Then I thread the ribbon through a few more stitches and again pull the ribbon flat. I repeat these steps until I have the entire row finished.

Linda Lee Vivian

SERGER WEAVING

Made-to-order fabric is as close as your serger and your collection of fabric scraps. All you have to do is edge fabric strips with decorative stitching and then weave a brand-new fabric.

Even the simplest material can become an elegant focal point by turning it into a woven fabric. It's this type of creative detailing that transforms a basic garment into a showpiece.

There are so many ways you can change the personality of the "fabric." Use the same material throughout for a subtle approach, or combine two or more different fabrics to add pizzazz to an upscale garment. Introduce metallic fabrics to add a very dressy appearance.

Fabrics that have a slight color or surface variation on the right and wrong sides can be combined to add more interest to the completed garment.

If desired, you can also intersperse the fabric strips with lengths of ribbon, yarn, or even serger chain that's made with a rolled edge setting.

A pocket is a good first project for trying out this weaving technique because the square shape is easy to create. To showcase the weaving, seamstress Sue Nester followed the directions on pages 207–208 to make oversize patch pockets for a hip-length, loose-fitting jacket. The plain front made it easy to position the pockets. The jacket pattern is Sandra Betzina's, from her book *No Time to Sew.* (See page 244 for additional information.) Did you notice that the vertical fabric strips on the pocket are the same fabric as the shawl collar? Repeating the fabric strengthens the visual impact by continuing the color and pattern themes, while weaving with an alternate color adds variety.

SETTINGS & MATERIALS

Stitch: Rolled or narrow overlock

Stitch length: Short (1 to 2.5 mm)

Stitch width: Narrow (1 to 2 mm)

Needle position: Right (if possible)

Presser foot: Standard or rolled

Throat plate or stitch finger: Rolled (if necessary)

Needle thread: All-purpose

Upper looper thread: Decorative

Lower looper thread: All-purpose

Upper knife: Engaged

Differential feed: As needed to gather

Notions: Heavy cardboard, press cloth, rotary cutter, ruler, self-healing mat

Recommended fabric: Stay away from extremely ravel-prone or stretchy fabrics*

*For very lightweight fabrics, fuse a lightweight tricot interfacing to the wrong side before cutting the strips.

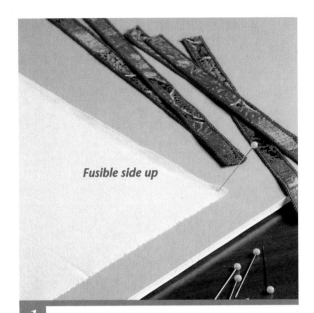

Fusible side up

1 Decide on the finished width and length of your woven fabric. Measure the garment piece if you plan to cut it from the woven fabric. Cut a piece of lightweight fusible interfacing 1½ to 2 inches (4 to 5 cm) larger. Pin the interfacing, resin (fusible) side up, on top of heavy cardboard.

Fast Fix

DOUBLE CROSS

If your weaving lacks body, the strips weren't stiff enough. Yet it is possible to serger-weave with even lightweight fabrics. The serger secret is to use more of the lightweight fabric in each single strip. For horizontal strips, start with a piece of fabric that's twice the width of the fusible interfacing. (Vertical strips need fabric that's twice as long as the interfacing.) Cut each strip 2¼ inches (6 cm) wide. Fold a strip in half lengthwise, with the wrong sides together. Serge the fold. Now serge the remaining lengthwise edge, catching both raw edges in the stitching.

Agnes Mercik

2 For the woven strips you need two fabric pieces, both the same size as the fusible interfacing. One is for the horizontal strips, the other for the vertical strips. It's best to overestimate the yardage. Quite often it's hit or miss on projects such as this. And typically, you use more fabric than you think you will. Serge-test the lengthwise and crosswise grain.

Use the least stretchy grain for the length of the strips. Cut your fabric strips 1⅛ inches (3 cm) wide. The width of the strips can vary, depending on your intended design and fabric weight. For example, cut lightweight fabric strips 1 inch (2.5 cm) wide. Serge all the lengthwise edges, trimming off ¼ inch (6 mm) of fabric.

3 Pin the lengthwise strips side by side and right side up on the fusible interfacing with the stitched edges butted together. Don't let them overlap each other. With your iron, lightly fuse both of the short ends of the strips to the interfacing to stabilize and immobilize the strips.

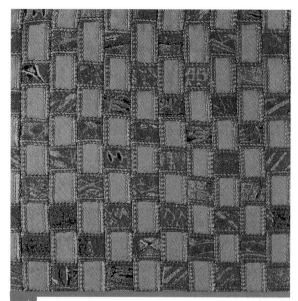

4 Weave the remaining horizontal fabric strips under and over the lengthwise strips. Butt the stitched edges of the strips. In this manner, cover the fusible interfacing so that none of the interfacing is visible. Periodically, stop and lightly press the woven strips to hold them in position.

5 Fuse the entire woven "fabric" to permanently secure the woven serger strips in place on the interfacing that's positioned underneath. The completed and pressed piece can now be handled as any other piece of fabric: inserted into a seam, cut into a garment piece, or serge-edged and topstitched (as a pocket) to a garment.

Fast Fix

STOP STRETCH MARKS

Serger weaving is easy and fun. Nevertheless, you may run into trouble because it's easy for the weaving to end up out of kilter, without perfectly vertical and horizontal lines. If the serger strips are stretched when cut or serged, you'll end up with inconsistent widths. This makes it very hard to obtain evenly woven, square fabric. I recommend serge-testing your fabric to find out which edge stretches the least. You then cut the length of your strips along the most stable grain on your fabric. The alternative is to adjust the differential feed toward gather before serging the lengthwise edges.

Agnes Mercik

Zippers

There are many reasons to insert a zipper with your serger. The fabric is simultaneously neatened, it's easier to avoid the slider because the presser foot is long, and the stitching looks great.

COVER-STITCHED ZIPPER

The cover stitch does more than add pretty topstitch detailing to garments. In fact, you can insert a zipper—from start to finish—with this stitch. In addition to being a very easy process, the extra rows of stitching (and the looper thread on the wrong side) ensure that the zipper stays secure for a long, long time.

This is an ideal treatment for clothes meant for an active lifestyle; pockets on sportswear and the front neck opening of a windbreaker are perfect locations. Add detail with contrasting thread in the needles.

While other serger zipper insertions leave the coils exposed, as shown here, you can also adapt this technique to resemble a centered zipper. For covered coils, simply fold the fabric over the zipper so that it meets or butts together directly over the coils rather than next to them. In either case, always remember that the zipper must be secured by an intersecting seam, or else you can bartack the zipper at the top edge to prevent the pull from coming off. During construction, if you do "lose" the coil, just remove the metal zipper stop from the bottom of the zipper, and slide the zipper pull back on.

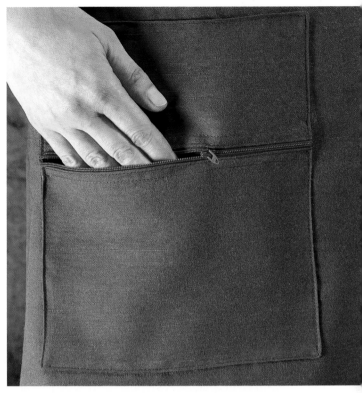

The cover-stitched zipper is an innovative and quick way to add zippers to a garment. The one on this pocket is both functional and fun and can be applied to any patch pocket. For a playful look, try making pockets in offbeat shapes like circles and triangles, or use a contrasting color zipper. This zipper application is also useful when constructing sporty accessories like duffel bags.

Simply cut the pocket pattern piece apart and add seam allowances at the desired zipper location, then topstitch the pocket to the garment after inserting the zipper.

SETTINGS & MATERIALS

Stitch: Cover
Stitch length: 3 mm
Needle position: Wide
Presser foot: Cover
Throat plate: Cover (if necessary)
Thread: All-purpose
Notions: Zipper, at least 4 inches (10 cm) longer than the zipper opening

1 Place the open zipper face down on the right side of the fabric. The outside edge of the zipper tape is on the raw edge of the fabric, and the end extends 2 inches (5 cm) above the top of the fabric. Cover stitch in place. Serge the remaining side of the zipper to the other garment piece.

2 Fold the fabric away from the zipper along the seamlines so that the fabric is right side up. Close the zipper. The zipper coil is now exposed. Place the zipper and attached garment pieces on your ironing surface. Press your work lightly to hold the fabric in place.

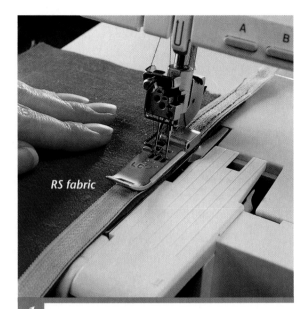

3 Open the zipper. Begin cover-stitch topstitching on the zipper tape, and then continue onto the fabric. Keep the edge of the presser foot even with the edge of the coil. Stitch off the fabric and onto the bottom of the zipper tape to ensure a smooth ending to the cover stitching on the fabric.

Fast Fix

HELP IN A JAM

Getting the cover stitch started is sometimes a chore. I bet that there have been times when the stitches jammed on you when the fabric was just under the toe at the front of the presser foot. I've been caught this way a few times, even though I know better. If jamming is a problem, then make sure your fabric is directly under the needle whenever you begin sewing a cover-stitched seam. Here's another serger secret: Don't even think about starting by pressing down on the foot pedal. Instead, turn the handwheel in order to lower the needle into the fabric. Now you can begin sewing.

Pam Hastings

FAUX FLATLOCKED ZIPPER

Here's the solution for inserting a separating zipper using your serger.

What's the problem? Separating zippers are more cumbersome, and the bottom of the zipper tab is difficult to work with. In addition, some teeth on separating zippers are so large that catching enough of the tape in the stitching is awkward.

There are several other situations where faux flatlocking is the best zipper insertion method to use.

If your serger can't make a 2-thread flatlock because you don't have a converter to block the thread hole in the upper looper, then the 3-thread faux flatlock is the way to go. You can flatlock a zipper using a 3-thread stitch (See "Flatlocked Zipper" on page 215), but you may be disappointed with the results and frustrated trying to obtain a flat, attractive flatlock.

In addition, some heavier varieties of decorative threads perform better in a balanced stitch. Finally, this is the first method you should try if you're serger-zipper shy.

It's nice to have alternatives to get through those frustrating moments and impossible situations.

You may recognize the edging on the sleeves and collar of this jacket, because the same treatment was recently shown on the fashion runways.

The stitching on the jacket is Woolly Nylon Metallic to complement the surface texture of the wool fabric. The wide, balanced overlocking on the sleeve and collar edges has Woolly Nylon only in the upper looper since the other side isn't visible. This echoes the faux stitching along the zipper, thus pulling the look together by matching the decorative threads on both sides of the zipper.

SETTINGS & MATERIALS

Stitch: 3-thread overlock
Stitch length: Narrow (1 mm)
Needle position: Left (if possible)
Needle thread: All-purpose
Upper looper thread: Decorative
Lower looper thread: All-purpose
Presser foot: Multipurpose*
Upper knife: Engaged
Notions: Zipper 4 inches (10 cm) longer than the zipper opening

*The multipurpose foot has a deep tunnel on the bottom, which prevents the zipper coil from wandering. Since this tunnel is also used for serging piping, this presser foot is often referred to as a piping foot.

1 Edge-finish the garment seam allowances for the zipper opening. The easiest way is to use a 3-thread overlock stitch and use all-purpose serger thread in the needle and both loopers. Now fold under the seam allowances on both sides of the garment's zipper opening.

2 Serge over the entire length of the fold on one of the garment pieces. Serge along the fold of the second garment piece in the same manner. It's important to serge the edges on both of the pieces with the garment pieces right side up so that the seam allowance is closest to the serger bed.

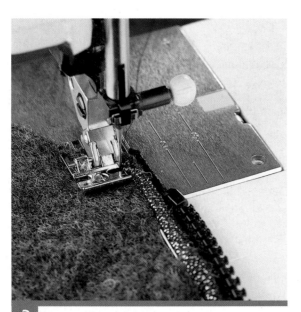

3 Place one of the two decoratively serged edges onto a side of the open zipper tape. Place it right side up about ⅛ to ¼ inch (3 to 6 mm) away from the coil, which is also right side up. At your sewing machine, edge-stitch the tape to the fabric with monofilament thread in the needle. Stitch as close as possible to the edge of the serging.

Fast Fix

USE TOP TOOLS

I'd like to share some of my sewing tricks. A zipper foot with an attached guide ensures perfect straight stitching alongside the overlock stitching. At my sewing machine I use the needle position that gets me as close as possible to the decorative overlocking. Or if the tape is very wide, I find that an open-toe embroidery foot often does the trick. Use a smoke-colored monofilament thread for dark fabrics and clear thread for light to medium fabric. Be aware of the bottom tab, which is usually thick and at times is difficult for a machine needle to penetrate. Stitch slowly, and use a sharp 90/14 needle.

Agnes Mercik

FAUX PIPED ZIPPER

Add an unexpected design element to a zipper by adding "piping" to the edges. The upscale treatment is easily achieved because the piping is made by serging along the folded edge of the garment's seamline. There's no basting and no fussing with separate strips of piping.

There are many types of piping to choose from for this unique touch. The quickest option is to buy ready-made piping and serge it on to the seam with a multipurpose presser foot. Since colors and widths can be limited, this isn't always the best solution.

Instead, you can customize piping on your serger; the piping color is limited only by the decorative thread that's available. For the simplest approach, serge over bias tricot. (See "Stretch Piping" on page 176.)

Whenever piping is used on jacket fronts, the top of a pocket, or any other straight edge, eliminate the bias tricot in favor of faux piping.

The piping isn't a separate seamline insertion. Instead, the effect is achieved with serger edge stitching along a fabric fold positioned at the seamline.

Faux piping is used in many locations to enhance the effect of seams on yokes, paneled skirts, and color-blocked insertions. However, faux piping is most suitable for a straight-line application. The sides of a zipper are ideal locations.

Unless someone is familiar with this serger technique, they'll think you painstakingly stitched piping to the edges of your zipper before inserting it.

Serger expert Agnes Mercik pulled this jacket together by echoing the piped zipper accent on the collar and top edge of the pocket.

SETTINGS & MATERIALS

Stitch: 3-thread overlock, then rolled*

Stitch length: As short as possible without overlapping threads

Stitch width: Narrow to medium (1 to 2.5 mm)

Presser foot: Standard

Throat plate or stitch finger: Rolled (if necessary)

Needle thread: All-purpose

Upper looper thread: All-purpose, then decorative

Lower looper thread: All-purpose

Upper knife: Disengaged

Notions: Zipper, length as specified in the pattern instructions

*Try both stitches along the fold of a scrap of fashion fabric, and choose the most appealing one for the piping.

1 Overlock the garment seam allowances for the zipper opening using all-purpose serger thread in all positions. Fold under the seam allowance of one side of the zipper opening. Serge the fold. For additional guidance on this procedure, see "Mock Piping" on page 174.

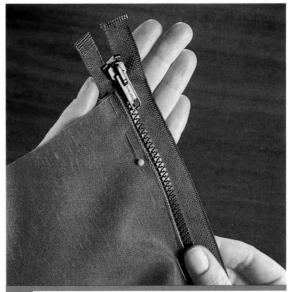

2 Place the serged fold right side up on the right side of the zipper tape ¼ inch (6 mm) from the outer edge of one side of the nylon coils. Pin the zipper tape in place. Securing the serged edge prevents it from getting caught in the zipper tab when the zipper is opened or closed.

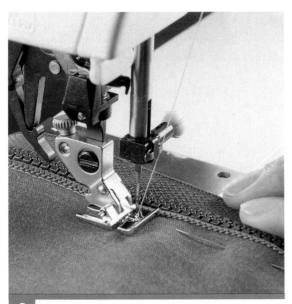

3 At your sewing machine, switch to a piping or zipper presser foot. Thread the machine's needle with monofilament thread, and thread the bobbin with all-purpose polyester sewing thread. Straight stitch the fabric to the zipper tape. Repeat both Steps 2 and 3 on the remaining, unattached, side of the zipper.

Fast Fix

RAISE THE EDGE

Sometimes I want the faux piping to be really visible along the edges of the zipper that I'm attaching.

While I can use a thread color that contrasts with the fabric, I can also obtain a subtler effect by making a type of "raised" piping.

In this case, the piping needs to be thicker than a single fabric fold. I place fingering yarn (a fine baby yarn) or several pieces of pearl cotton thread inside the fold that I made in the fabric and then serge over it. If I think the yarn is going to wander, I use a glue stick to hold it in place, and I serge with a cording foot.

Agnes Mercik

FLATLOCKED ZIPPER

Casual tops and dresses look great with this design detail. You can use the technique anywhere, but you'll especially enjoy it if you plan to insert a zipper along a seamline rather than at the top or bottom of a garment. (In other words, don't consider it for a zipper that starts at a skirt waistband unless it ends at the bottom of a yoke that attaches to a skirt.) If you've inserted an invisible zipper you'll be comfortable with this procedure because the tape is attached to the garment pieces before sewing the seamline.

As indicated below in "Settings and Materials," a flatlocked zipper calls for a 2- or 3-thread stitch. A 2-thread is best.

The results are disappointing when stitched with a 3-thread flatlock. The stitch isn't wide enough because you can't use a left needle position. Consequently, the security and stability of the stitch is minimal. You can, however, switch to a 3-thread overlock, as explained in "Faux Flatlocked Zipper" on page 211.

Why hide your zipper? It can be a focal point for your garment, especially when you insert it with decorative thread and a flatlock stitch.

Since the zipper on the front of this jumper is so prominent, serger expert Agnes Mercik decided to work with thick thread to make it even more distinctive.

SETTINGS & MATERIALS

Stitch: 2- or 3-thread flatlock
Stitch length: Medium (2 to 3 mm)
Stitch width: Wide
Needle position: Left
Presser foot: Multipurpose*
Upper looper converter: (For 2-thread flatlock only) engaged or attached
Needle thread: Decorative
Upper looper thread: (For 2-thread flatlock only) all-purpose or decorative
Lower looper thread: All-purpose
Upper knife: Engaged
Notions: Press cloth, zipper 4 inches (10 cm) longer than the garment opening†

*The multipurpose foot has a deep tunnel on the bottom, which prevents the zipper coil from wandering. Since this tunnel is also used for serging piping, this presser foot is often referred to as a piping foot.

†Lightweight nylon coil zippers are the easiest to work with and are available in a variety of fashionable colors.

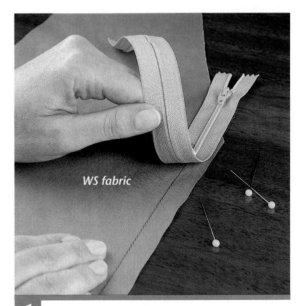

WS fabric

1 With wrong sides together, pin the zipper on the fabric with the tape in the seam allowance and the coil on the seamline. (The seamline is thread-traced only for visibility in this photo.) Let the knife trim the excess fabric and tape while serging. The zipper can be closed or open.

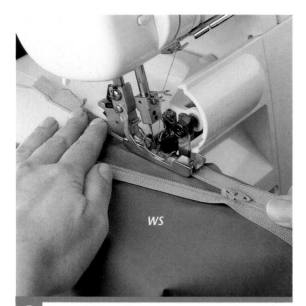

2 Place the top of the zipper coil directly under the tunnel of the presser foot. Now stitch the tape to the fabric, continuing to serge until the zipper is stitched to the fabric along the entire length of the zipper opening in the garment. End by serging off the fabric.

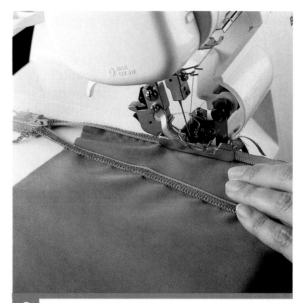

3 Serge the remaining zipper tape, but start at the bottom. If the zipper is closed, the stitches will probably be closer to the coil than they will be with the zipper open. On some zippers this position makes it hard to open and close the zipper. Serge either with the zipper either open or closed in both directions.

4 Close the zipper if you serged it in the open position in the previous steps. From the right side, gently pull the zipper and fabric apart until they're flat. Make sure that there isn't a tiny fabric tuck underneath the needle threads. Press with a pressing cloth, making sure that the iron doesn't touch the zipper coils or the flatlocking.

5 At your sewing machine, bartack both ends of the zipper tape. The zipper is longer than the opening, so the bartacks are your new "stops" at the bottom and top of the coils. Cut off the excess tape. Hide the bartacks in a seam allowance, if desired. Stitch with the presser foot mounted. It was removed in this photo for better visibility.

SPORTSWEAR ZIPPER

You can finish your seam allowances at the very same time that you're inserting a zipper. This procedure is a great time-saver when you're making a casual garment, where the zipper will be crossed by another seam, as in a zippered yoke that's attached to the body of a top with a horizontal seam.

Since the overlock stitching and zipper tape are visible on the wrong side, you may want to consider another method for inserting a zipper into a high-end garment. This technique is ideal for casual clothes, especially if the garment fabric has some "give." With Wooly Nylon in all positions your stitches will have some elasticity.

SETTINGS & MATERIALS

Stitch: 3- or 4-thread overlock
Stitch length: Medium (3 to 4 mm)
Stitch width: Medium (3 to 4 mm)
Presser foot: Piping*
Thread: All-purpose
Upper knife: Engaged
Notions: Zipper, at least 4 inches (10 cm) longer than the garment opening

*You can use an all-purpose foot, but stitching is smoother with a piping foot because the zipper coil rides through the channel on the bottom of the foot.

An exposed zipper looks great in activewear like this pull-on top. It's a fun, casual look. Like several items featured in this book, this garment was stitched by seamstress Sue Nester. Before working on this top, she had never used a serger to insert a zipper. Yet Sue found it relatively easy to do. She simply followed the instructions here and on the next page, which were written by serger expert Barbara Weiland. As Sue says, the process for an exposed zipper isn't all that tricky. The serger secret is to use a zipper that's several inches longer than the intended opening. After inserting the zipper, the top and bottom of the coils are trimmed off to fit the garment piece.

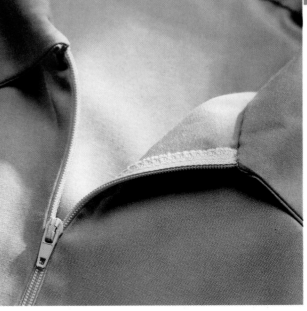

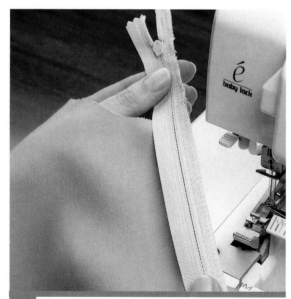

1 Insert the zipper before sewing any seams. Chalk-mark the zipper seamline on the right side of the garment pieces. Pin the zipper face down on the right side of one garment piece with the teeth on the seamline. Extend the zipper above and below the edges.

Fast Fix

PLAN AHEAD

You can't serge with the bulk of your garment to the right of the needle. You'll know this as soon as you place the fabric on the serger's bed because you'll see how the knife will cut into your garment fabric. This means you need to plan how you'll attach each zipper tape, because it isn't a very good idea to simply flip over your garment and zipper. I always recommend against stitching with the zipper underneath the fabric for one simple reason: It's easier to see and guide the zipper when it's on top of the fabric.

Agnes Mercik

2 Serge the pinned zipper tape in place. As with most serging, it's best to let the knives cut off a bit of the fabric edge. This results in a clean finish. Trim off at least 1/8 inch (3 mm) of the tape as you stitch. If you're using a novelty zipper with a wider tape, you need to trim away more than 1/8 inch (3 mm) of the tape.

3 Fold the garment piece away from the zipper so that both are right side up. Press the fabric away from the zipper coil. With some fabrics, the seam allowance may leave an imprint on the right side of the garment piece. To avoid this, slide an envelope or piece of heavier paper between the seam allowance and the wrong side of the garment piece.

4 With right sides facing, place the closed zipper on the remaining garment piece. Carefully align the raw edges of the remaining half of the garment with the other half of the zipper. Serge the zipper tape to the fabric in the same manner the first half was attached in Steps 1 and 2.

5 If needed, serge any intersecting seam at the bottom of the zipper. Don't worry if the bottom of the zipper is cut off, but make sure that the bottom of the zipper is caught in—and trimmed—during stitching. For strength, bartack across the zipper bottom even if you're joining it to another garment piece.

Fast Fix

CLEAN 'EM UP

Are the undersides of your bartacks messy? This tip is for your sewing machine, but it's worth repeating since you need to finish your sportswear zipper. Try lowering the feed dogs and use either a button sew-on stitch or a simple zigzag stitch to make the bartacks. For a zipper that has to spread apart at the top, bartack the top of the coil on each tape. But bartack both coils together at the bottom. If your zipper is inserted in a seam, and the tip doesn't need to open, then bartack both coils together at the top and the bottom of the tape.

Agnes Mercik

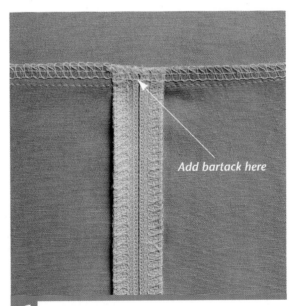

Add bartack here

6 To complete the technique and make the zipper as secure as possible, it's best to go to your sewing machine and machine- or hand-bartack over the zipper coil or teeth at the top and bottom. If the upper end of the zipper opens in the finished garment, bartack across the bottom and on each half of the top.

Problem Solver

Your serger—no matter what brand or model—is a complex machine. So things are bound to go wrong. You can always turn to the experts at the shop where you purchased the serger. But there are a number of non-technical problems you can easily deal with on your own. As an educator, serger expert Pam Hastings is frequently asked to troubleshoot.

To save you time and money, she and editor Susan Huxley compiled 40 of the more commonly asked—or more difficult to solve— questions.

DILEMMA
Fabric threads poke out of the rolled hem.

TRY THIS
- Widen the stitch length
- Use Woolly Nylon
- Use tricot binding

THE EXPERTS EXPLAIN
Widening the stitch length or bite allows more fabric to be turned under, thus preventing the "pokies." If the problem persists, try using Woolly Nylon and the shortest stitch length. This thread fluffs to fill the spaces between stitches. If all else fails, serge tricot binding, like Seams Great, to the right side along the fabric edge. The tricot rolls over the ravelly edge, encasing it. Trim away the excess tricot.

DILEMMA
The stitch quality is poor.

TRY THIS
- Change the needles
- Check all of the tensions
- Check the threading sequence
- Switch to better-quality thread

THE EXPERTS EXPLAIN
A burr or bent needle won't penetrate your fabric properly, thus causing a variety of problems.

A missed thread guide or tangled thread may be the culprit. Check thread paths carefully, or better yet, unthread your serger and start over. This problem is often difficult to locate—it takes less time to rethread than to find where the multiple threading went wrong.

Quality thread that feeds smoothly gives much better results than a bargain brand with thick and thin spots.

DILEMMA
The stitches hang off the edge of the fabric.

TRY THIS
- Change the bite or width of the stitch
- Adjust the position of the upper knife

THE EXPERTS EXPLAIN
When set too wide, stitches "hang" off the edge of your fabric. Refer to the instruction manual for your serger to find the location of your stitch-width dial and how to adjust the width.

While you're at it, read up on the cutting width and stitch finger. If your machine doesn't make automatic adjustments, this could be the problem.

DILEMMA
The differential feed isn't gathering enough.

TRY THIS
- Increase the stitch length
- Increase the needle tension
- Stitch over the same area a second time

THE EXPERTS EXPLAIN
If the stitch length is too short, the fabric has no place to go when it's gathered. Select the longest stitch possible when using the differential feed. If you've tried everything and still aren't pleased with the results, simply stitch over the same area a second time. Your gathers are "gathered" again. This only works with single layers of fabric.

DILEMMA

The 3-thread rolled hem is stiff or stretched.

TRY THIS
- Use a lighter-weight thread
- Place Woolly Nylon in both loopers
- Switch to a 2-thread rolled edge stitch
- Turn the differential slightly toward gather ("+" or number above 0)
- Increase the stitch length

THE EXPERTS EXPLAIN

When sewing rolled hems on lightweight fabrics, a 2-thread rolled hem with an embroidery-weight thread produces excellent results. Decorative thread, such as metallic, is a bit more challenging. Before deciding to use a decorative thread, check its weight and pliability by doing some test stitching on a swatch of your selected fabric. Some types are stiffer and thicker than others.

DILEMMA

The thread is breaking.

TRY THIS
- Check the thread paths
- Loosen the needle tension
- Look for caught or tangled threads
- Check the needle insertion

THE EXPERTS EXPLAIN

If thread constantly breaks, the first thing you should do is check thread paths and the spool pins. When you're using a spool of thread, rather than a cone, be sure to use spool caps so the thread doesn't catch on the top of the spool.

DILEMMA

Stitches separate from the fabric edge.

TRY THIS
- Increase the stitch length
- Use a smaller needle
- Use tricot binding, like Seams Great
- Run a line of straight stitching along the edge of the fabric, and serge over this

THE EXPERTS EXPLAIN

Rolled edge hems on sheer fabrics need a slightly longer stitch. A smaller needle helps because it decreases the number and size of needle penetrations on the fabric edge. If stitches still separate, place a tricot binding on the right side of the fabric, and roll-hem over both layers. Trim off the excess.

If you're using a very loosely woven fabric and a regular serger stitch for edge-finishing, run a row of straight stitching to hold the fabric in place, and then serge-finish the edge.

DILEMMA

The fabric bunches underneath the stitches.

TRY THIS
- Adjust the bite or stitch width
- Check the upper knife

THE EXPERTS EXPLAIN

It's most likely that the setting on your serger for the stitch width, or bite, is too narrow for the fabric you're working with.

You'll also experience bunching fabric if you disengaged the upper knife and didn't adjust it for your next serger technique.

If you're trying to trim a seam, and the knife is disengaged, the seam allowance isn't cut; instead it bunches under the right-hand side of the stitches.

DILEMMA
After serging elastic, the stitches bunch.

TRY THIS
- Do not overstretch the elastic
- Increase the stitch length

THE EXPERTS EXPLAIN
When elastic is stretched out, so are your serger stitches. Consequently, when the elastic relaxes, so do the stitches. Use the longest stitch length possible when serging the elastic.

DILEMMA
The fabric puckers.

TRY THIS
- Use the differential feed
- Loosen the needle thread tension(s)
- Lengthen the stitch
- Decrease the presser foot pressure on lightweight fabrics
- Check the thread paths for caught or tangled threads

THE EXPERTS EXPLAIN
If you're experiencing puckering in your fabric, the best option (if you have this option) is adjusting the differential feed. Adjust the setting toward stretch ("—" or number below 0) a little at a time until your seam flattens out. If you don't have differential feed, or if the feed isn't helping, it's time to check the needle and looper tensions and thread paths as well as to lengthen the stitch.

DILEMMA
The fishline hem doesn't curl or wave.

TRY THIS
- Use a heavier-weight fishing line
- Stretch the fabric as you serge
- Cut the fabric on the bias, or in the direction with the most stretch
- Stretch the fabric over the fishing line after you have completed the hem

THE EXPERTS EXPLAIN
When sewing a fishline hem, remember to use a fishing line that's heavier than your fabric. This is important because the line needs to maintain its curl. It's best to serge a test swatch, and as you serge, stretch the fabric the desired amount.

If the fabric isn't stretching, then the hem needs to be cut on the bias or in the direction with the most stretch. When you finish serging, smooth the fabric over the fishing line. See pages 113–114 for complete step-by-step instructions.

DILEMMA
The serger stitches are hard to remove.

TRY THIS
- Pull out the needle thread
- Use a serger seam ripper

THE EXPERTS EXPLAIN
Unravel the tail of your serger stitch; notice that the threads are various lengths. The longest is the needle thread. If you pull out the needle thread, the chain then comes apart easily.

A serger seam ripper has a curved blade on the end that easily fits under the loops. Simply run the ripper along the loops and remove the stitches.

DILEMMA
Decorative thread isn't feeding properly.

TRY THIS
• Use a horizontal spool holder

THE EXPERTS EXPLAIN
The ideal remedy for ensuring proper feeding of decorative threads is a horizontal spool pin. This accessory attaches to the back of your serger and, as the name implies, allows thread to rest horizontally as it feeds into the serger.

DILEMMA
The fabric layers shift when you're starting to serge.

TRY THIS
• Lift the presser foot at the start of the seam
• Baste the layers together

THE EXPERTS EXPLAIN
One of the nice things about the serger is sewing a seam without lifting the presser foot. This works perfectly almost all the time. But on occasion, bulky or slippery fabric layers shift. If this happens, simply lift the presser foot, and slide the fabric under the foot and up to the blade. Lower the foot and begin serging.

DILEMMA
The rolled hem is too wide.

TRY THIS
• Make sure you're using the correct throat plate, stitch finger, or presser foot
• Adjust the width for a rolled hem setting
• Use Woolly Nylon
• Adjust the lower looper tension
• Make sure that the knife is engaged (if you're trimming the seam)

THE EXPERTS EXPLAIN
All sergers require some type of adjustment that changes the normal stitch finger to a narrow (pin) stitch finger to make a rolled edge. Some sergers require an adjustment to the stitch width as well. If you made the adjustments and the hem is still too wide, try using Woolly Nylon in both loopers. This thread is stretchy, so it will pull the hem in a bit. Also, be sure to drastically increase the lower tension, to pull the upper looper thread around to the back of the fabric.

DILEMMA
The serger won't start.

TRY THIS
• Close the door
• Check the power switch
• Check the plug
• Ensure that you're pressing the correct foot pedal

THE EXPERTS EXPLAIN
Many of today's sergers are equipped with a safety feature. If the looper door is open, the serger won't run. Some sergers have a power switch that only turns the light on, or both power and the light, so make sure you turn the power switch completely to the "on" position.

While this seems silly, many of us use our sergers on the same table as our sewing machines, and sometimes the serger doesn't run because we just stepped on the wrong foot control!

DILEMMA
The cover stitch unravels at the end of the seam.

TRY THIS
• Leave a longer thread tail
• Tie off the ends

THE EXPERTS EXPLAIN
The cover stitch is formed very much like a chain stitch, so it unravels easily. When you complete a seam, be sure to leave a bit of chain before cutting it off. You can also tie a small knot in the chain, close to the end of your fabric.

DILEMMA
The ribbing is uneven or stretched out.

TRY THIS
• Cut the ribbing to the proper size
• Divide both the ribbing and neckline into quarters

THE EXPERTS EXPLAIN
While ribbing does stretch, its ability to expand is limited. If you cut the ribbing too short for your neckline, and then stretch it way out of shape in order to fit, it won't recover. Be sure to divide both your ribbing and neckline into quarters, and mark them before serging. Match the markings as you sew to ensure evenly inserted ribbing. Keep in mind that the shoulder seam isn't a suitable quarter mark.

DILEMMA
The needle thread is too tight.

TRY THIS
• Check the thread path
• Place a spool cap over the spool of thread
• Adjust the tension

THE EXPERTS EXPLAIN
Check your threading to ensure that the thread isn't caught on anything. If you're using a spool of thread, use a spool cap so the thread won't catch in the notch on the spool. Loosen the needle tension if threading is correct and the stitch still seems a bit tight.

DILEMMA
The upper knife isn't cutting the fabric.

TRY THIS
• Check the upper blade
• Check the lower blade
• Replace the lower blade

THE EXPERTS EXPLAIN
If your serger doesn't cut fabric, first ensure that both knives are in the correct positions. The upper knife must be engaged for cutting and the lower knife must be even with the top of the throat plate.

If the knives are in the correct position but leave a jagged edge, it's time for replacements. Generally speaking, your knives should last many years.

DILEMMA
The stitches are too loose.

TRY THIS
- Ensure the tensions are correct for the stitch and the fabric
- Check the thread paths

THE EXPERTS EXPLAIN
When threading, be sure to pull the threads tightly into the tension disks. Likewise, if you miss any thread guides, the stitch will be loose. If you see loops on the reverse side of your fabric along the needle line, simply tighten the needle tension.

DILEMMA
There are holes on the knit fabric seamline.

TRY THIS
- Use a smaller needle
- Switch to a ballpoint needle
- Stitch with a finer thread
- Adjust the serger for a longer stitch length

THE EXPERTS EXPLAIN
Quite often on seams in interlock knits, there are cuts on the seamline where the stitches enter the fabric. Usually this is caused by a needle that's either damaged or too large. For best results, use a ballpoint or universal needle. If your serger uses only industrial needles, ask your dealer to special-order industrial ballpoint needles for you.

DILEMMA
When opened, the flatlocking won't flatten.

TRY THIS
- Use a 2-thread flatlock rather than a 3-thread overlock version of the stitch
- Check the tension settings
- Make sure that your fabric isn't too flimsy for flatlocking
- Switch to another type of needle thread

THE EXPERTS EXPLAIN
A 2-thread flatlock stitch is your best choice because it's the nature of this stitch to always flatten. A 3-thread overlock can be adjusted for flatlocking by turning the needle to the lowest tension setting and the lower looper to the highest setting. The flatlock works best on medium-weight, stable fabrics. If you're using a very loosely woven fabric, it stretches with the stitch when you try to flatten it.

DILEMMA
There are skipped stitches on heavy fabric.

TRY THIS
- Elongate the stitch length
- Increase the stitch width
- Increase the pressure on the presser foot
- Use a larger needle

THE EXPERTS EXPLAIN
When sewing a heavy fabric or several layers of fabric, you need to make the thread loops "larger" so they encase the edge of the seam. Lengthening the stitch and increasing the width will do this. Also adjust the pressure on the presser foot. By increasing the pressure, the presser foot compresses the fabric even more, so that the loops go around the edge of the fabric more easily.

DILEMMA
Needle breaks while stitching.

TRY THIS
- Ensure that the replacement needle isn't bent
- Insert the needle properly
- Insert the needle all the way into the needle shaft

THE EXPERTS EXPLAIN
A bent or incorrectly inserted needle won't move properly through the range of motion. It may hit the needle plate or upper looper, thus messing up the timing so that your stitching is unbalanced.

There's a good chance that a bent needle will break. When replacing a needle, be sure to discard the old one so it doesn't get mixed in with the new needles. Make sure you loosen the needle set screw enough to insert the needle all the way into the needle shaft.

In the future, don't pull the fabric through the machine when you're serging. This undue stress will bend or break the machine needle.

DILEMMA
Loose needle tension.

TRY THIS
- Adjust the tension dials, one at a time, in increments of .5
- Check the thread path
- Ensure that the threading path for the needle tension is suitable for the needle

THE EXPERTS EXPLAIN
Nothing is more frustrating than unsuccessful tension adjustments. When adjusting dials, turn the tension setting .5 up or down, and sew a swatch. Continue adjusting in small increments until you're satisfied. If you get too high or low on the tension dial, the problem may be caused by another thread. Switch to another dial, and repeat the same procedure.

Also make sure you're using the correct threading sequence for your needle. When switching a needle from the left or right position, it's very tempting to skip the rethreading process. Don't. You must rethread the entire path to avoid tension problems.

DILEMMA
Fabric stretches.

TRY THIS
- Adjust the differential feed
- Stabilize the seam
- Decrease the presser foot pressure

THE EXPERTS EXPLAIN
If the fabric is stretching while you serge it, turn the differential feed dial toward gather by one notch or number. If your machine doesn't have this option, you can try stabilizing the seam. Place twill tape over the seamline, and serge through all of the layers. Sometimes the culprit is the pressure that the presser foot is exerting on the fabric. Tighten the pressure for lightweight fabrics.

DILEMMA
Fabric jams in the serger.

TRY THIS
- Check for tangled thread
- Make sure that fabric that's trimmed off isn't going into the machine
- Match the stitch length and thread weight
- Ensure the knife is engaged

THE EXPERTS EXPLAIN
Thread can really pull fabric into a machine. Watch for tangles, and check the tension settings when you switch thread. Heavy, decorative threads work best with a longer stitch length. You will pull fabric into the serger's lower mechanisms if the length is too short.

When trimming fabric when you're serging, make sure that the knife is engaged, the machine's front door is closed all the way, and scraps aren't caught in the loopers.

DILEMMA
Stitches show at the seamline.

TRY THIS
- Tighten the needle tension
- Use Woolly Nylon in the needle

THE EXPERTS EXPLAIN
Threads that show at the seamline are most likely caused by a loose needle tension. (If you're using two needles, the left needle is the culprit.) Ensure that the needle is properly threaded and pulled all the way into the tension dials.

DILEMMA
Stitching bunches under the presser foot.

TRY THIS
- Use the correct throat plate

THE EXPERTS EXPLAIN
It's important to use the proper throat plate for the selected technique. For example, in most cases a rolled hem plate will mess up your stitching if you've switched your needle to the left position. Likewise, setting up the serger for a rolled hem but not attaching the rolled hem plate will create tight stitches that have no place to go—they don't easily slide off the stitch finger of the regular throat plate.

DILEMMA
The 3-thread flatlock stitching unravels.

TRY THIS
- Tighten the needle tension
- Start and end with a thread tail
- Hold the fabric taut as you sew

THE EXPERTS EXPLAIN
Generally the needle tension is turned down to one or zero for flatlocking with a 3-thread stitch. However, with little—or no—tension on the needle thread, the stitching can easily pull out when you open the fabric along the seamline. Tightening the tension even by a very small increment (like .5) will help. It also helps to start with a 3-inch (7.5-cm)-thread tail and hold it behind the presser foot when your fabric begins feeding through the serger. Also end the stitching with another long tail. Tie a knot in both of the tails before opening your flatlocked seam.

DILEMMA
Blind hem does not lie flat.

TRY THIS
- Adjust the blind-hem guide
- Increase the stitch length
- Loosen the needle tension
- Switch to the longest stitch length possible

THE EXPERTS EXPLAIN
Line up the inside (right) edge of the guide on the presser foot with the outside (left) edge of the needle so that the needle just pierces the fold. Loosening the needle tension results in slightly looser stitches.

DILEMMA
Thread tail catches in the stitching.

TRY THIS
- Stitch a 2-inch (5-cm) thread tail after threading and before serging on fabric
- Pull the chain out from under the presser foot after completing each seam

PAM EXPLAINS
Before beginning each seam, make sure that enough thread is pulled out from under the presser foot. The chain left from your previous seam can curl around the presser foot and tangle in the loopers or the needle stitching.

DILEMMA
The 3-thread overlock stitch won't form.

TRY THIS
- Ensure that the needle is straight
- Rethread the loopers
- Check the looper tensions
- Check the timing

PAM EXPLAINS
If the timing is wrong, each stitch won't form properly because the looper and needle threads are wrapping around each other. Most often, the problem is the upper looper or the needle thread. When the timing is correct, the upper looper thread is "thrown" on top of the fabric, just to the left of the seamline. The needle comes down into the fabric so that the needle thread locks the upper looper thread in position. If the looper moves too fast or the needle is bent, the two threads miss each other.

If the lower looper is the problem, the needle thread won't lock underneath the fabric, and the line of needle stitching will be missing.

DILEMMA
Overlocked fabric under the loopers is slightly curled.

TRY THIS
- Increase the stitch width
- Decrease the cutting width
- Loosen the looper tensions
- Make sure the knives are engaged
- Serge both seam allowances together rather than separately

THE EXPERTS EXPLAIN
This is an easy problem to resolve. Usually, trying only one of the suggestions at left is enough. It's best to increase the stitch width or decrease the cutting width by small increments until you're happy with the results. The same goes for the looper tensions.

DILEMMA
The serged raw edges are too bulky.

TRY THIS
- Switch to a finer thread
- Use a stitch that calls for one less looper or needle thread
- Serge each seam allowance separately, then press them open along the seamline

THE EXPERTS EXPLAIN
Overlocking and making a rolled edge both add more weight and thickness to a fabric because there are more threads in each stitch. To counter this problem, serger thread is thinner than versions intended for a sewing machine. (This doesn't apply to decorative threads.) However, you may find that the serged fabric is still too thick, heavy, and bulky for the fabric.

DILEMMA
Needle insertion is difficult.

TRY THIS
- Use a Two-Needle Installer
- Tip the serger back or onto its side
- Install the left needle first

THE EXPERTS EXPLAIN
This may be cold comfort, but the next time you upgrade to a new serger, look for one with a presser foot that swings to the side. With it out of the way, there's more room for your fingers, tweezers, or tool to position and hold the needles. In the meantime, give one of the suggestions at left a try. You may find one solution is more suitable for you and your machine.

DILEMMA
Stitch length is inconsistent when inserting a flatlocked zipper.

TRY THIS
- Use a 90/14 sharp needle
- Make sure you have the recommended needle type for your machine

THE EXPERTS EXPLAIN
Stitch quality is very, very important when inserting this type of zipper because the serger stitches are featured so prominently. Inconsistent stitch length and skipped stitches can interfere with your beautiful zipper application. If you can't get a top-notch stitch, try replacing the needle that's in your machine. Since zipper tapes are thick and densely woven, a 90/14 sharp needle is the best choice.

DILEMMA
Fabric stretches at the rounded edges on a facing.

TRY THIS
- Adjust the fabric position
- Don't pull on the fabric
- Engage the differential feed just on the curve

THE EXPERTS EXPLAIN
Even though your tension and differential feed settings are perfect for your fabric, you can run into trouble when you enter a curved edge. Since rounded shapes are so common on garment pieces (facing, sleeve cap, shirttail hem, and inseam pockets), it's important to master serging this shape. If the rounded edge is stretched, you're probably pulling the fabric too much as you try to position it for the line of stitching. Relax your hold on the fabric, and try the start-and-stop technique described at the bottom of page 53.

Writers' Contributions

MARY GRIFFIN

At the Improv: the entire chapter
Exploring Stitches and Tension:
    Understanding Stitches, Taming Tension
Beading: *Flatlocked Pearls*
Braid: *Customized Trim*
Cording: *Reinforced Belt Carriers*
Edgings: *Lettuce-Leaf Edging*
Gathering: *Gathering for the Real World,*
    Skirting the Issue
Hems: *Blind Hem*

PAM HASTINGS

Nuts and Bolts: *Feeding the Dogs*
Decorative Stitching: *Cover Stitching*
Seams Incredible: *Using the Right Seam*
Skill Building: the entire chapter
Buyers' Guide: the entire chapter, except
    Getting a Notion
Casings: *Quick Casing*
Edgings: *Fishline Edge Finish, 2-Thread*
    Rolled Edge
Hems: *Bound to Be Rolled, Cover-Stitched*
    Hem
Neck Bands: *Cover-Stitched Band,*
    V-Neck Perfection
Shirring: *Painless Shirring*
Waistband: *Stitch-in-the-Ditch Waistband*
Zippers: *Cover-Stitched Zipper*
Problem Solver

AGNES MERCIK

Nuts and Bolts: *Cutting Widths*
Needles: the entire chapter
Glorious Thread: *Selecting the Best,*
    Understanding Thread
Seams Incredible: *Making Choices*
Beading: *Free-Motion Beading*
Buttons and Bows: *Beautiful Bow*
Casings: *Cover-Stitched Casing*

Edgings: *Reversible Wrapped Edge*
Fagoting: *Decorative Wide Fagoting,*
    Narrow Fagoting
Lace: *Cover-Stitched Lace, Rosette*
Neck Bands: *Double Ribbing*
Piping: *Mock Piping, Zipper Coil Seaming*
Reversible Garments: *Double-Layer Blouse*
Tucks: *Aggie's Tucks, Chain-Stitch Tucks,*
    Soutache Tucks
Weaving: *Serger Weaving*
Zippers: *Faux Flatlocked Zipper, Faux Piped*
    Zipper, Flatlocked Zipper

LINDA LEE VIVIAN

Decorative Stitching: *Chain Stitching*
Couching: *Flatlock Couching*
Heirloom Serging: *Understanding Heirloom*
    Serging, Creating "New" Fabric, Entredeux
    to Fabric, Entredeux to Lace, French Serged
    Seam, Lace to Fabric, Lace to Lace,
    Pintucks, Puffing
Placket: *Dart-Stitched Placket*
Quilting: *Curved Flatlock Piecing*
Weaving: *Ribbon Weaving*

BARBARA WEILAND

Exploring Stitches and Tension: *Easing*
    the Tension
Decorative Stitching: *Rolled Edge Chain*
Buttons and Bows: *Button Toggle, Decorative*
    Bound Buttonhole
Edgings: *Wired Edging*
Gathering: *No-Frills Easing*
Lace: *Overlocked Lace Edging*
Piping: *Stretch Piping*
Quilting: *Reversible Channel Quilting*
Zippers: *Sportswear Zipper*

Acknowledgments

The skill and talents of many people and companies contributed to the success of this innovative book.

A special thank-you is extended to the machine companies who so generously loaned us the sergers: Bernina of America, Inc. (model 2000DE), Pfaff American Sales Corporation (sewing machine model 7570 and Hobbylock serger model 4870), Singer Sewing Company (model 14U555), Tacony Corporation (the baby lock Éclipse LX), and Husqvarna Viking Sewing Machine Company (models White Superlock 2000 electronic and also the Viking Huskylock 1002LCD).

If you own *Sewing Secrets from the Fashion Industry*, then you know that this is the second time Rodale Press has created a step-by-step sewing book with many hundreds of photographs. This exciting project would not have been accomplished without the vision of Vice President and Editorial Director Margaret Lydic.

To create the photographs, much advice, samples, plus boxes of notions and many, many yards of fabric were provided by the following companies:

Allentown Sewing Machine Outlet
Central Penn Sewing Machine Co., Inc.
Handler Textile Corporation
Hobbs Bonded Fibers
Kimberly Design Studio
Loose Ends
Madeira Threads
Sawyer Brook Distinctive Fabrics
Schmetz Needle Corporation
The Souder Store

The editor would also like to give great big hugs to her boss, Cheryl Winters-Tetreau, for her patience. The authors are also greatly appreciated: Agnes (the Serge-On General) for her sense of humor, Linda for her attention to detail, Pam for always

coming through in the crunch, Mary for her calm and professional manner, and Barbara for her inspiration.

A very talented group of people helped the editor, Susan Huxley (in the center), with this book. Mitch Mandel, the photographer, (center back) and his partner in crime, stylist and book designer Stan Green (back, left), created every photo and kept the team in good spirits. (Even though they wouldn't let Susan play dance music at 9:00 A.M., at least Stan did the East Coast Swing with hand model Anne Cassar.) Anne is standing in the back on the right. This is one of the few times you'll see Anne's face, rather than her hands, in a published photo. In front of Anne is Jen Hornsby, the copy editor who patiently dealt with Susan's idiosyncracies. Last, but certainly not least, is Sue Nester at bottom left. An integral part of the team, Sue helped sew garments and ensure technical sewing accuracy in the photos. Interestingly, this photo was taken on one of the few days that the team wasn't garbed in matching colors.

Shopping Guide

Allentown Sewing Machine Outlet
725 N. 15th St., rear
Allentown, PA 18102
(800) 290-8484
http://www.Allentownsewing.com
Sewing machines, fabric, and notions

American & Efird, Inc.
P.O. Box 507
Mt. Holly, NC 28120
(800) 847-3235
Threads and stabilizers

Bernina of America
3500 Thayer Ct.
Aurora, IL 60504-6182
(630) 978-2500
*Sewing machines and sergers,
and accessories*

Capitol Imports
P.O. Box 13002
Tallahassee, FL 32317
(800) 521-7647
(800) 433-5457
*Fine cotton embroideries and laces, fabrics for
heirloom clothing*

Coats & Clark
30 Patewood Dr., Ste. 351
Greenville, SC 29615
(864) 234-0331
Threads

HTC-Handler Textile Corp.
24 Empire Blvd., Dept. RP
Moonachie, NJ 07074
(201) 641-4500
Interfacing

Hobbs Bonded Fibers
P.O. Box 2521
Waco, TX 76702-2521
(254) 741-0040
Thermore by Hobbs

Kelsul, Inc.
3205 Foxgrove Ln.
Chesapeake, VA 23321
*Quilter's Dream Cotton
100 percent cotton batting*

Linda Lee Originals
2480 Riniel Rd.
Lennon, MI 48449
(810) 621-4665
http://www.lindaleeoriginals.com
*Serger-specific patterns (including her
serger coat shown on pages 32 and 76)
and educational materials*

Londa's Sewing Etc., Inc.
404 S. Duncan
Champaign, IL 61821
(217) 352-2378
Heirloom patterns and fine fabrics

K1C2 Solutions!
2220 Eastman Ave. #105
Ventura, CA 93003
(800) 607-2462
Rainbow Elastic

Loose Ends
P.O. Box 20310
Keizer, OR 97307
(503) 390-7457
Handmade paper

Madeira-SCS U.S.A.
9631 N.E. Colfax St.
Portland, OR 97220-1232
(800) 547-8025
*Decorative threads: Burmilana, Decor 6,
and Glamour*

Pfaff American Sales Corp.
610 Winters Avenue
Paramus, NJ 07653-0566
Sewing machines and sergers

Rhode Island Textile Co.
P.O. Box 999
Pawtucket, RI 02862
(401) 722-3700
Threads and stabilizers

Rupert, Gibbon, & Spider
P.O. Box 425
Healdsburg, CA 95448
(800) 442-0455
Fine silk fabrics and Jacquard Acid Dye

Singer Sewing Co.
Consumer Products Division
4500 Singer Rd.
Murfreesboro, TN 37129
(800) 4SINGER
Sewing machines and sergers

Speed Stitch, Inc.
(SULKY of America)
3113 Broadpoint Dr.
Harbor Heights, FL 33983
(800) 874-4115
Threads and stabilizers

Sullivans USA, Inc.
5221 Thatcher Rd.
Downers Grove, IL 60515
(630) 435-1530
*Fray Stop, Spray Fabric
Stabilizer, and
Quilt Basting Spray*

Tacony Corp.
1760 Gilsinn Ln.
Fenton, MI 63026
(314) 349-3000
Sewing machines and sergers

**Husqvarna Viking Sewing
Machine Co.**
11760 Berea Rd.
Cleveland, OH 44111
(800) 301-0001
Sewing machines and sergers

White Sewing Machine Co.
11760 Berea Rd.
Cleveland, OH 44111
(800) 301-1110
Sewing machines and sergers

YLI Corp.
161 W. Main St.
Rock Hill, SC 29730
(800) 296-8139
*Decorative threads, such as Candlelight, Pearl
Crown Rayon, Jeans Stitch, Designer 6, and
Silk Stitch*

Index

Fantastic Fit for Every Body

How to Alter Patterns to Flatter Any Figure

by Gale Grigg Hazen

Learn to create garments that fit and complement your body—no matter what your shape. Nationally known sewing, fitting, and machine expert Gale Grigg Hazen knows what it is like to sew for a less-than-perfect figure, yet her clothes always fit, and she always looks fabulous. Now Gale shares her unique fitting process with you, using real people with real fitting problems.

Hardcover ISBN 0-87596-792-2

High-Fashion Sewing Secrets from the World's Best Designers

A Step-by-Step Guide to Sewing Stylish Seams, Buttonholes, Pockets, Collars, Hems, and More

by Claire Shaeffer

Nationally known sewing expert Claire Shaeffer reveals the sewing secrets of fashion industry legends from Ralph Lauren to Yves Saint Laurent. You'll also discover that high-fashion sewing does not have to be difficult!

Hardcover ISBN 0-87596-717-5

No Time to Sew

Fast & Fabulous Patterns & Techniques for Sewing a Figure-Flattering Wardrobe

by Sandra Betzina

Sandra Betzina, star of the television series "Sew Perfect," helps you to sew in record time, offering stylish patterns, step-by-step instructions, timesaving tips, and wardrobe advice. Whatever your skill level, you'll find intriguing techniques for your next garment. Plus, you'll receive a complete set of multisize patterns for several garments when you buy this book.

Hardcover ISBN 0-87596-744-2

Secrets for Successful Sewing

Techniques for Mastering Your Sewing Machine and Serger

by Barbara Weiland

The ultimate owner's manual, full of tips and techniques for mastering a machine—regardless of brand. Includes a comprehensive look at machines and their accessories, plus step-by-step instructions for the most popular and unique serger and sewing machine techniques. Barbara Weiland is a former editor of *Sew News*.

Hardcover ISBN 0-87596-776-0

Sew Fast, Faster, Fastest

Timesaving Techniques and Shortcuts for Busy Sewers

by Sue Hausmann

Sue Hausmann, star of the PBS series "America Sews," lets you in on her secrets for faster fabric selection, quicker cutting techniques, and speed work at the sewing machine and serger. You choose from three methods to complete any technique, each one taking even shorter amounts of time to complete. Pick the one that fits your schedule. Learn great ways to finish seams; attach waistbands; sew casings; finish hems; sew collars, sleeves, and cuffs; make jacket linings, and much more.

Hardcover ISBN 0-87596-793-0
Available October 1998

Sewing Secrets from the Fashion Industry

Proven Methods to Help You Sew Like the Pros

edited by Susan Huxley

Learn the same tips and techniques that the industry professionals use in their sample rooms and production factories. Over 800 full-color photographs accompany the step-by-step instructions.

Hardcover ISBN 0-87596-719-1